ESTONIA, LATVIA, LITHUANIA, AND POLAND

ESTONIA, LATVIA, LITHUANIA, AND POLAND

EDITED BY AMY MCKENNA, SENIOR EDITOR, GEOGRAPHY

Britannica
Educational Publishing

IN ASSOCIATION WITH

ROSEN
EDUCATIONAL SERVICES

Published in 2014 by Britannica Educational Publishing
(a trademark of Encyclopædia Britannica, Inc.)
in association with Rosen Educational Services, LLC
29 East 21st Street, New York, NY 10010.

Distributed exclusively by Rosen Educational Services.
For a listing of additional Britannica Educational Publishing titles, call toll free (800) 237-9932.

First Edition

Britannica Educational Publishing
J.E. Luebering: Director, Core Reference Group
Adam Augustyn, Assistant Manager, Core Reference Group
Marilyn L. Barton: Senior Coordinator, Production Control
Steven Bosco: Director, Editorial Technologies
Lisa S. Braucher: Senior Producer and Data Editor
Yvette Charboneau: Senior Copy Editor
Kathy Nakamura: Manager, Media Acquisition
Edited by: Amy McKenna, Senior Editor, Geography

Rosen Educational Services
Nicholas Croce: Editor
Nelson Sá: Art Director
Brian Garvey: Designer, Cover Design
Introduction by Richard Barrington

Library of Congress Cataloging-in-Publication Data

Estonia, Latvia, Lithuania, and Poland/edited by Amy McKenna.
    pages cm.—(The Britannica guide to countries of the European Union)
"In association with Britannica Educational Publishing, Rosen Educational Services."
Includes bibliographical references and index.
ISBN 978-1-61530-971-9 (library binding)
1. Baltic States—Juvenile literature. 2. Estonia—Juvenile literature. 3. Latvia—
Juvenile literature. 4. Lithuania—Juvenile literature. 5. Poland—Juvenile literature.
I. McKenna, Amy, 1969– editor.
DK502.35.E87 2014
947.9—dc23

                                                            2012047989

Manufactured in the United States of America

On the cover: A composite image of the European Union Information Centre in Warsaw,
Poland, and the Wrocław Fountain in western Poland. © *iStockphoto.com/Jakub Kalaska
(building),* © *iStockphoto.com/Karolina Paszkiewicz (fountain)*

Cover, p. iii (map and stars), back cover, multiple interior pages (stars) © iStockphoto.
com/pop_jop; cover, multiple interior pages (background graphic) Mina De La O/Digital
Vision/Getty Images

On page xv: Map of Eastern Europe, showing the countries covered in this book: Estonia,
Latvia, Lithuania, and Poland. © *GeoAtlas*

CONTENTS

Faroe Islands
DENMARK

Suduroy

and Islands
U.K.

Trondheimfjorden

Trondheim

Ålesund

Bergen

Boknafjorden
Stavanger

Kristiansand

Orkney
Islands

Wick

SCOTLAND

Aberdeen

Perth

Glasgow Edinburg

ULSTER
ast

UNITED

Great

Britain

NORTH
SEA

Skagerrak

OSLO
Drammen

STOCKHOLM

SWEDEN

Luleå

Umeå

Sundsvall

Vaasa

Gulf of Bothnia

Pori

Turku

Åland

F

Hiiumaa

Saaremaa

G. of
Riga

BALTIC SEA

Gulf of

Vänern

Vättern

Norrköping

Göteborg

Kattegat

Gotland

Oland

Kalmar

RIGA

LITHU

Kaliningr
RUSSIAN F

Lof Man

ENGLAND

Liverpool   Manchester

N

KINGDOM

WALES

Cardiff

Southampton

Plymouth

English Channel

Channel
Islands

Ushant I.

Brest

Belle-Île

Newcastle

Bristol LONDON

Le Havre

NETHERLANDS
AMSTERDAM

Rotterdam

Antwerp

Lille

BEL.
BRUSSELS

LUXEMBOURG

Seine

Rennes

PARIS

FRANCE

Frisian Is.

Weser

DENMARK

COPENHAGEN

Bornholm

Malmö

G. of
Gdansk

Hamburg

BERLIN

Elbe

Dusseldorf

Leipzig

GERMANY

Frankfurt

Rhine

Stuttgart

Strasbourg

Munich

Danube

Oder

Gdansk

POLAND

WARSAW

Vistula

PRAGUE

CZECH REPUBLIC

Krakow

SLOVAKIA

VIENNA   BRATISLAVA

AUSTRIA   BUDAPEST

BERNE LIECHT

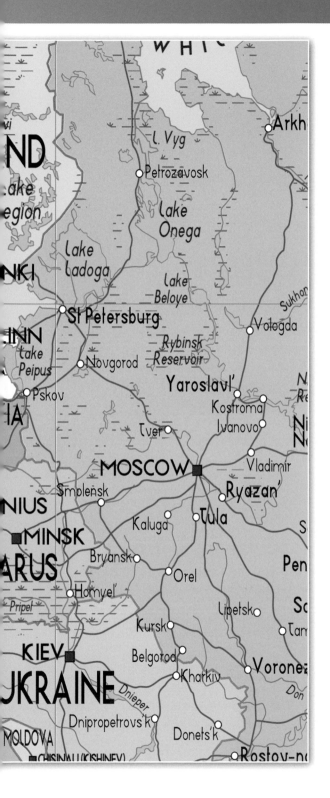

Some of the most important battles of the past century have been fought in the eastern and central European countries of Estonia, Latvia, Lithuania, and Poland. That includes both the territorial battles of two world wars and the ideological battle between capitalism and communism. Indeed, two things these countries have in common is that they were all once under the dominating influence of the Soviet Union, and today they are all members of the European Union (EU).

Of course, the contrast between those two associations that these countries share could not be greater. Subservience to the Soviet Union was imposed on these countries from the outside, while belonging to the EU was a voluntary choice. The Soviet era was marked by violent repression, while the EU has done a great deal to promote freedom within countries and ease tensions between countries. In fact, the EU was awarded the Nobel Peace Prize in 2012 for its efforts.

The prospect of a peaceful Europe is in many ways a departure from history, but nonetheless a prospect that has been hard-earned by the Baltic states (Estonia, Latvia, and Lithuania) as well as by their neighbour Poland. The path these countries have taken from an often turbulent past to the peaceful present is a fascinating story, and this book will tell that story while also providing insights into the individual characteristics of each of these countries.

Estonia has been a leading example of a successful transition from Soviet domination to a free, independent, and thriving society. After the U.S.S.R. dissolved in 1991, Estonia was one of the quickest of its former members to liberalize its markets and privatize most of its industries. While industry and agriculture once dominated its economy, the free market economy has allowed Estonia to become more diversified. The country also has a more diverse population than most European countries, due in particular to immigrants from Russia and other countries that were once part of the U.S.S.R.

In addition to freeing its markets, Estonia was also quick to embrace a democratic system, and it now has a parliamentary republic in which multiple parties vie for legislative seats and the leadership post of president. Because of its success in reforming both its economy and its government after leaving the U.S.S.R., Estonia was one of the first members of the former communist bloc to be considered for membership in the EU. It was admitted to that body in 2004 and adopted the euro as its currency in 2011.

Estonia's transition to freedom and independence is not just a triumph because it meant the end of Soviet domination, but because it represents an emergence from a history in which foreign oppression has been the rule rather than the exception. Germans, Swedes, and Danes have all invaded Estonia at one time or another, but Russia—starting well before the communist era—repeatedly sought control over the region. Russian incursions into Estonia date back to the 11th century, but it wasn't until the early 1700s that Russia finally wrested the area from Sweden. Russian rule continued until the early 20th century; Estonia then enjoyed a brief period of independence between the world wars, before being forced to join the U.S.S.R. in 1940. After achieving independence from the Soviet Union in 1991, Estonia was able to enter the 21st century well positioned and with strong hope that it would be the first fully independent century of its history.

In many ways, Latvia's story is similar to Estonia's, but if anything Latvia's challenges are even steeper than those that its neighbour to the north has faced. Indeed, Latvia's population has been shaped by oppression: a thriving Jewish population was reduced to nearly nothing by Nazi persecution during World War II, and Soviet occupation reduced the proportion of ethnic Latvians. Even following the dissolution of the U.S.S.R., economic difficulties have contributed to low birth rates that have suppressed population growth.

Economically, Latvia became the most heavily industrialized of the Baltic states in the 20th century, and since the end of the Soviet era it has largely succeeded in privatizing its industries and agriculture. However, energy remains a nagging economic problem, as the country is highly dependent on imported petroleum and electric energy.

Demographics and economics are modern problems faced by Latvia, but the country has also had its share of other problems throughout history. Like Estonia, Latvia has frequently been trampled on by foreign invaders. Slavs and Swedes raided Latvian territory during the 10th and 11th centuries, and then Germany ruled the country through the latter Middle Ages and the Renaissance. After Russia took control in the 1700s, Latvia found itself under Russian rule, while its people often worked on farms still owned by German landlords. However, in the 19th century, a combination of political reforms and the spread of information led to a growing sense of Latvian identity, and with it, a new spirit of nationalism.

Like Estonia, Latvia had a couple decades of independence between World War I and World War II, before spending the second war largely as a battleground between the Germans and the Russians. The outcome was that Latvia emerged from the war as part of the U.S.S.R., which is how it remained until Latvia declared independence in 1991. Tensions between Latvia and Russia continue to run high over a variety of issues, from the prosecution of former Soviet officials for human rights violations to the treatment of the ethnic Russian minority in Latvia. With Russia controlling a major portion of Latvia's petroleum imports, Russian influence on the country can still be heavy-handed even though the Soviet Union is long gone.

While Lithuania's story has some similarities with those of its Baltic neighbours Latvia and Estonia, there are also some significant differences. Latvia and Estonia were each frequently invaded throughout the centuries; in contrast, in its early history Lithuania was more often the invader of other countries rather than the one to be invaded. This is one reason Lithuania's population remains less ethnically mixed than those of the other Baltic states. Another distinguishing aspect of Lithuania is that it was the last country in Europe to embrace Christianity, though today the country is heavily Roman Catholic.

Aside from those differences, some prominent aspects of Lithuania's story closely mirror those of Latvia and Estonia. Lithuania came under Russian domination in the late 18th century. It had a short-lived period of independence between the world wars, before becoming a member of the U.S.S.R. in 1940. Since becoming independent again in the early 1990s, Lithuania has become a parliamentary democracy. As has been the experience of several former Soviet republics, Lithuania has struggled at times with the transition to a free market economy, but it achieved a sufficient level of privatization and stability to be admitted to the EU in 2004.

Sitting to the south and west of the Baltic states, Poland is at the geographical centre of Europe, and its history has felt the pull of both the east and the west. Indeed, its history generally is a study in contrasts: at various times, Poland has been the largest country in Europe but also was once temporarily partitioned out of existence; it has been a leading light of democracy in some instances, but was also a totalitarian state for a while. Out of such contrasts, Poland has produced major artists including Frédéric Chopin and prominent global figures such as Pope John Paul II. With roughly one out of every three Poles now living outside the country, Poland's influence has been felt in many parts of the globe.

Poland evolved out of a tribal culture in the 10th century, and the Roman Catholic Church became a strong influence at about the same time. The presence of the Roman Catholic Church also brought elements of western civilization and culture to Poland. Though early Poland developed into a monarchy, the system was not particularly stable and depended largely on the strength and skill of whoever was ruling Poland at the time.

In the 13th century, Poland had become a thriving economic force as well as something of a safe haven where Jews fleeing persecution in western Europe could enjoy religious freedom. Even so, the Roman Catholic Church remained not only the dominant religion in Poland, but the strongest institution of any kind in a country where divided regional rulers were often more powerful than the central government.

This divided state continued until King Casimir III unified the country and established a common code of law and currency in the mid-1300s. Later

in that century, Poland's evolution took yet another turn when the monarchy was linked by marriage to neighbouring Lithuania. The combined military strength of Poland and Lithuania greatly improved their position relative to their foreign rivals.

However, while an allied Lithuania and Poland had military might, the power of its sovereigns was undermined by the growing power of landowners. By the 16th century, these landowners had earned parliamentary representation for themselves, though the country was far from a democracy—the landowners used their power to restrict the rights of the peasantry, widening the division between the classes.

The growing territorial reach of the combined Polish and Lithuanian entity inevitably brought them into regular conflict with their large rival to the east, Russia. A series of armed conflicts ensued, beginning in the 16th century, and established a tradition of resentment between Russians and Poles. Those conflicts plus internal divisions weakened the Poland-Lithuania Commonwealth enough to expose it to foreign invasions in the 17th century.

By the 18th century, the combination of internal and external conflicts weakened Poland to the point where it faced perhaps the greatest threat to its existence. Through a series of partitions, Poland's territory was systematically annexed by the Russians, Prussians, and Austrians. Ironically, it was also during this period that Poland adopted what is now Europe's oldest constitution, but by the end of the 18th century Poland had ceased to exist as a separate and independent country.

A sense of Polish nationalism, often with the Roman Catholic Church as a rallying point, survived during the period of 123 years when Poland was partitioned, and there were a series of uprisings against foreign rulers during the 19th century. However, it was not until 1918 and the end of World War I that Poland was restored as an independent country.

Polish independence wasn't to last very long. In 1939 the country was invaded and quickly conquered by Germany from the west and Russia from the east, and Poland spent much of World War II as a battleground. During the German occupation, the Holocaust decimated Poland's Jewish population, and as the war drew to a close Russia's premier Joseph Stalin laid the groundwork to manipulate a weakened Poland into adopting a communist government.

Unlike the Baltic states, Poland did not become part of the Soviet Union, but in the decades that followed World War II it was known as one of the communist "satellite" countries, which were countries that were both dominated by and often dependent upon the U.S.S.R. However, in the early 1980s a popular protest movement known as Solidarity began to rise up, and this movement grew strong enough to force reforms on the government. When the Soviet Union collapsed in the early 1990s, the transition to a free Poland became complete. Today, the country is a republic that was admitted to the EU in 2004.

Estonia, Latvia, Lithuania, and Poland are all many centuries old, yet in a sense they are also very young countries, having only recently emerged from the shadow of the Soviet Union and from long histories of foreign domination. This makes them particularly interesting examples of living history, as they are still evolving, still trying to establish themselves. By tracing the history and national characteristics that led these countries to this point, this book will provide a background for understanding the continuing challenges they face.

CHAPTER 1

ESTONIA: THE LAND AND ITS PEOPLE

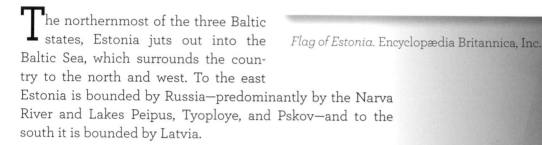

Flag of Estonia. Encyclopædia Britannica, Inc.

The northernmost of the three Baltic states, Estonia juts out into the Baltic Sea, which surrounds the country to the north and west. To the east Estonia is bounded by Russia—predominantly by the Narva River and Lakes Peipus, Tyoploye, and Pskov—and to the south it is bounded by Latvia.

RELIEF AND DRAINAGE

The Estonian landscape is largely the product of glacial activity; the south is covered with moraine hills, and the central part of the country abounds in elongated hills with flat tops.

BALTIC STATES

The republics of Lithuania, Latvia, and Estonia are commonly referred to as the Baltic states because of their location on the eastern shore of the Baltic Sea. The name has sometimes been used to include Finland and Poland.

Lithuania, Latvia, and Estonia were created as independent states in 1917 from the Baltic provinces of Russia, the city of Kovno, and part of the Polish department of Wilno (later Lithuania). With the aid of German and Allied forces, the Baltic states repelled a Bolshevik invasion in 1919. In 1940 they were forcibly occupied by the Soviet Union and incorporated as constituent republics. In 1944 Soviet troops recovered the territory, which had been overrun by German forces in 1941. The Baltic states gained independence on the breakup of the Soviet Union in 1991.

Estonia is located in northeastern Europe. The country's area includes some 1,500 islands and islets; the two largest of these islands, Saaremaa and Hiiumaa, are off mainland Estonia's west coast. The country's capital is Tallinn. Encyclopaedia Britannica, Inc.

Northern Estonia is characterized by long narrow swells consisting of deposits left by glacial rivers that formed during the melting of ice. Extensive sandy areas mark what was once the glacier's edge. Estonia's relief is thus generally undulating, with small hills and numerous lakes, rivers, and forests lending a mild and picturesque aspect to the scene, particularly in the south.

The mean elevation is 164 feet (50 metres) above sea level; only about one-tenth of the territory lies at elevations exceeding 300 feet (90 m). In the southeast is the Haanja Upland, containing Suur Munamägi (Great Egg Hill), which, at 1,043 feet (318 m), is the highest point in Estonia.

Estonia abounds in rivers, which flow to the Gulf of Finland, to the Gulf

HAANJA

The Haanja morainal region of southeastern Estonia is steep on the north but slopes more gently toward the south, extending slightly into Latvia. Deeply incised valleys separate the hills, and there are many lakes. Haanja is the highest and most irregular part of Estonia. The natural vegetation of the region is field and meadow. Haanja is now covered with woods and farms, and flax is an important traditional crop. Gypsum deposits are present at the southeastern edge of the moraine.

of Riga, and into Lake Peipus. The longest river, the Pärnu, stretches for about 90 miles (145 km); other important rivers are the Pedja, Narva, and Kasari. The country's largest lake is Peipus, with a surface area of about 1,370 square miles (3,550 square km), which is shared with Russia. Lake Võrts is situated in south-central Estonia.

CLIMATE

The temperate and humid climate of Estonia differs sharply from the climates of regions to the east (in Russia) at the same latitude. The country lies in the path of air masses borne by cyclonic winds that originate in the North Atlantic Ocean and carry warm

LAKE PEIPUS

Lake Peipus (Estonian: Peipsi Järv; Russian: Chudskoye Ozero) forms part of the boundary between Estonia and Pskov oblast (province) of Russia. It is connected by the narrow Lake Tyoploye to a southern extension, Lake Pskov. Lake Peipus has an area of 1,370 square miles (3,550 square km), although this varies. The lake bottom, reaching a depth of about 50 feet (15 m), consists of gray mud; only in the south is it sandy. The banks are predominantly low-lying. The lake, which is frozen for six months of the year, forms the headwaters of the Narva River.

Lake Peipus was the scene of a historic battle in 1242, when the Russians under Alexander Nevsky defeated the Teutonic Knights on the frozen lake. In 1239 the Livonian Knights (Order of the Brothers of the Sword) had begun a military campaign in northwestern Russia to expand their territory and convert the Russians to Roman Catholicism. Interrupted by the Mongol invasion of Poland and Silesia (1241), the campaign was resumed by the Teutonic Knights (with whom the Livonian Knights were affiliated). In 1241 the Knights captured Pskov, then proceeded against Novgorod in March 1242. But Nevsky led an army against them. Recovering all the territory seized by the Knights, he engaged them in battle on the frozen Lake Peipus, known as the "Battle on the Ice" (Ledovoye Poboishche). His victory (April 5) forced the grand master of the Knights to relinquish all claims to the Russian lands that he had conquered and substantially reduced the Teutonic threat to northwestern Russia.

air in winter and cool air in summer. The northern and western coastal areas tend to be milder than the country's inland regions, while the eastern and southeastern regions tend to have a continental climate. The mean temperature is 17 to 23 °F (–8 to –5 °C) in January and 61 to 63 °F (16 to 17 °C) in July. Annual precipitation is about 24 to 28 inches (600 to 700 millimetres), which, coupled with negligible evaporation and low relief, leads to waterlogging. The Estonian climate is generally favourable for agriculture.

PLANT AND ANIMAL LIFE

Mixed forests, with about 90 native species of trees and shrubs, cover almost half of Estonia's territory. Most widespread are pines, firs, birches, and aspens; less common are oaks, maples, elms, and ashes. Scots pine is the most common native tree. Meadows occupy a large area, as do marshes and swamps, where one-quarter of Estonia's 1,500 plant species are found.

About 60 species of mammals live in Estonia. The largest of these is the elk; roe deer, red deer, and wild pigs also are found. In the deep forests of the northeast, bears and lynx are encountered. Foxes, badgers, otters, rabbits, hare, and—along the riverbanks—mink and nutria (coypu) are fairly common. Fish (cod, herring, salmon, eel, plaice, and others) are of commercial importance. Birds are numerous and migratory; more than 300 species have been identified, few of which are year-round residents.

With the restoration of the independent republic in 1991, Estonia made strides in improving the health of its environment. Air and water pollution have been reduced, and the percentage of forestlands has been enlarged. About one-tenth of the country is set aside as a nature preserve.

ETHNIC GROUPS

Compared with other European countries, Estonia has a large percentage of foreign-born residents and their children. Only about two-thirds of the population are ethnic Estonians. Russians are the most significant minority, comprising about one-fourth of the citizenry. Prominent among other ethnic minorities are Ukrainians, Belarusians, and Finns. There are some regional linguistic and cultural differences among the ethnic Estonians; notably, the Seto people in southeastern Estonia speak a distinct dialect of Estonian and are part of an Eastern Orthodox religious tradition, while the islanders of the Muhu archipelago in the west also have their own dialect and share a number of cultural affinities with the people of Scandinavia.

LANGUAGE

Estonian, the official language of the country, is a member of the Finno-Ugric branch of the Uralic language family. More than two-thirds of the populace speak Estonian as a first language; about

TALLINN

The capital of Estonia, Tallinn (Russian: Tallin; German: Reval), is located on Tallinn Bay of the Gulf of Finland. Until 1918, the city was known as Revel.

A fortified settlement existed on the site from the late 1st millennium BCE until the 10th–11th century CE, and there was a town there in the 12th century. In 1219 it was captured by the Danes, who built a new fortress on Toompea hill. Trade flourished, especially after Tallinn joined the Hanseatic League in

A street in the old city centre of Tallinn, Est. Kurt Scholz/SuperStock

1285. In 1346 it was sold to the Teutonic Knights, and on the dissolution of the order in 1561 it passed to Sweden. Peter I (the Great) captured Tallinn in 1710, and it remained a Russian city until it became the capital of independent Estonia from 1918 to 1940. (Estonia was annexed to the Union of Soviet Socialist Republics from 1940 to 1991.) The city was occupied by German forces from 1941 to 1944 and was severely damaged. After the Supreme Soviet of Estonia declared independence in 1991, Tallinn became the capital of the newly independent state.

Both in 1940 and again in 1944–49, many Estonian citizens of Tallinn were deported and imprisoned by Soviet forces for alleged conspiracy, collaboration with the Germans, and opposition to collectivization. Of those exiled, a large proportion settled in Sweden or North America. Russians immigrated to the Estonian capital and now comprise two-fifths of the population. Ethnic Estonians make up roughly half of the city's population.

Many relics of Tallinn's long history survive or have been restored, especially on Toompea hill and in the old, walled Lower Town. They include the 13th-century Toom Church, the Gothic Oleviste and Niguliste churches, the Great Guildhall of 1410, the 14th-century Rathus, and much of the old castle. The city's historic centre was designated a UNESCO World Heritage site in 1997.

Today Tallinn is a major commercial and fishing port and industrial centre. Shipbuilding and machine building head a range of engineering industries, and many consumer goods are produced. The cultural centre of Estonia, Tallinn has an academy of sciences; polytechnic, fine-arts, and teacher-training institutes; a music conservatory; and several theatres and museums. Tallinn Airport, servicing both domestic and international flights, is the biggest airport in the Baltic states.

an additional one-fourth speak Russian as their first language (mostly in the northeast), though few Estonians over age 60 or under age 20 speak the language.

RELIGION

There is no state religion in Estonia, and many of the people are either non-religious or atheist. The Christian majority includes a large slice of unaffiliated Christians, along with significant Evangelical Lutheran and Eastern Orthodox communities, as well as lesser numbers of Baptists, Methodists, and Roman Catholics.

SETTLEMENT PATTERNS

As in the other Baltic states, Estonia's population is predominantly urban (more than two-thirds). Ethnic Estonians make up the vast majority of the rural population, while the urban population has a preponderance of non-Estonians.

Tallinn and Tartu are the two largest cities, though Helsinki, across the Gulf of Finland, is closer to Tallinn than Tartu is. Other cities of significance are Narva, Kohtla-Järve, and Pärnu.

DEMOGRAPHIC TRENDS

During the last half of the 20th century, Estonia experienced both considerable internal migration and, following Soviet annexation in 1940, extensive immigration from the other republics of the Soviet Union, especially Russia. In the process, the population in the industrially advanced northern part of the country increased appreciably at the expense of the southern and western regions, which remained primarily agrarian. Following independence, immigration slowed greatly, and many Russians left the country. Moreover, as the birth rate slowed dramatically at the end of the 20th century and life expectancy increased, Estonia's overall population began to age.

CHAPTER 2

THE ESTONIAN ECONOMY

As part of the interrelated Soviet economy, Estonia was basically an industrial region, with agriculture making a smaller contribution. Industry and agriculture remain important components of the economy of independent Estonia, but their portion of gross domestic product (GDP) and of the labour force have declined, while those of commerce and the service industry have grown. The Estonian economy experienced an initial downturn during its transition to a market economy (characterized by declining production, inflation, and unemployment), but by the mid-1990s it had rebounded, with some improvement across the decade following. Moreover, the Estonian economy has been cited as one of the most liberal in Europe; it has a balanced national budget, flat-rate income tax, and very few customs tariffs. Estonia was among the first eastern and central European countries with which the European Union (EU) started accession negotiations. It gained membership in 2004. Privatization of state-owned businesses was virtually complete by the beginning of the 21st century, though government controls remain over some energy and seaport activities.

AGRICULTURE AND FORESTRY

During Estonia's tenure as a Soviet republic, its agriculture was collectivized. Instead of some 120,000 small peasant farms that existed in 1945, there were by the 1990s about 190

KOLKHOZ

In the former Soviet Union, a cooperative agricultural initiative known as the kolkhoz (plural: kolkhozy) was the dominant form of agricultural organization. A kolkhoz was operated on state-owned land by peasants from a number of households who belonged to the collective and who were paid as salaried employees on the basis of quality and quantity of labour contributed. Conceived as a voluntary union of peasants, the kolkhoz became the primary form of agricultural enterprise as the result of a state program of expropriation of private holdings embarked on in 1929. Operational control was maintained by state authorities through the appointment of kolkhoz chairmen (nominally elected) and (until 1958) through political units in the machine-tractor stations (MTSs), which provided heavy equipment to kolkhozy in return for payments in kind of agricultural produce. Individual households were retained in the kolkhozy, and in 1935 they were allowed garden plots.

An amalgamation drive beginning in 1949 increased the pre-World War II average of about 75 households per kolkhoz to about 340 households by 1960. In 1958 the MTSs were abolished, and the kolkhozy became responsible for investing in their own heavy equipment. By 1961 their production quotas were established by contracts negotiated with the State Procurement Committee, in accordance with centrally planned goals for each region; the kolkhozy sold their products to state agencies at determined prices. Produce in surplus of quotas and from garden plots was sold on the kolkhoz market, where prices were determined according to supply and demand. With the collapse of communism and the breakup of the Soviet Union in 1990–91, the kolkhozy began to be privatized.

collectivized farms and more than 120 state farms. Decollectivization became a government goal in the post-Soviet period, and privatization proceeded quickly. Within the first year, Estonia had twice as many private farmers as either Latvia or Lithuania. Agriculture is the foundation of Estonia's significant food-processing industry. Principal crops include potatoes, barley, and hay. Livestock farming, notably of cattle and pigs, is also important.

Timber and woodworking constitute one of the oldest industries of Estonia, and the country's wood products include paper, pulp, plywood, matches, and furniture. The main production centres are Tallinn, Tartu, Narva, Pärnu, Kehra, Kuressaare (Kingissepa), and Viljandi.

RESOURCES AND POWER

The country's most important mineral is oil shale, of which Estonia is a significant world producer. Reserves and production of peat also are substantial, and large deposits of high-quality phosphorites, limestone, dolomites, marl, and clay exist.

Electric-power generation has great significance both for the economy of Estonia and for the surrounding region. Estonia supplies much of the power requirements of Latvia and parts of north-western Russia. Most of the electricity produced in the country is generated by thermal power plants fired with oil shale. Two of those plants, located near Narva, account for much of the electricity produced for the Baltic states. There is also another major power station, the peat-fired plant at Ellamaa, as well as other smaller stations. Like the power industry, the large shale-processing industry is a major employer in Estonia. It produces great quantities of fuel gas, much of which is transported to Russia by pipelines extending from Kohtla-Järve to St. Petersburg. There has been, however, growing concern about the environmental impact of both groundwater pollution from oil shale mining and sulfur dioxide emissions from the Narva power plants. Similarly, the phosphorite-mining industry has become the focus of environmental concerns. Oil shale satisfies about nine-tenths of Estonia's electrical needs, with alternative energy (peat, wood, and biomass) providing most of the remainder.

MANUFACTURING

Like agriculture, industry in Estonia underwent a period of adjustment during the transition to a market economy. Raw materials, previously inexpensive owing to the Soviet system, are now acquired at world market prices. In addition to imported raw materials, Estonian industry uses local resources, such as those that provide the base materials for the construction industry, including cement, mural blocks, and panels made from either shale ash or reinforced concrete. The main centres of this industry are Tallinn, Kunda, Tartu, and Aseri.

Much of the industrial labour force is engaged in the food-processing and forestry industries, machine building, and energy production. The chemical and mining industries, once significant employers, have declined in importance. On the other hand, Estonia's information technology and telecommunications industries began to blossom at the end of the 20th century. Among consumer-goods industries, textiles are highly developed, though they provided a diminishing share of total exports in the early 21st century. Still, most of the cotton cloth produced in the Baltic states is manufactured in Estonia. The country also produces wool, silk, linen, knitted and woven garments, and shoes.

FINANCE

In the period immediately following independence, Estonia continued to use the Russian ruble as its currency. Beginning in June 1992, the republic issued its own currency, the kroon, which was replaced by the euro in January 2011. At the centre of the republic's banking system is the Bank of Estonia (extant before the Soviet period and reestablished in 1990). In addition to a number of commercial banks, there is also the state-owned Savings Bank, and the Estonian Investment Bank offers financing for private companies. Sweden and Finland are the biggest foreign investors, providing three-fourths of external investment in the early 21st century. There is a stock exchange in Tallinn.

TRADE

The introduction of the kroon contributed to the stabilization of foreign trade, which was initially focused overwhelmingly on Russia and the countries of the Commonwealth of Independent States but later expanded to include nations of the EU. Estonia's major trading partners are Finland, Sweden, Germany, Russia, and Latvia. Principal exports include machinery and equipment, timber, textiles, metal and metal products, and processed foodstuffs. Principal imports include machinery and equipment, vehicles and transport equipment, and chemicals. The Russian oil industry, which makes heavy use of Baltic ports, distributes large amounts of oil through Estonia to the rest of Europe.

In addition to membership in the EU, Estonia had joined the World Trade Organization (WTO) in 1999.

SERVICES

By the early 21st century, the service sector was the largest component of the Estonian economy, employing about two-thirds of the workforce and contributing about two-thirds of the annual GDP. Following independence, foreign tourism grew steadily, primarily from Finland and predominantly in the summer months.

LABOUR AND TAXATION

During the Soviet era, trade unions were official organs of the state. In 1990–92 the groundwork was laid for the creation of independent labour associations with the formation of the Association of Estonian Trade Unions and the Estonian Employees' Unions' Association, the country's two main trade unions. Although the constitution, adopted in 1992, allowed employees to freely join and form independent unions, legislation enacted in 2000 cemented these rights and provided guidelines for trade union activities. Estonia employs a flat income tax rate (both for corporations and for individuals), a value-added tax (VAT), and property taxes but has neither inheritance nor gift taxes.

TRANSPORT AND TELECOMMUNICATIONS

Major highways link Tallinn with St. Petersburg and Riga, Latvia. The majority of the republic's freight is carried by road, but freight also is transported by rail and sea. Estonia's main rail lines connect

NARVA

The Estonian city of Narva lies along the Narva River, 9 miles (14 km) above the river's outflow into the Gulf of Finland. It was founded in the 13th century and quickly became a substantial commercial city. Occupied first by Russia (1558–81) and then by Sweden, it was important as the scene of Peter I the Great's defeat by the Swedes in 1700 and his subsequent victory, reconquering Narva for Russia, by means of a siege in 1704.

Since the 1850s Narva has been a major cotton textile centre. It also manufactures jute and hemp products and furniture. It has a technical school and a historical museum.

Tallinn with Tartu and Narva. There are three commercial ports near Tallinn and another inland port at Narva. Estonia has a state-owned shipping company and a state-owned airline. The country's major airport is at Tallinn, but there are also airports at Tartu and Pärnu. River transport is of local significance only.

At the beginning of the 21st century, cell phone use was high in Estonia, and Estonians, like Lithuanians, were more likely to own cell phones than were citizens of many other European countries. On the other hand, Estonians were less likely than many of their European neighbours to have personal computers.

CHAPTER 3

ESTONIAN GOVERNMENT AND SOCIETY

A mong the many initiatives of the Estonian government after independence from the U.S.S.R. was declared in August 1991 were preparation of a constitution, including the protection of minority group rights; proposed negotiations with Russia over territory lost during border adjustments following the Soviet occupation of 1940; and the development of legislation that would assist in the conversion to a market economy. A new constitution, based largely on the 1938 document that provided the basis for Estonia's pre-Soviet government structure, was approved by voters in a June 1992 referendum and came into effect in early July.

Guaranteeing the preservation of the Estonian nation and its culture, this document established a unicameral legislature, the Riigikogu (parliament), whose members are directly elected through proportional representation to four-year terms. The president, who serves as the head of state and supreme commander of the armed forces, is elected to not more than two consecutive five-year terms by the Riigikogu. Executive power rests with the prime minister, who is nominated by the president, and with the Council of Ministers. The government is responsible for implementing domestic and foreign policies and for coordinating the work of government institutions.

LOCAL GOVERNMENT

Estonia is divided into 15 *maakonnad* (counties), which are further divided into *vallad* (parishes). In addition to parish governments, there are administrative bodies for a number of towns and independent municipalities. The parishes are further divided into *külad* (villages) and *asulad* (townships).

JUSTICE

The judiciary comprises rural, city, administrative, and criminal courts, regional and appellate courts, and the National Court, which is the court of final appeal. A legal chancellor is appointed by the Riigikogu to provide guidance on constitutional matters.

POLITICAL PROCESS

Estonia has proportional representation and universal suffrage at age 18. In 1990 the government—no longer under the domination of the Communist Party of Estonia, which previously had controlled all aspects of political life—approved a multiparty system.

At the forefront of the many political groups formed in the postindependence period was the Estonian Centre Party (an offshoot of the Estonian Popular Front), the organization whose leader, Edgar Savisaar, was independent Estonia's first prime minister. It was soon joined by a wide variety of parties from across the political spectrum, including a number of single-issue parties. Shifting coalitions of these parties came to dominate not only the formation of governments in the Riigikogu but also the slates organized to contest elections. Since

2005, however, the centre-right Estonian Reform Party has led coalition national governments, most prominently in partnership with Pro Patria and Res Publica Union. Among the other important parties are the generally conservative Estonian People's Union, which includes many former communists; the Social Democratic Party; and the Estonian Greens.

SECURITY

Although military service is compulsory for men aged 19–28, women may choose to serve in the military. Volunteers can join at age 17, and reservists are eligible until age 60. The Estonian military includes land, air, and naval forces. Estonia became a member of the North Atlantic Treaty Organization (NATO) in 2004.

HEALTH AND WELFARE

Benefiting from their country's advantaged position in the Soviet economic system, from comparatively high levels of productivity, and from very low rates of net natural population increase that suggested a tendency to trade increased family size for material benefits, Estonians had the highest monthly salaries and the highest per capita housing allocation in the Soviet Union on the eve of independence. Moreover, during the Soviet period health care was available free of charge and was administered by the executive branch of the government.

TARTU

Tartu (German and Swedish: Dorpat), an old university city, lies on the Emajogi River in southeastern Estonia. The city was known as Derpt until 1893 and then as Yuryev from 1893 to 1918.

The original settlement, known as Tarbatu, dates from the 5th century; in 1030 the Russians built a fort there called Yuryev. From the 13th to the 16th century, the town was a prosperous member of the Hanseatic League. Then held in turn by Poles (1582–1600, 1603–25) and Swedes (1600–03, 1625–1704), it was finally annexed to Russia by Peter I the Great in 1704. The city was devastated by fire in 1775 and was largely rebuilt in classical style. It suffered heavily again during World War II. Its university, founded in 1632 by Gustavus II Adolphus of Sweden, was evacuated to Parnu in 1699 and closed in 1710, but it was reopened in Tartu in 1802.

The university is noted for its observatory, art museum, botanical garden, and library. In 1951 an agricultural college was established. In addition to its academic role, modern Tartu is a city of factories producing instruments, agricultural machinery, footwear, foodstuffs, and other goods. The ruins of the 13th-century cathedral remain on Toomemjagi Hill.

After independence a new law on health insurance (1992) established a decentralized system of medical funding under the aegis of the Riigikogu that operated primarily on the county and municipal level.

EDUCATION

A law enacted in 1993 restructured education in Estonia and raised the level of compulsory attendance to age 17 or completion of the 9th grade. Education is conducted primarily in Estonian, but Russian continues to be the language of instruction in a number of schools. Higher education, which under the 1993 law was restructured along Western lines, is both public and private. Notable institutions include Tartu University (founded 1632) and Tallinn Technical University (founded 1918). Scientific research has been centred at the Estonian Academy of Sciences, founded in 1938.

HOUSING

More than two-thirds of Estonian households live in apartment buildings. About five-sixths of the housing stock in Estonia was built after World War II, and of that about one-fourth was constructed after 1981.

CHAPTER 4

ESTONIAN CULTURAL LIFE

Because Estonia sits along the divide of western and eastern Europe—looking west, across the Baltic, toward Sweden, and east, across Lake Peipus, to Russia—it has long been influenced by both of those cultural traditions. Traditionally, northern Estonia, especially Tallinn, has been more open to outside influences (including Germanic Christianity, the Reformation, and Russification) than has southern Estonia, which has been more insular and provincial. The Estonian nationalist revival of the 19th century helped bridge this gap to create a national culture that for a long time had the country's agricultural heritage as common denominator. Central to that heritage was the barn dwelling, a multipurpose farmhouse that has no real equivalent in other countries (save for northern Latvia). Estonian farm families both lived and worked in these buildings, which typically included the living quarters, a threshing room (for drying grain), a threshing/work area, and sometimes animal pens.

DAILY LIFE AND SOCIAL CUSTOMS

Barn dwellings are now historical curiosities, but other elements of Estonian folk culture remain alive. Although the traditional costumes that were once everyday wear began to disappear in the last half of the 19th century as a result of increasing urbanization, they are still worn for festive occasions, and song and dance remain central to Estonian identity. Traditional cuisine in Estonia includes leavened rye bread, stews, berry jams, pickled gherkins, pearl barley, potato porridge, brawn (headcheese), and salt herring, among other dishes. Holiday meals may include roast goose or pork, ale, black pudding, apples, nuts, and gingerbread.

Among the main holidays are New Year's Day, Easter Sunday, Labour (or Spring) Day (May 1), and Christmas (December 25), as well as the summer holidays of Victory Day (June 23; Võidupüha) and St. John's (or Midsummer) Day (June 24; Jaanipäev). Celebrated February 24, Independence Day honours the 1918 declaration of independence from Soviet Russia, while the 1991 declaration of independence from the Soviet Union is observed on August 20 and known as Restoration Day. Other national holidays commemorate the Tartu Peace Treaty of 1920 (February 2) and the Soviet deportation of some 10,000 Estonians on a single night in 1941 (June 14).

THE ARTS

The scope and importance of Estonian literature have steadily increased since the period of national awakening in the 19th century. Open to cultural and literary influences of western Europe, Estonian literature developed a diversity of styles, ranging from Neoclassicism to bold experimentation. In the 20th century, Estonian writers represented three different epochs: Anton Hansen Tammsaare was the leading novelist of the former Republic of Estonia (1920–40); Jaan Kross wrote in an allegorical style during the period of Soviet occupation; and Tõnu Õnnepalu, whose work fits comfortably in the broader European context, became internationally recognized in the 1990s. Both Estonian classics and the works of contemporary authors have been translated into many languages.

KALEVIPOEG

Kalevipoeg (Estonian: "The Son of Kalevi"), the Estonian national epic, was compiled in 1857–61 by Estonian folklorist and poet F. Reinhold Kreutzwald. The work became the focus of the nascent 19th-century Estonian nationalism and independence movement and subsequently exercised considerable influence on the country's literature, art, and music. It was translated as *Kalevipoeg: An Ancient Estonian Tale* (1982).

In response to growing nationalistic feelings in his country, F.R. Faehlmann (Fählmann) consciously set about to produce an Estonian nationalist epic. He and many others collected thousands of Estonian folktales and folk songs. Kreutzwald combined these accumulated materials with original poetry, wrote its more than 19,000 verses, and published it as *Kalevipoeg*. Kalevipoeg, the hero of the epic, is the symbol of ancient Estonian independence, and the plot revolves around his romantic adventures.

The beginning of professional theatrical art in Estonia is closely connected with the creation of the Vanemuine Theatre in Tartu in 1870. Tallinn has several theatres, including the national opera theatre, a youth theatre, and a puppet theatre. The festival Baltoscandal, which presents alternative theatre, started in Parnu in 1990.

Estonian visual art came of age in the middle of the 19th century, when Johann Köler was among the leading portrait painters. The graphic art of Eduard Wiiralt symbolized bohemian art in the country in the 1920s and '30s. The international reputation of Estonian art has grown beyond these origins with the work of sculptor Juri Ojaver, ceramicists Leo Rohlin and Kaido Kask, digital media artist Mare Tralla, and graphic artist Urmo Raus.

An early expression of Estonian nationalism dating from the mid-19th century, song and dance festivals

ARVO PÄRT

Arvo Pärt (born September 11, 1935, Paide, Estonia) is an Estonian composer of international renown. A devout Orthodox Christian, he developed a style based on the slow modulation of sounds such as those produced by bells and pure voice tones, a technique reminiscent of the medieval Notre-Dame school and the sacred music of Eastern Orthodoxy. His major works include the violin concerto *Tabula Rasa* (1977), *Cantus in Memory of Benjamin Britten* (1977), *Magnificat-Antiphones* (1988), *The Beatitudes* (1991), and *Lamentate* (first performed 2003). His medieval liturgical sound won him a wide audience in the West during the late 1990s.

Pärt showed an early interest in music. In 1958, after finishing requisite military service, he enrolled at the music conservatory in Tallinn, Estonia. From 1958 to 1967 he worked for the music division of Estonian Radio. He won recognition in eastern Europe by taking first place in the All-Union Young Composers' Competition for an early popular work, *Meie aed* (1959; "Our Garden"), a cantata for children's choir and orchestra, and also for the oratorio *Maailma samm* (1960; "The World's Stride").

Developing an interest in the contemporary 12-tone system, he experimented with it in his own striking composition *Nekrolog* (1960), the first 12-tone piece written in Estonia. Pärt graduated from the conservatory in 1963. Soon afterward he composed his *Symphony No. 1* (1964) and *Symphony No. 2* (1966), the latter including quotations from the music of other composers. He also used this collage technique in *Credo* (1968), a work for piano, mixed chorus, and orchestra. Banned in the Soviet Union because of its religious text, *Credo* signaled the end of Pärt's experimentation with the 12-tone system.

Eight years of intensive music study followed. Pärt composed little but film scores during this time, immersing himself in the examination of such forms as the Gregorian chant and

Orthodox liturgical music. The first sign of his new musical direction was his *Symphony No. 3* (1971), one of the few works he produced during his "years of silence." But it was with the release of his works for strings during the late 1970s—especially *Fratres* (1977)—that his compositions began to take on a distinctly Pärtian sound.

Pärt's first work written in this new, austere style was a piano piece titled *Für Alina* (1976), the work in which he discovered the triad series, which he made his "simple, little guiding rule." Describing the sound of the triad as like that of pealing bells, he called his new method of composition "tintinnabuli style." It did not, however, win the approval of the authorities, and in 1980 Pärt moved with his family to Vienna; later he settled in West Berlin.

In 1996 Pärt was elected a foreign honorary member of the American Academy of Arts and Letters. He continued to write orchestral and choral works, many of which were recorded. The music of his later period was characterized by slow tempi, long stretches of silence, medieval tonal and rhythmic devices, and the controlled use of dissonance, among other features. In 2009, the year in which his fourth symphony (*Los Angeles*) premiered, the Arvo Pärt Archive was established in Harjumaa, Estonia.

continue to be extremely popular. The first national song festival was held in Tartu in 1869, and today the Song and Dance Celebration remains a linchpin of national identity. Classical composers and conductors of note include Rudolf Tobias (*Jonah's Mission*, 1908), Arvo Pärt (*Fratres*, 1977), and Neeme Järvi.

CULTURAL INSTITUTIONS

Known for its historic architecture, the old city centre of Tallinn was designated a UNESCO World Heritage site in 1997. The Museum of Estonian Architecture in Tallinn celebrates that and other national architectural traditions, from the multipurpose barn dwellings, with their enormous hatched roofs, that are a distinctive feature of the countryside to modern urban structures.

Founded in Tartu in 1909 as a comprehensive repository of Estonia's cultural heritage, the Estonian National Museum now takes a primarily anthropological approach, while its offshoot institution, the Estonian Literary Museum, also located in Tartu, is the country's archive of literature and folklore. Among Estonia's other museums and galleries are the Centre for Contemporary Arts in Tallinn, the Museum of New Art in Pärnu, and the Estonian Open Air Museum, a reconstruction of an 18th-century village, at Rocca-al-Mare.

SPORTS AND RECREATION

Boating is a passion in Estonia, with yacht clubs dotting the coastline of the mainland and the islands of Saaremaa and Hiiumaa. In fact, the yachting events of the 1980 Moscow Olympic Games were held in the waters off Tallinn. Canoeing is also popular, principally on the Võhandu, Piusa, and Ahja rivers in the southern part of the country. Bog walking is widely enjoyed, and bird-watchers frequent Estonia's nature reserves. In the summer, city dwellers flee to country cottages or the country's many sandy beaches to swim and sailboard. After Estonia entered the EU in 2004, tourists from across the continent flocked to the country's Baltic Sea resorts, and Tallinn became one of Europe's most popular weekend getaway destinations. In winter, many Estonians cross-country ski. Other popular sports are athletics (track and field), football (soccer), and basketball. Estonia made its Olympic debut at the 1920 Games in Antwerp, Belgium.

MEDIA AND PUBLISHING

Estonia has a number of television stations and daily newspapers (most prominently, *Today*), and the FM band is crowded with radio stations. Prior to the restoration of the republic, the media were state-owned and controlled by the Communist Party, mainly through state censors. Since independence, the media have been greatly liberalized. Both deregulation and consolidation were trends of the early 21st century.

CHAPTER 5

ESTONIA: PAST AND PRESENT

The Estonians are first mentioned by the Roman historian Tacitus (1st century CE) in *Germania*. Their political system was patriarchal, based on clans headed by elders. The first invaders of the country were Vikings, who from the mid-9th century passed through Estonia and Latvia on their way to the Slavonic hinterland. In the 11th and 12th centuries, the Danes and the Swedes tried to Christianize the Estonians, without success. Between 1030 and 1192, the Russians made 13 incursions into Estonia but failed to establish supremacy.

GERMAN CONQUEST

Meinhard, a monk from Holstein, landed in 1180 on what is now the Latvian coast and for 16 years preached Christianity to the Livs, a Finno-Ugric tribe. His successor, Berthold of Hanover, appointed bishop of Livonia, decided that the sword had to be used against the recalcitrant pagans. He was killed in 1198 in battle. Albert of Buxhoevden, who succeeded him as bishop, proved himself a shrewd colonizer, pacifying the "treacherous Livs" and forcing them to build the fortress of Riga. To popularize recruitment for his army, Albert dedicated Livonia to the Virgin Mary. In 1202 he established the Order of the Brothers of the Sword.

By 1208 the knights were firmly established on both banks of the Western Dvina (Daugava) River, and Albert felt strong enough to proceed northward to the conquest of Estonia. In the following years, the Estonians decreased steadily in manpower, while the knights replenished theirs with new Crusaders from Germany. The Russian princes of Novgorod and Pskov also raided Estonia on many occasions, penetrating especially deep in 1212 and 1216. Finally, in a major battle in 1217, the knights defeated the Estonians and killed their commander, Lembitu. Northern Estonia and the islands, however, remained free for another 10 years. To complete the conquest, Albert concluded an alliance with King Valdemar II of Denmark, who in 1219 landed with a strong army on the northern coast, on the site of Tallinn.

In 1237 the Order of the Brothers of the Sword suffered a crushing defeat and was absorbed by the Teutonic Order, which assumed control of Livonia. Northern Estonia and the islands were under Danish rule; Livonia (i.e., southern Estonia and Latvia) was shared between the Teutonic Order and the bishops. The terms under which the Estonian localities submitted were not severe, but the conquerors violated them as their position became stronger, provoking a series of revolts. After major risings in 1343–45, the Danish crown sold its sovereignty over northern Estonia to the Livonian branch of the Teutonic Order in 1346. The Germans became the masters in the "Land of the Virgin" and, with minor exceptions, dominated its government, its commerce, and the church for the next five centuries. The Estonians, the Latvians, and the Livs became the serfs of their conquerors, with little to sustain national feeling save their folklore and traditional crafts.

SWEDISH PERIOD

By the end of the 15th century, two major powers were emerging around Livonia: Poland-Lithuania, already united in the south, and Muscovy, which had conquered Novgorod, in the east. More by diplomacy than by victory in battle, Lithuania gained Livonia on the dissolution of the Teutonic Order in 1561. Three years before, northern Estonia had capitulated to the king of Sweden. The Muscovite tsar Ivan IV (the Terrible) had captured Narva in 1558 and penetrated deep into Estonia, bringing devastation with him, and it was not until 1581 that the Russians were expelled by the Swedes. In 1559 the bishop of Saaremaa had sold the Estonian islands to Denmark, but in 1645 they became part of the Swedish province. By the Truce of Altmark (1629), which ended the first Polish-Swedish war, the Polish-Lithuanian Commonwealth surrendered to Sweden the major part of Livonia, so that all Estonian lands then came under Swedish rule.

Prolonged wars left the country devastated, and many farms were unoccupied. The vacancies were partly filled by foreign settlers who were soon assimilated. This also gave the German nobility the opportunity to enlarge its estates, increase taxes, and exact more unpaid labour. The Swedish kings attempted to curb the power of the nobility and improve the lot of the peasants. Soon after Charles XI of Sweden came of age (1672), the nobles of Livonia were forced to show their title deeds, and those who failed to do so became tenants of the crown.

RUSSIAN CONQUEST

The "good old Swedish days" for Estonia were more a legend than reality, and they ended with the Second Northern War (Great Northern War). The Russian tsar, Peter I (the Great), was finally able to achieve the dream of his predecessors and conquer the Baltic provinces. After the defeat of Charles XII of Sweden at the Battle of Poltava (1709), Russian armies seized Livonia. The barons did not resist, angered as they were at the Swedish crown for its policy of reversion of estates. By the Peace of Nystad in 1721, Sweden ceded to Russia all its Baltic provinces.

The peasants' lot became the worst ever. In 1804, however, under Tsar Alexander I, the peasants of Livonia were given the right of private property and inheritance; a bill abolishing serfdom was passed in Estonia in 1816 and in 1819. Other agrarian laws followed—in particular that of 1863 establishing the peasants' right of free movement, that of 1866 abolishing the landowners' right of jurisdiction on their estates, including the right to flog, and that of 1868 abolishing the corvée.

ESTONIAN NATIONAL AWAKENING

The Estonian peasants benefited from these reforms, and, at the end of the 19th century, they possessed two-fifths of the privately owned land of the country. With the growth of urban prosperity as a result of industrialization, the population increased. Improvement in education was such that by 1886 only about 2 percent of the Estonian army recruits were unable to read. National consciousness also increased.

The accession of Alexander III marked the beginning of a period of more rigid Russification. The Russian municipal constitution was introduced in 1882. Russian criminal and civil codes replaced the old Baltic ones. In 1887 Russian was made the language of instruction, instead of German and Estonian. In 1893 the University of Dorpat (now Tartu), which was then an important centre of German learning, was Russified. The first reaction of the Estonians was that poetic justice was being administered to their age-old oppressors, but they also feared reactionary Pan-Slavism. In 1901 in Tallinn (Revel), Konstantin Päts founded the moderately radical newspaper *Teataja*. In 1904, thanks to Päts, the Estonians won a clear victory on the Tallinn town council.

In January 1905 the revolution that started in Russia spread immediately to Estonia. Jaan Tönisson founded a National Liberal Party and organized its first congress in Tallinn on November 27. The 800 delegates soon split into a Liberal and a Radical wing, but both voted for resolutions demanding political autonomy for Estonia. In December Päts

KONSTANTIN PÄTS

Konstantin Päts (born February 11 [February 23, New Style], 1874, Pärnu district, Estonia, Russian Empire—died January 18, 1956, Kalinin [now Tver] oblast, Russia, U.S.S.R.) was an Estonian nationalist and statesman. He served as the last president of Estonia (1938–40) before its incorporation into the Soviet Union in 1940.

Päts was educated in the law but began a career in journalism in 1901, when he founded the Estonian-language newspaper *Teataja* ("Announcer"), which reflected Päts's socialistic leanings. In 1904 Päts became deputy mayor of Tallinn. During an Estonian rising in connection with the 1905 Russian Revolution, Päts, although he had called for restraint, was sentenced to death and had to flee Estonia. He was not able to return until 1910, at which time he served a brief prison term.

Active in the movement for Estonian independence after 1917, Päts became head of a provisional government when independence was declared in February 1918. Almost immediately, Päts was arrested by Estonia's German occupiers, but he resumed his post after the November 1918 armistice. In 1921–22, 1923, and 1932–33 Päts served as *riigivanem* (equivalent to president and prime minister) of Estonia. After a new constitution providing for a stronger executive was approved in a 1933 referendum, Päts learned of a planned coup d'état by the fascist "Vap" movement, which had sponsored the constitution. He arrested the leaders of the movement and assumed dictatorial powers. Päts's authoritarian regime lasted until the Soviet Union occupied Estonia in June 1940. He was deported to the U.S.S.R. at the start of the occupation and died there.

summoned a peasant congress in Tallinn. The Russian government responded by declaring martial law; this prompted parties of workers to scatter into the countryside, where they looted and burned manor houses. In the repression that followed, 328 Estonians were shot or hanged, and Päts and the Radical leader Jaan Teemant fled abroad, both having been sentenced—in contumacy—to death. (Päts returned in 1910.) At the elections to the first and the second Russian Duma, Estonian voters returned five deputies to the council.

INDEPENDENCE

The Russian Revolution of 1917 during World War I brought autonomy to Estonia. An Estonian National Council, which came to be known as the Maapäev, met on July 14 and on October 12 appointed a provisional government with Päts as premier. The November coup d'état that brought the Bolsheviks into power in Petrograd (St. Petersburg) made itself felt in Estonia. On November 28, 1917, the Estonian Diet decided to break away from the Russian state, but on December 8 the

JAAN TÖNISSON

Jaan Tönisson (born December 22, 1868—died 1941 or after) was an Estonian statesman, lawyer, newspaper editor, and civic leader. He opposed Russian (tsarist and communist) domination of his country.

In 1905, after a revolution had broken out in Russia, Tönisson founded the National Liberal Party in Estonia and in 1906 sat in the first Russian Duma (legislative assembly). Although he was expelled from Estonia by the Bolsheviks late in 1917, he took part in negotiations for Allied recognition of Estonian independence. During his term as prime minister (1919–20), Estonia, having repulsed the Red Army, obtained favourable peace terms from the Soviet Union. He later served Estonia as president (1927–28, 1933) and foreign minister (1931–32). Arrested by Soviet occupation forces in 1940, he was last heard of in a Tartu jail the following year.

Russian Council of People's Commissars appointed a puppet communist government headed by Jaan Anvelt, who seized power in Tallinn but never obtained control of the whole country. In February 1918, German forces entered Estonia. The communists fled, and on February 24 the Maapäev declared Estonia independent. The following day German troops entered Tallinn. Päts was briefly arrested, and other Estonian leaders went abroad or underground. On March 3 the Treaty of Brest-Litovsk was signed; sovereignty over the Baltic countries was transferred from Russia to Germany.

German rule lasted until Germany's capitulation to the Allies on November 11, 1918. The Estonian provisional government, again headed by Päts, immediately proclaimed independence, but the Soviet government declared the Treaty of Brest-Litovsk null and void, and on November 28 the Red Army took Narva and entered

Estonia. Col. (later Gen.) Johan Laidoner opened a counteroffensive in January 1919, supported by weapons and war matériel from the Allies, a British naval squadron, and a Finnish voluntary force of 2,700 men. By the end of February, all Estonian territory had been freed, and the Estonian army penetrated into Soviet and Latvian territory.

On June 15, 1920, the constituent assembly (elected in April 1919), with August Rei as president, adopted a new constitution providing for a single-chamber Parliament (Riigikogu) of 100 members elected for three years, a system of proportional representation, and a chief of state (riigivanem), who was also the premier. Because no party had an absolute majority, government by coalition became the rule, and, from May 1919, when the first constitutional cabinet was formed, to May 1933, Estonia had 20 coalitions headed by 10 statesmen.

JOHAN LAIDONER

The Estonian soldier and patriot Johan Laidoner (born February 12, 1884, Viiratsi, near Viljandi, Estonia, Russian Empire—died March 13, 1953, Penza, Russia, U.S.S.R.) was educated in Russia for a military career and earned the rank of lieutenant colonel in Russian service. He served in World War I (1914–18) as an intelligence officer and then as a divisional chief of staff. In 1918 Laidoner became commander in chief of the new Estonian army, which drove the German and Russian occupiers out of Estonia in 1918–19. He left the army in 1920 but returned to it in 1924 to put down an attempted communist coup d'état. In 1925 he headed a League of Nations commission that dealt with a British–Turkish Mosul frontier dispute. In 1934 Laidoner again led the Estonian army in putting down an attempted government takeover by the right-wing "Vap" movement, and thereafter he headed the military support of President Päts's authoritarian regime. Laidoner was deported to the Soviet Union when the Soviets occupied Estonia in June 1940, and he died there.

On December 1, 1924, 300 conspirators, mostly Russians working on the transit base at Tallinn or smuggled in, tried to seize communications and call in Soviet troops but failed ignominiously. The Communist Party was outlawed, and the movement became virtually extinct. The Great Depression of the early 1930s resulted in unemployment and falling agricultural prices. The strong government action necessary to cope with the situation was precluded under the 1920 constitution. A new constitution in 1933 gave sweeping powers to the president. Päts became acting president and was expected to prepare the ground for the first presidential election. Instead, after learning of a fascist plot to overthrow the government, he proclaimed a state of emergency on March 12, 1934.

Opposition leaders were arrested; the political activities of all parties were forbidden; and Päts assumed dictatorial powers. In December 1936, a new constituent assembly was elected. It prepared a third constitution calling for the creation of a chamber of 80 deputies elected by the majority system and a national council of 40 members. A legislative election was held in February 1938. In April Päts was elected president for a term of six years.

INDEPENDENCE LOST

The fate of Estonia was decided by the German-Soviet Nonaggression Pact of August 1939 between Nazi Germany and the U.S.S.R. On September 28 the Soviet government imposed on Estonia a treaty of mutual assistance that conceded to the Soviet Union several Estonian military bases, which were occupied forthwith. A broadly based nonpolitical government under Prime Minister Juri Uluots was appointed, but on June 16, 1940, a Soviet ultimatum demanded a new Estonian government, "able and willing to secure the honest application of the Soviet-Estonia mutual assistance treaty." The following day, Soviet forces occupied the whole country. On July 21 the Chamber of Deputies was presented with a resolution to join the U.S.S.R.; it was unanimously adopted the next day in spite of being contrary to constitutional procedure. On August 6 the Moscow Supreme Soviet incorporated Estonia into the U.S.S.R. as one of its constituent republics. Meanwhile, Päts, Laidoner, and many other political leaders were arrested and deported to the U.S.S.R. In the first 12 months of Soviet occupation, more than 60,000 persons were killed or deported; more than 10,000 were removed in a mass deportation during the night of June 13–14, 1941.

On June 22, 1941, Germany attacked the U.S.S.R. Large areas of Estonia were freed from Soviet forces by improvised Estonian units before the German army reached Estonia. For three years Estonia was under German occupation, becoming part of the Ostland province. By February 1944, however, the Russians were back on the Narva front. About 30,000 Estonians escaped by sea to Sweden and 33,000 to Germany; many thousands perished at sea. On September 22, 1944, Soviet troops took Tallinn.

SOVIET REPUBLIC

The first postwar decade was a particularly difficult period of repression and

GERMAN-SOVIET NONAGGRESSION PACT

On August 23, 1939, the Soviet Union and Germany signed the German-Soviet Nonaggression Pact (also known as the Nazi-Soviet Nonaggression Pact), an agreement stipulating mutual nonaggression. The Soviet Union, whose proposed collective security agreement with Britain and France was rebuffed, approached Germany, and in the pact the two states pledged publicly not to attack each other. Its secret provisions divided Poland between them and gave the Soviet Union control of Latvia, Lithuania, Estonia, and Finland. The Soviets hoped to buy time to build up their forces to face German expansionism; Germany wished to proceed with its invasion of Poland and the countries to its west without having to worry about the Red Army. News of the pact shocked and horrified the world. Nine days after its signing, Germany began World War II by invading Poland. The agreement was voided by the German attack on the Soviet Union in 1941. Until 1989 the Soviet Union denied the existence of the secret protocols because they were considered evidence of its involuntary annexation of the Baltic states.

Russification. The efforts of the regime to restructure the country in a Soviet mold rendered national political and cultural life virtually impossible. Mass deportations occurred in several waves, most significantly in 1949 during the campaign to collectivize agriculture. It has been estimated that as many as 80,000 Estonians were deported between 1945 and 1953. Massive immigration from Russia and other parts of the U.S.S.R. decreased the indigenous proportion of the population. Before the war ethnic Estonians made up almost 90 percent of the population. By 1990 the proportion had sunk to about 60 percent. The ruling Communist Party was disproportionately immigrant in character. A large-scale purge in 1950–51 left virtually no native Estonian officials in the highest positions. The situation changed somewhat in the late 1950s and early 1960s, but by the late 1980s the ruling elite was still heavily immigrant.

The Soviet liberalization campaign of the late 1980s provided an opportunity for a national renaissance. In April 1988 an opposition Popular Front emerged. On June 16 the incumbent first party secretary, Karl Vaino, an immigrant, was dismissed. In the fall of 1988 the Popular Front pushed his successor, Vaino Väljas, to guide a resolution on sovereignty through the legislature. In the face of Soviet protests and warnings, Estonian law took precedence over Soviet legislation.

INDEPENDENCE RESTORED

Proponents of independence won a clear victory in the March 1990 elections. On March 30, 1990, the Estonian legislature declared a transitional phase to independence. Independence was declared formally in August 1991 and was recognized by the Soviet Union the following month.

In June 1992 a new constitution was adopted, and in September legislative and presidential elections were held, with Lennart Meri, who was supported by the Isamaa (Fatherland) alliance, elected president. Among the key issues for independent Estonia were the rights of those residents of the republic who had immigrated after the Soviet annexation of Estonia in 1940. These nonethnic Estonians (mostly ethnic Russians) were required to apply for citizenship, with naturalization requirements including proficiency in the Estonian language. Relations between Russia and Estonia were strained over this issue and over the continued presence in Estonia of Russian troops, which finally left the country in August 1994.

Despite allegations of corruption and abuse of power by some top officials, by the end of the 1990s Estonia had developed a stable democracy. In 2006 Toomas Hendrik Ilves became president. Although affected by the Russian financial crisis of 1998, Estonia's economy was fairly robust

TOOMAS HENDRIK ILVES

The Estonian politician Toomas Hendrik Ilves (born December 26, 1953, Stockholm, Sweden), who was elected president in 2006, took an atypical path to that office. He spent much of his life outside of the country, only moving to Estonia in 1996.

Ilves was born to Estonian refugees and raised in the United States. He completed a B.A. in psychology at New York City's Columbia University in 1976. Two years later he graduated from the University of Pennsylvania with an M.A. in psychology. After holding several jobs in the United States and Canada, Ilves moved to Munich in 1984 to work as an analyst and researcher for Radio Free Europe, eventually becoming head of the radio's Estonian desk. In 1984 he also made his first visit to Estonia. From 1993 to 1996 he served as Estonia's ambassador to the United States, Canada, and Mexico. In 1996 Ilves moved to Estonia and began serving as the country's minister of foreign affairs, a post he held until 1998 and again from 1999 to 2002.

Ilves's political career advanced when he was elected to the Riigikogu, the Estonian national legislature, in 2002. He was elected to the European Parliament in 2004 and began negotiations that resulted in Estonia's admittance to the EU in 2004. He ran for the presidency of Estonia as the candidate of the Social Democratic Party and was elected in September 2006.

Ilves's supporters expected him to use his office to further integrate Estonia into the EU and to strengthen the country's ties to the United States. Critics, however, worried that he did not have a sufficiently thorough understanding of domestic issues because he had spent most of his life abroad. Detractors also claimed that he was not well-equipped to manage the country's difficult relations with neighbouring Russia.

throughout much of the late 1990s, and it strengthened even more in the opening years of the 21st century. Ruled since 2005 by a coalition led by the Estonian Reform Party and Prime Minister Andrus Ansip, the government responded to the challenges of the world financial crisis of 2008 with an austerity program that kept the country's economy strong enough for Estonia to join the euro zone in 2011.

In foreign affairs, the country sought to improve its often tense relations with Russia and reoriented itself toward the West. In 1999 Estonia joined the World Trade Organization (WTO), and in 2004 it became a full member of both NATO and the EU.

CHAPTER 6

LATVIA: THE LAND AND ITS PEOPLE

Flag of Latvia. Encyclopædia Britannica, Inc.

The northeastern European country of Latvia lies along the shores of the Baltic Sea and the Gulf of Riga. It is bounded by Estonia to the north, Russia to the east, Belarus to the southeast, and Lithuania to the south. Latvia's capital and chief city is Riga.

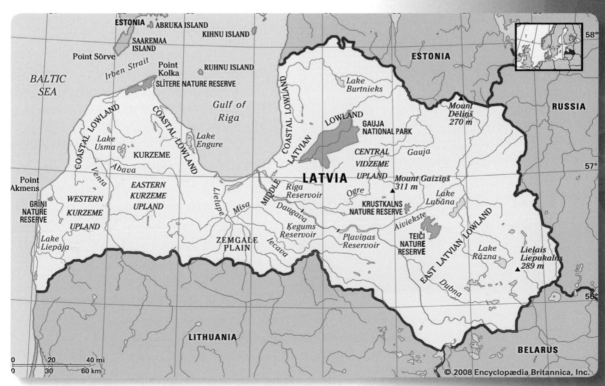

Physical map of Latvia. Encyclopædia Britannica, Inc.

RELIEF, DRAINAGE, AND SOILS

Latvia is essentially an undulating plain, with fairly flat lowlands alternating with hills. The eastern part of the country is more elevated, its most prominent feature being the Central Vidzeme Upland, which reaches a maximum elevation of 1,020 feet (311 m). In the southeast the highest point is Lielais Liepukalns (947 feet [289 m]), which is part of the Rāzna

The Amata River in Gauja National Park in the Middle Latvian Lowland. © Mr. Janis Miglavs

National Park territory. The Kurzeme (Courland) Upland in the west is divided by the Venta River into western and eastern parts. Between the Central Vidzeme and Latgale uplands in the southeast lies the East Latvian Lowland, partly crossed by moraine ridges that impede drainage. There are numerous peat bogs in this area.

Latvia contains a multitude of rivers that drain into the Baltic Sea. The largest are the Western Dvina, locally called the Daugava (with a total length of 222 miles [357 km] in Latvia), the Gauja (Russian: Gauya), the Venta, and the Lielupe. Amid the hills, many of which are forested, are numerous lakes, some measuring up to about 12 square miles (30 square km). Latvia's soils are predominantly podzolic, though calcareous soils characterize the Semigallia (Zemgale) Plain, located just east of the Eastern Kurzeme Uplands. Swampy soils are found in some areas, particularly the East Latvian Lowland. Erosion is a problem in the more intensely cultivated hilly areas.

CLIMATE

The climate is influenced by the prevailing southwesterly winds coming from the Atlantic. Humidity is high, and the skies are usually cloudy; there are only about 30 to 40 days of sunshine per year. Average precipitation usually exceeds 20 inches (about 500 mm) on the lowlands and may approach or exceed 30 inches (about 760 mm) on

WESTERN DVINA RIVER

The Western Dvina River (Latvian: Daugava; Belarusian: Dzvina; Russian: Zapadnaya Dvina) is the major river of Latvia and northern Belarus. It rises in the Valdai Hills and flows 632 miles (1,020 km) in a great arc south and southwest through Russia and Belarus and then turns northwest prior to crossing Latvia. It discharges into the Gulf of Riga on the Baltic Sea. Its tributaries include the Mezha, Kasplya, Ula, and Dzisna entering from the left and the Toropa, Drysa, Aiviekste (with its tributary the Pededze), and Ogre entering from the right.

The Western Dvina drains an area of approximately 34,000 square miles (88,000 square km). Most of the river basin is between 300 and 700 feet (100 and 200 m) above sea level—a rolling plain with numerous swamps and forests. The basin also has more than 5,000 lakes, most quite small. The basin has a humid climate with warm summers and mild winters.

The Western Dvina draws much of its water from melting snow, and consequently, like other rivers of the eastern European plains, it has high spring floodwaters. It also floods after heavy rains. In spring the water level rises by 20 to 35 feet (6 to 11 m) or more at various places. Its average discharge is about 25,000 cubic feet (700 cubic m) per second. The icebound period begins in the upper reaches in late November or early December and somewhat later in the middle part of the course. Thawing begins near the mouth of the river about the end of March, and in the upper reaches the water is open by about the middle of April.

The Western Dvina has been an important water route since early times. Connected in its upper reaches by easy portages to the basins of the Dnieper, Volga, and Volkhov rivers, it constituted part of the great trade route from the Baltic region to Byzantium and to the Arabic east. At the beginning of the 19th century the Western Dvina was joined by canals through its tributary, the Ula, to the Byarezina (Berezina) River and thus to the Dnieper, but this system was never much used except for rafting timber. Through another tributary, the Drysa, it is connected with Lake Sebezha, and a small canal unites the Western Dvina with the Gavya River.

The abundance of rapids and, in the 20th century, the presence of dams have restricted navigation on the river to a few separate stretches. The main items carried are lumber, construction materials, and grain. Seagoing vessels navigate the mouth of the river as far as Riga, 9 miles (15 km) from the sea. Hydroelectric stations have been built at Kegums, Plavinas, and Riga.

the uplands. The frost-free season lasts about 125 to 155 days. Summers are often cool and rainy. The mean temperature in June is in the mid-60s F (about 17 °C), with occasional jumps into the mid-90s F (about 34 °C). Winter sets in slowly and lasts from the middle of December to the middle of March. The mean January temperature ranges from the upper 20s F (near -2 °C) on the coast to the lower 20s F (about -7 °C) in the east. There are occasional extreme temperature drops into the -40s F (about -40 °C).

PLANT AND ANIMAL LIFE

More than half of Latvia is covered with forests, meadows, pastures, swamps, and wasteland. Forests account for more than one-third of the total area, and about one-tenth of the forests are cultivated. The larger forest tracts are in the northern part of the Kurzeme Peninsula, along the banks of the Western Dvina, and in the northeast, where conifers (pine and spruce) predominate. Of the deciduous species, birch, aspen, and alder are the most prevalent. Meadows are found both in the river valleys and among the hills.

Latvia's fauna consists of squirrels, foxes, hare, lynx, and badgers. Somewhat less common are ermines and weasels. Conservation measures have resulted in an increase in the number of deer and elk, and beavers have been reintroduced to Latvia. The country's bird population includes the nightingale, oriole, blackbird, woodpecker, owl, grouse, partridge, finch, tomtit, quail, and lark. Storks and herons are usually found in the marshes and meadows.

ETHNIC GROUPS, LANGUAGES, AND RELIGION

Before Soviet occupation in 1940, ethnic Latvians constituted about three-fourths of the country's population. Today they make up about three-fifths of the population, and Russians account for about one-third. There are small groups of Belarusians, Ukrainians, Poles, Lithuanians, and others. The official language of Latvia is Latvian; however, nearly one-third of the population speaks Russian. Smaller numbers speak Romany, the Indo-Aryan language of the Roma (Gypsies), and Yiddish, a Germanic language. The majority of Latvians adhere to Christianity—mainly Lutheranism, Roman Catholicism, and Eastern Orthodoxy. About one-fourth of Latvians consider themselves nonreligious.

Latvia had a significant Jewish population—estimated at more than 90,000 in the 1930s—until the Soviet and German occupations during World War II, when tens of thousands of Latvian Jews fled the country, were deported to prison camps or concentration camps, or were killed. Nazi forces were responsible for between 65,000 and 75,000 of these deaths. By war's end, only several thousand Latvian Jews remained.

SETTLEMENT PATTERNS

Latvia's rural population decreased after World War II, largely because of poor socioeconomic and political conditions, while its urban population increased steadily. By the early 2000s more than two-thirds of the country's population lived in urban areas. Riga is the most populous city, followed by Daugavpils and Liepāja.

DEMOGRAPHIC TRENDS

A major challenge for Latvia in the early 1990s was to offset the aging of its population, a serious problem that had existed

RIGA

The capital of Latvia is Riga (Latvian: Rīga). The city occupies both banks of the Western Dvina River 9 miles (15 km) above its mouth on the Gulf of Riga.

An ancient settlement of the Livs where the Ridzene River joins the Western Dvina, Riga was founded in 1201 by Bishop Albert I of Livonia, who had landed at the mouth of the Western Dvina two years earlier with 23 ships of Crusaders. He made Riga the seat of his bishopric (raised to an archbishopric in 1253) and founded there the Order of the Brothers of the Sword (1201; attached as a branch unit to the Teutonic Knights in 1237). Riga joined the Hanseatic League in 1282 and became one of the most important centres of trade on the Baltic. Its episcopal privileges allowed the town to act with considerable independence; but on the dissolution of the Teutonic Knights in 1561, the surrounding territory passed to Poland, and Riga itself passed to Poland in 1581. In 1621 Gustavus II Adolphus of Sweden captured Riga, but both Poles and Swedes granted Riga autonomy of government. In 1709–10 the Russians took Riga, and Sweden formally ceded the city by the Treaty of Nystad in 1721. Under Russian rule, its trade grew considerably. By 1914 Riga was the third largest city of Russia.

In 1918 Riga became the capital of independent Latvia. It was occupied by the Russians and incorporated into the Soviet Union in 1940. Together with other parts of Latvia, Riga suffered in 1940–41 from the Soviet deportations and executions of thousands of Latvian citizens. From 1941 to 1944 the city underwent German occupation and sustained heavy damage, especially in the old central city, destroying the medieval church of St. Peter and the 14th-century headquarters of the Brothers of the Sword. Soviet deportations resumed after the war and again in 1948–49. Russian immigration filled the vacuum left by forced removal of Latvians and a low Latvian birth rate. In 1991 Latvia regained its independence.

Many historical buildings survived, including the castle on the waterfront, the Doma Cathedral (dating from c. 1215), and several medieval merchants' houses and warehouses. The canal around the old town was the medieval moat, though the former fortifications have been replaced by boulevards. The historic centre of Riga was designated a UNESCO World Heritage site in 1997.

Modern Riga is a major administrative, cultural, and industrial centre and port, although icebreakers are necessary from December to April. The city's many engineering industries build ships and manufacture electrical and electronic equipment, machine tools, rolling stock, diesel engines, streetcars, and other items. The chemical, glass, and textile industries are important, and there are varied consumer-goods and food-processing industries. Riga's cultural institutions include an academy of sciences; a university (founded 1919), a Polytechnic Institute, and other institutions of higher education; a conservatory; the Latvian Open-Air Ethnographical Museum (founded 1924); and numerous theatres. Along the Gulf of Riga is the resort suburb of Rīgas Jūrmala.

even before the country's independence and that was the result largely of birth rates that were not high enough to ensure population replacement. An attempt was also made to increase the percentage of the population made up of ethnic Latvians by encouraging them to have larger families and by instituting stronger immigration controls. However, because of the unstable political and economic situation of the early post-Soviet period, most families postponed having more children. In fact, at the onset of the 21st century, Latvia had the lowest birth rate of the Baltic states as well as one of the lowest life expectancies in all of Europe.

CHAPTER 7

THE LATVIAN ECONOMY

Industrialization in Latvia began in the latter part of the 19th century, and by the late 20th century the country was the most heavily industrialized of the Baltic states. Substantial economic changes occurred following Latvia's independence in 1991, as the country transitioned to a market economy. Starting in the mid-1990s, the economy diversified, and by the early 21st century most industry in Latvia had been privatized.

AGRICULTURE AND FISHING

About one-third of agricultural land in Latvia is used for crop cultivation, and about one-tenth is dedicated to pasture for livestock. Of the crops, grain (mainly rye) is the most important. Wheat, oats, flax, and barley are also significant. Potatoes, onions, carrots, and sugar beets are the main crops produced for export.

Collectivization of agriculture was accomplished, against resistance, in 1947–50, after Latvia was incorporated into the Soviet Union. Up to the time of independence, in 1991, there were collective farms (engaged mainly in the cultivation of grain crops and mixed farming) and state farms (usually specializing in the cultivation and processing of a particular crop). Decollectivization became a goal of the newly independent government. During the Soviet period Latvia was a net importer of agricultural products, albeit on a small scale. After independence it was hoped that the privatization of agriculture would lead to higher levels of production and a

COLLECTIVIZATION

The Soviet government pursued a policy of collectivization to transform traditional agriculture in the Soviet Union and to reduce the economic power of the kulaks (prosperous peasants). Under collectivization the peasantry were forced to give up their individual farms and join large collective farms (kolkhozy). First begun in the late 1920s, the process was ultimately undertaken in conjunction with the campaign to industrialize the Soviet Union rapidly. Collectivization was introduced in the Baltic states in the late 1940s.

It was not a popular policy, as the peasants objected violently to abandoning their private farms. In many cases, before joining the kolkhozy they slaughtered their livestock and destroyed their equipment. Harsh measures—including land confiscations, arrests, and deportations to prison camps—were inflicted upon all peasants who resisted collectivization. In the case of Latvia, collectivization was no longer pursued as agricultural policy after independence was restored in 1991.

favourable balance of trade in agricultural commodities, but, as a result of the economic hardships of adjusting to a market economy and of the high cost of equipment required, agriculture contributed only a small percentage of the gross domestic product (GDP) in the early 1990s. By the early 21st century, agriculture had been completely privatized.

Latvia's fishing industry accounts for only a tiny percentage of the GDP, and fish products for export have decreased in importance. In general, sportfishing has contributed more to Latvia's annual catch from inland waters than has commercial fishing. Much of the catch from the Baltic is consumed domestically as a source of protein, most notably codfish and herring (sprats). The most common species of fish found in inland waters are pike, bream, carp, perch, eel, and lamprey. Some salmon and trout are bred artificially in nurseries and then released into rivers. Crayfish and carp have been raised successfully in ponds.

RESOURCES AND POWER

The principal mineral resources found in Latvia are sand, dolomite, limestone, gypsum, clay, and peat. Oil has been discovered in the Kurzeme Peninsula, and exploration of reserves has been undertaken. Latvia has hydropower plants on the Western Dvina River. Nonetheless, the country is highly dependent on imported sources of energy. Electric energy is supplied primarily by Estonia and Lithuania, and petroleum products are supplied by Russia and Lithuania. Beginning in the early 21st century, Latvia has attempted to diversify its domestic energy sources to reduce its dependence on foreign supply.

MANUFACTURING

The production of furniture, foodstuffs, beverages, and textiles had replaced machine building and metal engineering as Latvia's leading manufacturing activities by the late 1990s. The manufacture of chemicals and pharmaceuticals became important in the 21st century.

FINANCE

Under Soviet rule, Latvia used the Russian ruble as its monetary unit, but by 1993 the country had adopted its own currency, the lats. The Central Bank of the Republic of Latvia is the centre of the banking system. There is a stock exchange in Riga. In the middle of the first decade of the 2000s, foreign direct investment, which came mainly from other EU countries, accounted for about one-third of GDP.

TRADE

Latvia's main trading partners are Germany, Lithuania, Estonia, Russia, Poland, and the United Kingdom. Exports include wood and wood products, metals, foodstuffs, and textiles. Latvia imports machinery, oil, foodstuffs, and chemical products.

SERVICES

By the early 21st century the service sector accounted for the largest percentage of Latvia's GDP and employed about one-fifth of the country's workforce. Latvia's tourist infrastructure, which was virtually

LIEPĀJA

The city and port of Liepāja (German: Libau; Russian: Libava) is located on the west (Baltic Sea) coast at the northern end of Lake Liepāja. First recorded in 1253, when it was a small Kurish settlement, Liepāja was the site of a fortress built by the knights of the Teutonic Order in 1263. It was created a town in 1625, and in 1697–1703 a canal was cut to the sea and a port was built. In 1701, during the Great Northern War, Liepāja was captured by Charles XII of Sweden, but the end of the war saw the city in Polish possession. It was taken by Russia in the Third Partition of Poland, in 1795.

Liepāja's importance as a port, especially for grain export, was greatly stimulated in 1876 by the construction of the railway from Romny in the Ukraine. In 1893 a naval port was built, and its function as a naval base persisted through World Wars I and II, when the city suffered heavy damage, to the present. Modern Liepāja has important industries, producing steel, agricultural machinery, linoleum, sugar, canned fish, textiles, and footwear. It is a deep-sea fishing base and has several schools including a college of navigation and a branch of the Riga Polytechnic Institute. After the accession of Latvia to the European Union (EU) in 2004, the city became a popular summer holiday destination for foreign tourists.

nonexistent in the early 1990s, contributed a small percentage to the GDP. Major tourist attractions include the historic centre of Riga, which was designated a UNESCO World Heritage site in 1997; the country's picturesque castles and monasteries; and its coastline and lakes. Improvements were made in the quality of tourist accommodations in the early 2000s, but Latvia's infrastructure was still not fully sufficient to cater to an influx of visitors.

TRANSPORTATION AND TELECOMMUNICATIONS

Latvia's favourable geographic location and temperate climate allow for year-round freight transport. Major ports are located in Riga, Ventspils, and Liepāja, and there are several smaller ports located along the coast. An east-west railway corridor allows for the easy passage of freight from inland Latvia out to its main ports. There is an international airport in Riga.

The telecommunications sector of Latvia is partially nationalized. The number of Internet users increased significantly from the late 1990s to the mid-2000s; however, it is still somewhat lower than the average for the EU. Cellular phone usage in Latvia is much higher than fixed-line phone usage.

CHAPTER 8

LATVIAN GOVERNMENT AND SOCIETY

The Latvian constitution of 1922 provided for a republic with a president and a unicameral parliament, the Saeima. From 1940 to 1991 Latvia was a republic of the Soviet Union. On August 21, 1991, the Latvian government declared independence, which the Soviet Union recognized shortly thereafter, and the 1922 constitution was restored. Latvia has a unitary form of government. The head of state is the president, who is elected by the Saiema for a four-year term (with a maximum of two consecutive terms) and who plays a largely ceremonial role. The government is headed by a prime minister, who appoints officials of the cabinet and is responsible to the Saiema. The Saiema consists of 100 members, who are elected to four-year terms.

LOCAL GOVERNMENT

Latvia is divided into 26 self-governed *rajons* (districts). Outside of this structure are seven major cities that are designated republican cities and have their own governments. The districts are further organized into *pilsétas* (towns), *pagasts* (rural municipalities), and *novads* (amalgamated towns and rural municipalities). Each of these local administrative units has its own governing body (a council elected by its citizens). Because the local administrative units are so numerous, many of them lack sufficient staffing and funds, and the Latvian government has attempted to consolidate the country's administrative structure.

JUSTICE

Latvia's judicial system includes district courts, regional courts, and a Supreme Court. Supreme Court justices serve life terms, and judges in the lower courts serve two-year terms. The Constitutional Court of the Republic of Latvia was established in 1994 and began sittings in 1996. Its jurisdiction extends to areas such as ensuring the constitutionality of proposed legislation and of international agreements and ensuring that national laws are in compliance with international agreements. Justices of the constitutional court serve 10-year terms and are confirmed by the Saeima.

POLITICAL PROCESS

Suffrage is universal for all Latvian citizens aged 18 and older. However, as part of the government's attempts to preserve and increase the dominance of Latvian culture in the face of the country's large non-ethnic Latvian population, those wishing to become citizens are required to pass a Latvian language test. Until the late 1980s, when several prodemocracy groups united as the Popular Front of Latvia, the Communist Party of Latvia (Latvijas Komunistu Partija; LKP), like its counterparts in the other republics of the Soviet Union, was the only source of political power, under the Communist Party of the Soviet Union. The party was dominated by non-Latvians (mainly Russians and other Slavs) and by Russified Latvians who had lived in Russia for large parts of their lives. The power of the Communist Party began to weaken by the late 1980s, and in 1990 Latvia adopted a multiparty system. The Communist Party was outlawed in 1991, and many new and revived parties developed under the Popular Front.

COMMUNIST PARTY

A communist party is a type of political party organized to facilitate the transition of society from capitalism through socialism to communism. Russia was the first country in which communists came to power (1917). In 1918 the Bolshevik party was renamed the All-Russian Communist Party; the name was taken to distinguish its members from the socialists of the Second International who had supported capitalist governments during World War I. Its basic unit was the workers' council (soviet), above which were district, city, regional, and republic committees. At the top was the party congress, which met only every few years; the delegates elected the members of the Central Committee, who in turn elected the members of the Politburo and the Secretariat, though those organizations were actually largely self-perpetuating. The Soviet Union dominated communist parties worldwide through World War II. Yugoslavia challenged that hegemony in 1948 and China went its own way in the 1950s and '60s. Communist parties have survived the demise of the Soviet Union (1991), but with reduced political influence. Cuba's party remains in control, as does a hereditary communist party in North Korea.

The legacy of the LKP was widespread distrust of large-scale centralized political parties. Thus, the political landscape in Latvia after independence was complex. The Latvian National Independence Movement, founded in 1988, garnered a measure of popular support, but there were many other parties similarly intent on broadening their membership. Parties espousing liberal philosophies, environmental principles, or particular interests, such as those of the growing number of private farmers, were part of the fast-changing political scene.

EDUCATION

General literacy was achieved in Latvia in the 1890s. Education is free and compulsory until age 16. A 1998 education law ensured that a certain amount of instruction be provided in the Latvian language in the country's minority schools. However, state financing is provided for minority schools that teach classes in Belarusian, Estonian, Hebrew, Lithuanian, Polish, Romany, Russian, and Ukrainian, to preserve each minority's heritage and culture. Notable institutions of higher learning include the University of Latvia (1919), the Latvia University of Agriculture (1939), and Riga Technical University (1990). The Stockholm School of Economics in Riga opened in 1994. The Latvian Academy of Sciences (1946) in Riga is one of the top research institutes in the country.

CHAPTER 9

LATVIAN CULTURAL LIFE

Because it has been invaded and occupied by neighbouring powers for much of its history, Latvia has had to struggle to preserve its distinctive language, folklore, and customs. The country's loss of political independence in the 13th century effectively halted the development of Latvian culture for centuries. Indeed, it is only since the end of the 19th century that Latvians have been able to openly and actively celebrate their cultural heritage.

DAILY LIFE AND SOCIAL CUSTOMS

Religious and folkloric festivals, which were banned under Soviet rule, are celebrated again in traditional style. The festivals, complete with dance, music, and song, are usually performed in colourful costumes that are typical of specific regions of the country. The most important annual festival is Jāņi, a midsummer tradition based on an ancient pagan ceremony that celebrates the summer solstice. It is considered bad luck to fall asleep before dawn during Jāņi. Huge bonfires are lit, and special foods and beverages are prepared. Staples of Latvian cuisine include *kimeņu siers* (caraway cheese), bacon, berries, potatoes, sausages, soups, and rye bread. Smoked or salted herring is also a common dish. Berry pies and tarts served with sour cream are favourite desserts.

SUMMER SOLSTICE

The summer solstice occurs twice during the year, when the path of the Sun in the sky is farthest north in the Northern Hemisphere (June 20 or 21) or farthest south in the Southern Hemisphere (December 21 or 22). This event has long been the basis of rituals and celebrations in many cultures; in Latvia, the summer solstice is celebrated with the Jāņi festival.

   At the summer solstice, the Sun travels the longest path through the sky, and that day therefore has the most daylight. When the summer solstice happens in the Northern Hemisphere, the North Pole is tilted about 23.4° (23°27´) toward the Sun. Because the Sun's rays are shifted

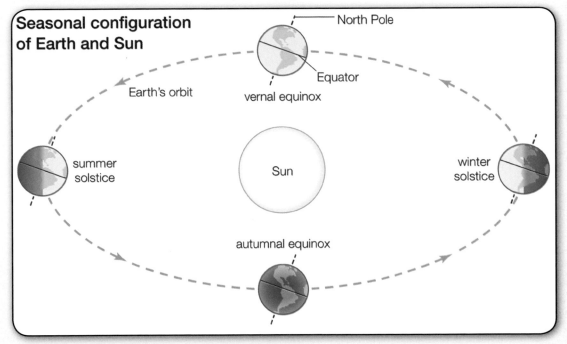

Diagram depicting the position of Earth in relation to the Sun at the beginning of each Northern Hemisphere season. Encyclopædia Britannica, Inc.

northward from the Equator by the same amount, the vertical noon rays are directly overhead at the Tropic of Cancer (23°27´ N). Six months later, the South Pole is inclined about 23.4° toward the Sun. On this day of the summer solstice in the Southern Hemisphere, the Sun's vertical overhead rays progress to their southernmost position, the Tropic of Capricorn (23°27´ S). According to the astronomical definition of the seasons, the summer solstice also marks the beginning of summer, which lasts until the autumnal equinox (September 22 or 23 in the Northern Hemisphere, or March 20 or 21 in the Southern Hemisphere).

THE ARTS

The Latvian folk song, or *daina*, is undoubtedly the heart of Latvian culture. *Dainas*, which are generally no more than four lines long, tend to be stories of family or love or are related to myths. Andrejs Pumpurs's literary epic *Lacplesis* (1888; *Bearslayer*) was inspired by the genre, as was the work of Rainis (pseudonym of Jānis Pliekšāns; 1865–1929), who is considered one of the great Latvian poets.

During the onset of the country's "national cultural awakening" in the mid-19th century, Latvians established their artistic independence, and for the first time an artists' community formed in Riga. An eminent poet of this period was Mikus Krogzemis, who took the pseudonym Auseklis, a god in Latvian mythology. Some of the best-known Latvian painters of that time were Janis Rozentāls and Vilhelms Purvītis, while Andrejs Jurjāns and Jazeps Vītols were highly regarded symphonic composers of the era.

CULTURAL INSTITUTIONS

Most of Latvia's major cultural sites are in the capital city of Riga. The Latvian National Symphony Orchestra (1926) and the Latvian National Opera are internationally renowned. The Riga Latvian Theatre was established in 1868, during the so-called Neo-Latvian movement of the 1860s and '70s, when Latvians strove to promote their identity in industry, trade, and the arts. Latvian ballet became prominent in the early 20th century, and the Latvian state ballet opened in 1932 in Riga; among its students were Mikhail Baryshnikov and Alexander Godunov.

RAINIS

The Latvian poet and dramatist Rainis (born Jānis Pliekšāns, September 11, 1865, Varslavani, Latvia, Russian Empire—died September 12, 1929, Majori, Latvia) produced works that were outstanding as literature and for their assertion of national freedom and social consciousness. He is also known for his efforts to translate important literary works into the Latvian language.

From 1891 to 1895 Rainis edited the newspaper *Dienas Lapa*, aimed at promoting social and class consciousness in the peasantry. Inspired by Marxist theory and writings, he began his literary career as a fighter for social justice and national freedom. His own philosophy, however, showed no trace of Marxist materialism—he regarded life as an incessant series of mutations of energy. Partly because of Russian censorship, he used symbols to express his ideal of political and personal freedom; but in 1897 he was banished to Pskov and, later, to Slobodsk for political activities. Returning in 1903, he took part in the unsuccessful revolution of 1905, after which he emigrated to Switzerland; he did not return until 1920, after Latvia had finally achieved independence. Enthusiastically welcomed, he was elected to the Saeima (Parliament) and was minister of education (December 1926–January 1928) and director of the national theatre (1921–25).

Monument commemorating the Latvian poet and dramatist Rainis (Jānis Pliekšāns) in Riga, Latvia. Vance Henry/Globe

Rainis' first volume of poetry, *Tālas noskanas zilā vakarā* (1903; "Far-Off Reflections on a Blue Evening"), displays his wide experience and contains some subtle love lyrics. Other books express the revolutionary struggle through Symbolism. *Gals un sākums* (1912; "End and Beginning") is imbued with the spirit of G.W.F. Hegel's dialectical philosophy. In his plays Rainis used motifs from folklore as symbols for his political ideals. Rainis also translated J.W. von Goethe's *Faust*, as well as works by William Shakespeare, Friedrich Schiller, Heinrich Heine, and Aleksandr Pushkin, which enlarged the vocabulary of literary Latvian and also introduced the use of shorter word forms.

The Latvian Open-Air Ethnographical Museum (1924) is one of the oldest open-air museums in Europe. It includes reproductions of typical 18th-century peasant dwellings, and artisans of all types produce and display their crafts there. The Castle Museum of Bauska, in southern Latvia near the Lithuanian border, is housed in the fortress built in 1443 by the Order of the Brothers of the Sword.

SPORTS AND RECREATION

Latvia's climate is conducive to winter sports, and bobsledding, skiing, ice skating, and ice hockey are popular. The Gauja valley is a well-known locale for winter sports. Canoeing on the Gauja and Abava rivers and the lakes in the Latgale region is a national pastime, as is bird-watching in the countryside. Latvia's Baltic coast is the site of numerous resorts, and its beaches are popular holiday destinations for tourists from across Europe.

Latvia made its first Olympic appearance at the 1924 Winter Games in Chamonix, France. After World War II, Latvian athletes competed for the Soviet Olympic team. Latvia competed at the 1992 Olympics as an independent country for the first time since 1936.

MEDIA AND PUBLISHING

Prior to independence, the media were state-owned and controlled by the Communist Party, mainly through state censors. Media censorship was abolished in 1989, and much of the media flourished as the economy became more liberalized. Latvia's print media is divided into Latvian- and Russian-language media. The daily *Diena* ("Day"), launched in 1990, is published in Latvian. The Latvian Telegraph Agency (Latvijas Telegrāfa Aģentūra; LETA) is the national news agency. The country's radio and television outlets mainly air programs in Latvian, Russian, and English; however, according to a 1998 law, at least half of the programming must be of European origin and at least two-fifths must be broadcast in the Latvian language.

CHAPTER 10

LATVIA: PAST AND PRESENT

The Latvians constitute a prominent division of the ancient group of peoples known as the Balts. The first historically documented connection between the Balts and the civilization of the Mediterranean world was based on the ancient amber trade; according to the Roman historian Tacitus (1st century CE), the Aestii (predecessors of the Old Prussians) developed an important trade with the Roman Empire.

During the 10th and 11th centuries, Latvian lands were subject to a double pressure: from the east there was Slavic penetration; from the west came the Swedish push toward the shores of Courland.

GERMAN RULE

During the time of the Crusades, German—or, more precisely, Saxon—overseas expansion reached the eastern shores of the Baltic. Because the people occupying the coast of Latvia were the Livs, the German invaders called the country Livland, a name rendered in Latin as Livonia. In the mid-12th century, German merchants from Lübeck and Bremen were visiting the estuary of the Western Dvina; these visits were followed by the arrival of German missionaries. Meinhard, a monk from Holstein, landed there in 1180 and was named bishop of Ikšķile ("one village") in 1186. The third bishop, Albert von Buxhoevden, founded the Order of the Brothers of the Sword in 1202. By the time they merged in 1237 with the Teutonic Order, they had conquered all the Latvian tribal kingdoms.

ORDER OF THE BROTHERS OF THE SWORD

The Order of the Brothers of the Sword (Latin: Fratres Militiae Christi; German: Schwertbrüderorden; also known as Knights of the Sword, Livonian Order, or Livonian Knights) was an organization of crusading knights that served as a permanent military body in Livonia to protect the church's conquests and to forcibly convert the native pagan tribes to Christianity. The order began the successful conquest and Christianization of Livonia (most of modern Latvia and Estonia) between 1202 and 1237.

The Order of the Brothers of the Sword was founded in 1202 by Livonia's third bishop, Albert von Buxhoevden, with Pope Innocent III's permission and was consecrated by the pope in 1204. The order's knights (called Knights of the Sword because their white cloaks were decorated with red crosses and swords) were required to be of noble birth and to take vows of obedience, poverty, and celibacy. They lived in district castles, each of which was ruled by its own council and a military chief, who was chosen by the order's grand master. The grand master, who served for life, was selected by the knights' general assembly, which also elected the order's other officials at its annual sessions. In addition to knights, the order's membership included soldiers, artisans, and clerics.

By 1206 the order had firmly established itself as the dominant power in the land of the Livs, the Finno-Ugrian people dwelling near the mouths of the Dvina and Gauja rivers, and by 1217 it had conquered not only the neighbouring Latvian tribes north of the Dvina but also southern Estonia. It then began the conquest of the lands south of the Dvina but encountered strong resistance from their inhabitants, the Curonians (Kurs) and the Semigallians. In September 1236 while the order's army, heavily burdened with booty, was returning through Semigallia from a raid in Lithuanian Samogitia, a combined force of Semigallians and Samogitians inflicted a disastrous defeat upon them (Battle of Saule), killing the grand master, Volquin, and effectively destroying the knights' military might. The order, which had been reprimanded by both the Holy Roman emperor and the pope for indiscriminately using brutal tactics against converts as well as heathens and which appeared by this time to be more concerned with establishing its own feudal domain than with gathering converts for the church, was then forced by the pope to disband and reorganize as a branch (1237) of the Teutonic Knights, whose main base was in Prussia and whose grand master thenceforth appointed the provincial master (*Landmeister*) of Livonia. The Livonian Knights continued the conquest of Livonia and ruled the region as an autonomous order again from 1525. Livonia, however, was divided and the order dissolved in 1561.

After the conquest, the Germans formed a so-called Livonian confederation, which lasted more than three centuries. This feudalistic organization was not a happy one, as its three components—the Teutonic Order, the archbishopric of Riga, and the free city of Riga—were in constant dispute with one another. Moreover, the vulnerability of its land frontiers forced the confederation into frequent foreign wars. However, the Latvians benefited from Riga's joining the Hanseatic League in 1282, as the league's trade brought prosperity. In general, however, the situation of the Latvians under German rule was that of any subject nation. The indigenous nobility was extinguished, apart from a few of its members who changed their allegiance, and the rural population was forced to pay tithes and taxes to their German conquerors and to provide corvée, or statute labour.

POLAND-LITHUANIA, SWEDEN, AND THE ENCROACHMENT OF RUSSIA

In 1561 the Latvian territory was partitioned: Courland, south of the Western Dvina, became an autonomous duchy under the suzerainty of the Lithuanian sovereign, and Livonia north of the river was incorporated into Lithuania. Riga was likewise incorporated into the Polish-Lithuanian Commonwealth in 1581 but was taken by the Swedish king Gustav II Adolf in 1621; Vidzeme, the greater part of Livonia north of the Western Dvina, was ceded to Sweden by the Truce of Altmark (1629), though Latgale, the southeastern area, remained under Lithuanian rule

The rulers of the Grand Principality of Moscow (Muscovy) had so far failed to reach the Baltic shores of the Latvian country, though Ivan III and Ivan IV (the

Terrible) had tried to do so. The Russian tsar Alexis renewed the attempt without success in his wars against Sweden and Poland (1653–67). Finally, however, Peter I (the Great) managed to "break the window" to the Baltic Sea. In the course of the Second Northern War, he took Riga from the Swedes in 1710, and at the end of the war he secured Vidzeme from Sweden under the Peace of Nystad (1721). Latgale was annexed by the Russians at the First Partition of Poland (1772), and Courland was acquired at the Third Partition (1795). By the end of the 18th century, therefore, the whole Latvian nation was subject to Russian rule.

RUSSIAN DOMINATION

In the period immediately following the Napoleonic Wars, the Russian tsar Alexander I was induced to grant personal freedom to the peasants of Courland in 1817 and to those of Vidzeme in 1819. This did not imply, however, that the peasants had any right to buy the land that their ancestors had tilled for centuries. Consequently, there was unrest in the Latvian lands until the emancipation of the serfs throughout the Russian Empire (1861) brought the right to buy land from the state and from the landlords, who were still mostly German.

During the last quarter of the 19th century, a national revival surged throughout Latvian territory. Universities and other national institutions were established. The idea of an independent

Latvian state was openly discussed during the Russian Revolution of 1905. This revolution, evoked as it was simultaneously by social and by national groups, bore further witness to the strength of the Latvian reaction to the economic and political pressures from German and Russian forces.

INDEPENDENCE

After the Russian Revolution of 1917, the Latvian National Political Conference of Riga asked for complete political autonomy. On September 3 of that year, however, the German army took Riga. After the Bolshevik coup of November 1917 in Petrograd (now St. Petersburg), the Latvian People's Council, representing peasant, bourgeois, and socialist groups, proclaimed independence on November 18, 1918, under the leadership of Kārlis Ulmanis, head of the Latvian Farmers' Union (Latvijas Zemnieku Savienība; LZS). The Soviet government established a communist government for Latvia at Valmiera, headed by Pēteris Stučka. The Red Army, which included Latvian units, captured Riga on January 3, 1919, and the Ulmanis government moved to Liepāja, where it was protected by a British naval squadron. But Liepāja was still occupied by German troops, whom the Allies were counting upon to defend East Prussia and Courland (Kurzeme) against the advancing Red Army. Their commander, Gen. Rüdiger von der Goltz, intended to build a German-controlled Latvia and to make it a German base of operation in the war against the Soviets. This intention caused a conflict with the government of independent Latvia supported by the Allies. On May 22, 1919, Goltz captured Riga. Pushing northward, the Germans were stopped near Cēsis by the Estonian army, which included 2,000 Latvians. The British forced the Germans to abandon Riga, to which the Ulmanis government returned in July. In the meantime, the Red Army, finding itself attacked from the north by the Estonians, had withdrawn from Latvia.

In July the British demanded that the German troops retreat to East Prussia. But Goltz now formed a "West Russian" army, systematically reinforced by units of German volunteers. These forces, headed by an anti-Bolshevik "White Russian" adventurer, Pavel Bermondt-Avalov, were to fight the Red Army, cooperating with the White Russian armies of commanders Aleksandr Vasilyevich Kolchak, Anton Ivanovich Denikin, and Nikolay Yudenich, supported by the Allies. But on October 8 Bermondt-Avalov attacked the Latvian troops and occupied the suburbs of Riga south of the river. By November 10, however, the Latvians, aided by the artillery of an Anglo-French naval squadron cooperating with Estonian forces, defeated Goltz's and Bermondt-Avalov's troops, attacked finally also by the Lithuanians. By December 1919 all German troops had abandoned Latvia and Lithuania. Only Latgale remained in Red hands, but it was soon after cleared of Red troops with military assistance from Poland.

KĀRLIS ULMANIS

Kārlis Ulmanis (born September 4, 1877, Berze, Latvia, Russian Empire—died 1942) was a leader in the fight for Latvian independence in the early decades of the 20th century. He was the first head of the Latvian Republic in 1918 and again in 1936–40 and was premier in 1918, 1919–21, 1925–26, 1931–32, and 1934–40.

Ulmanis studied agronomy in Germany as a young man and afterward worked to improve dairy farming and cattle breeding in Latvia. During the period of upheaval at the time of the Russian Revolution of 1905, he worked to promote freedom from Russia, which had controlled the country for more than a century. The defeat of the revolution forced Ulmanis to seek exile in the United States, where he taught in the agriculture department of the University of Nebraska.

In 1913 he was granted amnesty by the Russian government and returned to Latvia. At the time of the Russian Revolution of 1917, he founded the Latvian Farmers' Union to press for independence. Then with other nationalists he formed a Latvian national council that proclaimed independence on November 18, 1918, and appointed Ulmanis head of the provisional government.

He remained in power until June 1921, during the confused period immediately following the end of World War I, when the new nation was forced to fight to maintain itself in the face of threats, pressure, and military action from Russia, native Latvian Communists, and German forces. With a Latvian army formed by Gen. Jānis Balodis and supported on occasion by French and British naval forces and Polish troops, the new government was able to clear the country of opposition. Ulmanis organized the election of a constituent assembly, and the first Saeima (parliament) convened on August 11, 1920. That same month peace was concluded with the Soviet Union.

Ulmanis again served as premier from December 1925 to May 1926 and from March 1931 to December 1932. He came to power for the last time on March 17, 1934, during a period of great tension created by the demands of right-wing nationalists and the Nazified German minority. On May 15, 1934, Ulmanis and General Balodis declared a state of siege, dissolving the Saeima and all political parties, and instituting authoritarian rule. In June 1940, under an ultimatum backed by Soviet military forces, Ulmanis resigned, and Russian forces occupied the country. Ulmanis was arrested on July 21, 1940, by Soviet authorities and deported to Russia.

A Latvian constituent assembly, elected in April 1920, met in Riga on May 1, and on August 11 a Latvian-Soviet peace treaty was signed in Riga, under which the Soviet government renounced all claims to Latvia. The Latvian constitution of February 15, 1922, provided for a republic with a president and a unicameral parliament, the Saeima, of 100 members elected for three years.

The multiplicity of parties in the Saeima (22 in 1922 and 24 in 1931) made it impossible to form a permanent government; nevertheless, Latvia experienced a period of economic growth. One of the most significant achievements was the passage of an agrarian reform bill, which granted land to about 145,000 peasants. Still, democracy had not been instilled in Latvia, and in May 1934 Ulmanis, prime minister for the fourth time since 1918, dissolved the Saeima and all political parties and established authoritarian rule. On April 11, 1936, on the expiration of the second term of office of Pres. Alberts Kviesis, Ulmanis declared himself president.

THE SOVIET OCCUPATION AND INCORPORATION

When World War II started in September 1939, the fate of Latvia had already been decided in the secret protocol of the German-Soviet Nonaggression Pact of August 23. In October Latvia had to sign a dictated treaty of mutual assistance by which the U.S.S.R. obtained military, naval, and air bases on Latvian territory. On June 17, 1940, Latvia was invaded and occupied by the Red Army. On June 20 the formation of a new government was announced, and the Soviets organized elections in which only one list of candidates was allowed. Meanwhile, President Ulmanis was deported. On July 21 the new Saeima voted for the incorporation of Latvia into the U.S.S.R., and on August 5 the U.S.S.R. accepted this incorporation. After Latvia was annexed into the Soviet Union, a period known as the "year of terror" ensued. In the first year of Soviet occupation, about 35,000 Latvians, especially the intelligentsia, were deported to eastern portions of the U.S.S.R., many of them to prison camps in Siberia.

During the German invasion of the U.S.S.R., from July 1941 to October 1944, Latvia was a province of a larger Ostland, which included Estonia, Lithuania, and Belorussia (now Belarus). Many Latvians were recruited into German military units during the Nazi occupation. The Latvian Legion (a unit of the Waffen-SS troops) was formed under German order in 1943, and Latvian males were conscripted. A resistance movement against the German occupation was led by the Central Council of Latvia, with the participation of notable Latvian politicians. During the Nazi occupation of Latvia, between 65,000 and 75,000 Latvian Jews were killed.

By 1944 about two-thirds of the country was occupied by the Red Army. The Germans held out in Kurzeme until the end of the war. About 100,000 Latvians fled to Sweden and Germany before the arrival of Soviet forces.

The first postwar decade proved particularly difficult. The uncompromising effort of the regime to transform the country into a typical Soviet bailiwick compounded the devastation of the war. Severe political repression accompanied radical socioeconomic change. Extreme Russification numbed national cultural life. Several waves of mass deportation—of at least 140,000 people—to northern Russia and Siberia occurred, most notably in 1949 in connection with a campaign to collectivize agriculture. Large-scale immigration from Russia and other parts of the Soviet Union began and continued throughout the postwar period. In just over 40 years the proportion of Latvians in the population dropped from roughly three-fourths to little more than one-half, and the Russian language dominated both public and private life.

The ruling Communist Party of Latvia in the 1950s was disproportionately composed of immigrants. A concerted effort to nativize the party, especially its ruling cadres, triggered a purge in 1959 of Communist Party high-level officials who were accused of Latvian nationalism. These officials were replaced by First Secretary Arvīds Pelše and his successors Augusts Voss and Boriss Pugo, who remained in positions of power in the party during the following three decades.

A national renaissance developed in the late 1980s in connection with the Soviet campaigns for *glasnost* ("openness") and *perestroika* (economic and political restructuring). Some of the first opposition organizations included Helsinki-86, a group that sought to secure the basic human rights that had been established in the Helsinki Accords, and the Environmental Protection Club. Mass demonstrations on ecological questions in 1987 were the first nonofficial staged political gatherings in the country in postwar times.

INDEPENDENCE RESTORED

An opposition Latvian Popular Front emerged in 1988 and won the 1990 elections. On May 4 the legislature passed a declaration to renew independence after a transition period. Soviet efforts to restore the earlier situation culminated in violent incidents in Riga in January 1991. After a failed coup in Moscow in August, the Latvian legislature declared full independence, which was recognized by the Soviet Union on September 6.

The first post-Soviet elections, in which only pre-1940 citizens and their descendants were permitted to vote, were held in June 1993. The new legislature immediately restored the 1922 constitution. Among the new Latvian government's main concerns were its relations with non-ethnic Latvians (especially Russians), citizenship requirements, and the privatization of the economy. Allegations of discrimination against Russians in Latvia strained Latvian-Russian relations, which Latvia attempted to repair during much of the 1990s.

Another sensitive political issue that confronted the new government was what to do about the thousands of former Soviet military personnel still stationed within Latvia's borders (estimated at more than 50,000 in 1991). When the Russian armed forces finally withdrew in August 1994, Russia was given the right to station some hundreds of military and civilian employees at the early-warning radar station at Skrunda until 1998. By 1999 Russia had turned over full control of the radar station to Latvia.

Tensions between Latvia and Russia persisted into the early 21st century, however. Latvia continued to prosecute former Soviet officials for crimes committed during and after World War II. In 2002 Moscow temporarily stopped the flow of petroleum to Latvia in an attempt to gain control over the oil port at Ventspils; in 2004, after Russia opened a new oil port on the Baltic Sea, it again ordered its state-controlled pipeline agency to turn off the pipeline at Ventspils. Moreover, Russia accused Latvia of further violating the rights of its Russian-speaking minority when, in 2003, it was mandated that three-fifths of the public school curriculum be taught in Latvian. A longtime border dispute with Russia was resolved in 2007, helping warm relations between the two countries; however, the treaty remained controversial in Latvia because it affirmed Soviet-imposed boundaries that had incorporated Latvian border counties into the U.S.S.R.

Following independence, Latvia had quickly reoriented itself politically and economically toward western Europe. It joined the Council of Europe in the 1990s and gained full membership in the EU and the North Atlantic Treaty Organization (NATO) in 2004.

Latvia's economy expanded at a furious pace from 2005 to 2008, and double-digit GDP growth was the norm throughout that period. Skyrocketing inflation, soaring energy costs, and ripple effects from the global financial crisis of 2008, however, led to an economic contraction so severe that Latvia was forced to seek financial assistance from the International Monetary Fund. A basket of austerity measures—including tax increases, public sector wage cuts, and reductions in welfare payments—triggered a wave of popular discontent, and the government of Prime Minister Ivars Godmanis collapsed in February 2009. A shaky coalition was forged by former opposition leader Valdis Dombrovskis, and a series of economic reforms were pushed through the Saiema. With the Latvian economy showing signs of modest recovery, the Dombrovskis government survived a parliamentary general election in October 2010. A snap election in September 2011 resulted in the pro-Russia Harmony Centre party capturing the most seats, but it failed to win an absolute majority, and Dombrovskis was able to form a coalition government with the backing of the right-wing National Alliance.

The National Alliance then initiated a petition to establish Latvian as the sole language for education, but it failed to collect enough signatures to put the matter to a referendum. Pro-Russian parties responded with their own petition, with the goal of making Russian an official second language for Latvia. That petition generated sufficient support among registered voters to trigger a February 2012 referendum, and rhetoric on both sides of the debate became heated as the poll approached. In the event, turnout was around 70 percent, and the proposal was resoundingly rejected.

CHAPTER 11

LITHUANIA: THE LAND AND ITS PEOPLE

Flag of Lithuania. Encyclopædia Britannica, Inc.

The northeastern European country of Lithuania is the southernmost and largest of the three Baltic states. It is bounded by Latvia to the north, Belarus to the east and south, Poland and the detached Russian oblast of Kaliningrad to the southwest, and the Baltic Sea to the west. The capital is Vilnius.

RELIEF

Underlying rock structures are of little significance for the contemporary Lithuanian terrain, which basically is a low-lying plain scraped by Ice Age glaciers that left behind thick, ridgelike terminal deposits known as moraines. The Baltic coastal area is fringed by a region characterized by geographers as the maritime depression, which rises gradually eastward. Sand dunes line an attractive coast; the Curonian Lagoon (Lithuanian: Kuršiu Marios), almost cut off from the sea by the Curonian Spit, a thin 60-mile (100-km) sandspit, forms a distinctive feature. It is bounded by the Žemaičiai Upland to the east, which gives way to the flat expanses of the Middle Lithuanian Lowland.

The lowland, consisting of glacial lake clays and boulder-studded loams, stretches in a wide band across the country from north to south; some portions of it are heavily water-logged. The elevated Baltic Highlands, adjacent to the central lowland, thrust into the eastern and southeastern portions of

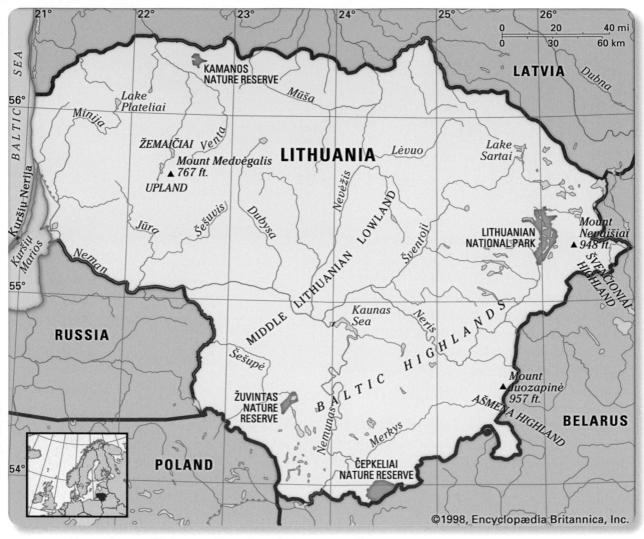

Physical map of Lithuania. Encyclopædia Britannica, Inc.

the country; their rumpled glacial relief includes a host of small hills and numerous small lakes. The Švenčioniai and the Ašmena highlands—the latter containing Mount Juozapinė, at 957 feet (292 metres) above sea level the highest point in Lithuania—are located in the extreme east and southeast.

DRAINAGE

Lithuanian rivers drain to the Baltic and generally have the slow, meandering characteristics of lowland rivers. The Neman River, cutting north and then west through the heart of the country, is the largest. Its main tributaries are the

CURONIAN LAGOON

The Curonian Lagoon (also called Courland Lagoon; Lithuanian: Kuršiu Marios; Russian: Kursky Zaliv; German: Kurisches Haff) lies along the gulf of the Baltic Sea at the mouth of the Neman River, in Lithuania and Russia. The lagoon, with an area of 625 square miles (1,619 square km), is separated from the Baltic Sea by a narrow, dune-covered sandspit, the Curonian Spit (Lithuanian: Kuršiu Nerija; Russian: Kurskaya Kosa), 60 miles (100 km) long and 1–2 miles (1.5–3 km) wide. A road along the spit connects resort and fishing villages. At its north end, the lagoon is connected to the Baltic Sea by a navigable strait, site of the Lithuanian port of Klaipėda. The east coast of the Curonian Lagoon is low, wooded marshland, part of which forms the Neman River delta. To

Merkys, Neris, Nevėžis, Dubysa, Jūra, Minija, and Šešupė. A distinctive feature of the Lithuanian landscape is the presence of about 3,000 lakes, mostly in the east and southeast. The boggy regions produce large quantities of peat that, dried by air, is used in both industry and agriculture.

SOILS

Lithuanian soils range from sands to heavy clays. In the northwest the soil is either loamy or sandy (and sometimes marshy) and is quite heavily podzolized, or leached out. In the central region, weakly podzolized loamy peats predominate, and it is there that the most fertile, and hence most cultivated, soils are found. In the southeast there are sandy soils, somewhat loamy and moderately podzolized. Sandy soils in fact cover one-fourth of Lithuania, and most of these are blanketed by woodlands.

CLIMATE

The climate of the country is transitional between the maritime type of

Trakai Castle, located on an island in Lake Galve, west of Vilnius, Lith. Itar—Tass/Sovfoto

NEMAN RIVER

The Neman River (Lithuanian: Nemunas) runs through Belarus and Lithuania. It is 582 miles (937 km) long and drains about 38,000 square miles (98,000 square km). It rises near Minsk in the Minsk Upland and flows west through a broad, swampy basin; it then turns north into Lithuania, cutting through terminal moraines in a narrow, sinuous valley. Near Kaunas, where there is a hydroelectric plant, it turns west and crosses another marshy basin to enter the Kurisches Gulf of the Baltic Sea south of Klaipeda. Navigation on the river is possible for 416 miles (670 km) to Belitsa; much timber is rafted.

western Europe and the continental type found farther east. As a result, damp air masses of Atlantic origin predominate, alternating with continental Eurasian and, more rarely, colder Arctic air or air with a southern, tropical origin. Baltic Sea influences dominate a comparatively narrow coastal zone. The mean temperature for January, the coldest month, is in the low 20s F (about -5 °C), while July, the warmest month, has an average temperature in the 60s F (about 17 °C). Average annual rainfall usually exceeds 30 inches (about 800 mm), diminishing inland. Rainfall reaches a peak in August, except in the maritime strip, where the maximum is reached two to three months later.

PLANT AND ANIMAL LIFE

Lithuanian vegetation falls into three separate regions. In the maritime regions, pine forests predominate, and wild rye and various bushy plants grow on the sand dunes. Spruce trees are prevalent in the hilly eastern portion. The central region is characterized by large tracts of oak trees, with elegant birch forests in the northern portions, as well as distinctive black alder and aspen groves. Pine forests prevail in the south. Indeed, about one-third of the country is forested, and about another one-fifth is taken up by meadowlands. Swamps and marshlands account for only a small percentage of the total land.

Wildlife is very diverse and includes numerous mammalian species. There are wolves, foxes, otters, badgers, ermine, wild boars, and many rodents. The deep forests harbour elk, stags, deer, beavers, mink, and water rats. Lithuania is also home to hundreds of species of birds, including white storks, ducks, geese, swans, cormorants, herons, hawks, and even an occasional bald eagle. There are many types of grouse and partridge as well.

ETHNIC GROUPS, LANGUAGES, AND RELIGION

Ethnic Lithuanians make up about four-fifths of the country's population; there are also Russians and Poles and lesser numbers of Belarusians, Ukrainians, Latvians, Tatars, Roma (Gypsies), and others. There was a significant Jewish community in Lithuania prior to World War II, and an influx of Jews from German-controlled Poland in 1941 boosted this population to nearly 250,000. By 1944, however, the majority of the population had been murdered, deported, or sent to concentration camps.

The official language of Lithuania is Lithuanian. Russian, Polish, Belarusian, Ukrainian, and other languages are spoken in the larger cities. Yiddish is commonly spoken by members of the tiny remaining Jewish community in Lithuania.

Lithuania was the last pagan country in Europe, accepting Roman Catholicism in the late 14th century. About four-fifths of the population is Roman Catholic; there are smaller groups of Evangelical Lutherans and other Protestants, as well as people of other faiths. Elements of the pagan religion have survived in the countryside.

SETTLEMENT PATTERNS

There has been a modest but steady movement of people to the cities since the 1990s, encouraged by the planning of regional centres, such as Alytus, Marijampolė, Utena, Plungė, and Mažeikiai. By the early 21st century about two-thirds of the total population lived in urban areas.

The largest city is Vilnius, followed by Kaunas, Klaipėda, Šiauliai, and Panevėžys.

VILNIUS

The capital of Lithuania is Vilnius (Russian: Vilnyus; Polish Wilno). The city is located at the confluence of the Neris and Vilnia rivers. A settlement existed on the site in the 10th century, and the first documentary reference to it dates from 1128. In 1323 the town became capital of Lithuania under Grand Duke Gediminas; it was destroyed in 1377 by the Teutonic Knights. Subsequently rebuilt, Vilnius received its charter of self-government in 1387, and a Roman Catholic bishopric was established there. The city underwent many calamities—Russian occupation in 1655–60, Swedish capture in 1702 and 1706, French occupation in 1812, and recurrent fires and plagues. In 1795 Vilnius passed to Russia in the Third Partition of Poland. It was occupied by the Germans in World Wars I and II and suffered heavy damage. From 1920 to 1939 it was included in Poland; it was taken by Soviet troops in 1939 and restored to Lithuania. The Soviets annexed Lithuania, including Vilnius, in June 1940. Soviet rule brought mass deportations (1940–41, 1946–50) of ethnic Lithuanians from Vilnius, and many Russians moved into the city. In 1991 Vilnius again became the capital of independent Lithuania.

A prominent feature of the city before World War II was its Jewish community, for nearly 150 years the centre of eastern European Jewish cultural life. In the 18th century, under the influence of Rabbi Elijah ben Solomon, it underwent a decisive religious and spiritual growth, becoming renowned for rabbinical studies that between 1799 and 1938 produced texts of the Mishna, Jerusalem Talmud, and other works that are still standard. In the 19th century the community became a centre for the Haskala (Enlightenment) and was the home also of the first Jewish socialists in Russia; by the beginning of the 20th century it had become the focus of the Zionist movement in Russia as well. A flourishing source of Hebrew and Yiddish literature, with numerous newspapers and literary, scientific, and cultural periodicals, it was the birthplace of the YIVO Institute for Jewish Research (founded 1924). The German occupation during World War II destroyed the community, reducing the city's Jewish population from 80,000 in 1941 to 6,000 by 1945.

Many historic buildings survive, representing the Gothic, Renaissance, Baroque, and classical styles of architecture. The ruins of the Castle of Gediminas on Castle Hill dominate the old town, with its narrow, winding streets that climb the wooded slopes surrounding the confluence of the rivers. There are a 16th-century Gothic Church of St. Anne and a dozen 17th-century Baroque churches, notably the Church of SS. Peter and Paul. The cathedral dates originally from 1387, but in its present form from 1801. Around the old town are the newer sectors of the city. The historic centre of Vilnius was designated a UNESCO World Heritage site in 1994.

Present-day Vilnius is an important industrial centre, producing machine tools, agricultural machinery, electronic calculators and other electrical and electronic apparatus, textiles, clothing, and foodstuffs. The city is the cultural centre of Lithuania and is home to the V. Kapsukas State University, the Vilnius Civil Engineering Institute, institutes of fine arts, teacher-training schools, and several theatres and museums.

DEMOGRAPHIC TRENDS

Natural increase, rather than immigration, has accounted for most of Lithuania's population growth in the early 21st century. The high birth rate distinguishes Lithuania from its Baltic neighbours, which have struggled to offset the aging of their populations.

The comparatively high level of ethnic homogeneity in Lithuania and the persistence of Roman Catholicism in the face of decades of Soviet promulgation of atheism as the official state ideology further distinguish Lithuania from Latvia and Estonia, where historically German-Scandinavian religious and cultural values have predominated.

CHAPTER 12

THE LITHUANIAN ECONOMY

Even before independence from the U.S.S.R. was formally established, the Lithuanian government had embarked on a program of dismantling the Soviet economic system. Beginning in February 1991, laws were passed to facilitate privatization. Complications marred the government's aspirations, however. Foremost, the bulk of Lithuania's trade was still closely linked to the former republics of the U.S.S.R., which were themselves in the throes of economic collapse. Second, Lithuania was dependent on critically important foreign oil and natural gas and industrial raw materials. Finally, the transition to a market economy had caused high rates of inflation and unemployment. Nevertheless, the succeeding governments continued to implement stringent stabilization policies; by 1995 inflation had been reduced, and the country's trade balance was positive for the first time since independence. Lithuania was admitted to the EU in 2004.

AGRICULTURE

The development of agriculture since 1991 has been closely linked to land reclamation and swamp-drainage schemes. By the early 21st century agriculture contributed only a small percentage to the gross national product (GNP) and employed only about one-tenth of the economically active population. The chief trend is toward the production of meat and milk and the cultivation of flax, sugar beets, potatoes, and vegetables. A significant portion of total production is made up of fodder crops, grain (barley and rye), and leguminous crops;

most of the rest consists of potatoes and vegetables. Livestock breeding is still the leading branch of agriculture, with an emphasis on dairy cattle and pigs. Most crop cultivation is mechanized, though during the autumn harvest large amounts of manual labour are still required.

Lithuania has long been a small net exporter of food products. The privatization of farming in the early 1990s began with the decision to liquidate all former collective and state farms. Some private farms emerged in the period immediately following independence, but the process was slow. Not only were there problems of financing, but equipment appropriate to smaller-scale farming operations was not readily available. By the late 1990s private farms had begun to outnumber state farms. The majority of these farms are not specialized and are involved in mixed production based on crops and livestock.

RESOURCES AND POWER

Lithuania possesses a range of useful mineral resources, including sulfates, notably gypsum; chalk and chalky marl; limestones; dolomites; various clays, sands, and gravels; peat; some iron ore and phosphorites; and mineral waters. Amber, which is a fossil tree resin, is found along the shore of the Baltic Sea.

Oil deposits have been detected in the offshore regions. A pipeline carries gas from Ukraine, and an oil pipeline transports crude oil from fields in western Siberia to the refinery at Mažeikiai, which was modernized in 2003. In 1999

AMBER

Amber is formed when fossil tree resin has achieved a stable state through loss of volatile constituents and chemical change after burial in the ground. Amber has been found throughout the world, but the largest and most significant deposits occur along the shores of the Baltic Sea in sands 40,000,000 to 60,000,000 years old.

Amber occurs as irregular nodules, rods, or droplike shapes in all shades of yellow with nuances of orange, brown, and, rarely, red. Milky-white opaque varieties are called bone amber. The turbidity of some amber is caused by inclusions of many minute air bubbles. Many hundreds of species of fossil insects and plants are found as inclusions. Deeply coloured translucent to transparent amber is prized as gem material.

Ornamental carved objects, beads, rosaries, cigarette holders, and pipe mouthpieces are made from amber. Amberoid, or "pressed amber," is produced by fusing together small pieces of amber under pressure. Parallel bands, or flow structure, in amberoid help to distinguish it from natural amber. Despite the introduction of numerous synthetic substitutes, the beauty of the real material has remained unexcelled.

a crude oil terminal at Būtingė was opened on the Baltic Sea. Almost all the oil that is exported through Būtingė comes from Russia.

Lithuania's rivers have the potential to generate electricity. Major power plants include a hydroelectric station on the Neman River and a thermal station at the town of Elektrėnai. After 1961 the country's power system became part of the unified network that also served the northwestern U.S.S.R. Upon entering the EU in 2004, Lithuania agreed to close its Soviet-era nuclear facility at Ignalina. The facility, which had been the country's only nuclear power plant as well as its largest domestic source of electricity, ceased operations in 2009.

MANUFACTURING

During the Soviet period Lithuanian economic policy emphasized manufacturing. After World War II the country's machinery, shipbuilding, electronic, electrical and radio engineering, chemical, cement, and fish-processing industries were overhauled. Traditional industries such as food processing and various branches of light industry also expanded significantly. Following independence in 1991, the textile, chemical, and food-processing sectors were the first to adapt to new market conditions. The manufacturing of communications equipment became a dominant economic activity. By the late 1990s much of Lithuania's manufacturing sector had been privatized.

FINANCE

The national currency, the litas, was introduced to Lithuania in 1922 and was restored in 1993. (During Soviet occupation Lithuania used the Russian ruble as its currency.) The litas is issued by the Bank of Lithuania, the country's central bank. All state-owned banks in Lithuania had been privatized by 2002. A stock exchange opened in Vilnius in 1993.

TRADE

Lithuania's chief trading partners include Russia, Latvia, Germany, Poland, Estonia, the Netherlands, and France. Imports include crude petroleum, machinery, foodstuffs, chemical products, and metals. Lithuania exports refined petroleum, foodstuffs, machinery, textiles, and transport equipment (mainly automotive parts).

SERVICES

By the early 21st century the service sector was the largest component of the Lithuanian economy, employing about half the workforce and contributing about two-fifths of the annual GNP. Tourism has grown in importance, and popular attractions in Lithuania include the Baroque-, Renaissance-, and Gothic-style mansions and castles in the historic centres of Vilnius, Kaunas, Klaipėda, and Kėdainiai, as well as in the former capitals of Kernavė and Trakai. The Kernavė archaeological site in eastern Lithuania, which dates from the Middle Ages, encompasses forts, settlements, and other historical monuments. It was designated a UNESCO World Heritage site in 2004. The countryside's lakes and forests, and the Baltic coastline's dune-covered Curonian Spit, which was added to the World Heritage list in 2000, are popular recreational areas.

LABOUR AND TAXATION

Lithuanians' salaries have generally been lower than those of workers in other EU member countries. For this reason, and because of high income taxes, many Lithuanian nationals were motivated to seek work in other EU countries after Lithuania joined the EU in 2004. Some of these emigrants started to return in 2007, however, when the government reduced income taxes and raised the minimum wage. Nearly half the women are economically active; however, employer discrimination against women has been a problem.

TRANSPORTATION AND TELECOMMUNICATIONS

Lithuania's geographic location has created favourable conditions for transit development. Railways are the main means of transport in Lithuania. Two major rail routes run through Lithuania— a north-south highway that connects Scandinavia with central Europe, as well as an east-west route linking Lithuania to the rest of Europe. Moreover, after

KLAIPĖDA

The Lithuanian city and port of Klaipeda (German: Memel) lies on the narrow channel by which the Curonian Lagoon and the Neman River connect with the Baltic Sea. Beside a small earlier settlement, the local population constructed a fortress in the early 13th century. In 1252 this fort was seized and destroyed by the Teutonic Knights, who built a new fortress called Memelburg. The town, later called Memel, and the adjacent territory were settled by Germans and formed part of the province of East Prussia. In 1923 Memel was given to Lithuania and renamed Klaipeda. The ice-free port expanded considerably and handled most of Lithuania's foreign trade. Ceded back to Germany in 1939, it passed to the U.S.S.R. from 1945 to 1991, at which time Lithuania became independent.

Modern-day Klaipeda has major shipbuilding and repair yards specializing in trawlers and floating docks. It is the base of a large deep-sea fishing fleet and has a fish cannery. Other industries include cotton textiles, pulp and papermaking, timber working, and the production of radio and telephone parts and amber jewelry. Klaipeda has become an increasingly popular tourist destination by virtue of its proximity to the white sand beaches of the Baltic coast. Lithuania's most popular coastal resort, Palanga, is nearby.

independence Lithuania emerged as a critical land bridge to Kaliningrad oblast, the region of the Russian Federation on the Baltic coast. A major rail route between Russia and the Kaliningrad region passes through Lithuania.

Sea transport is an important sector, with freight transportation showing a rapid increase since World War II. Klaipėda is the country's largest and most important port. River transport also is significant, and the country's hundreds of miles of waterways, which are navigable year-round, are used for internal shipping. Kaunas is a chief inland port.

Lithuania has international airports at Vilnius, Kaunas, and Palanga. Vilnius is the main air transportation centre, with links to many foreign cities. The independent Lithuanian Airlines began operating in 1991.

Lithuania's telecommunications sector is privatized. Fixed-line telephone use has decreased in Lithuania, but new technologies have been adopted quickly. The degree of cellular phone penetration is among the highest in the EU, and many Lithuanians have access to the Internet through their mobile phones

CHAPTER 13

LITHUANIAN GOVERNMENT AND SOCIETY

Lithuania's current constitution was approved by national referendum in 1992. The Republic of Lithuania, formerly the Lithuanian Soviet Socialist Republic, is administered by a president and a legislature, the Seimas, under a parliamentary system. The Seimas consists of 141 members, who are elected to four-year terms. The prime minister, formally appointed by the president, oversees the country's day-to-day affairs and is generally the leader of the Seimas's majority party. The president is popularly elected for a five-year term (with a maximum of two consecutive terms).

LOCAL GOVERNMENT

Lithuania is divided into *apskritys* (counties), which are then divided into *rajonas* (districts). The districts are further divided into *savivalbyde* (regional towns, urban settlements, and localities). The governor of each county is appointed by the national government. The districts are self-governing and elect local councils, which in turn elect the mayors.

JUSTICE AND SECURITY

Lithuania's judicial system is headed by a Supreme Court and a Constitutional Court, whose judges are selected by the parliament. There are also district and local courts whose judges are appointed by the president for five-year terms. Lithuania has an army, navy, and air force. Military service is mandatory for men and women ages 19 to 45 for one year and voluntary at age 18.

Map of Lithuania. Encyclopædia Britannica, Inc.

POLITICAL PROCESS

All Lithuanians age 18 and older are eligible to vote. During the Soviet period the Lithuanian Communist Party (Lietuvos Komunistu Partija; LKP) was the country's only political party. Its members and candidates for membership were supported by the activities of the Komsomol youth movement. In 1989, however, the legislature ended the Communist Party's monopoly on power by legalizing other political parties. The LKP began to lose power in

KOMSOMOL

The Komsomol (Russian abbreviation of Vsesoyuzny Leninsky Kommunistichesky Soyuz Molodyozhi; English: All-Union Leninist Communist League of Youth) was an organization for young people aged 14 to 28 in the Soviet Union that was primarily a political organ for spreading Communist teachings and preparing future members of the Communist Party. Closely associated with this organization were the Pioneers (All-Union Lenin Pioneer Organization, established in 1922), for ages 9 to 14, and the Little Octobrists, for the very young.

The Komsomol was organized in 1918 in order to band together various youth organizations that had previously been involved in the Russian Revolution; many of these groups had fought in the Civil War. When the military phase ended, a new purpose was set in 1922—to engage the members in health activities, sports, education, publishing activities, and various service and industrial projects. Komsomol membership reached a maximum of about 40 million in the 1970s and early '80s. In Soviet society, its members were frequently favoured over nonmembers in matters of employment and scholarships. Active participation in the Komsomol was also considered an important factor in gaining membership and eventual leadership positions in the Communist Party. All Komsomol cells were federated at levels paralleling those of the party. Reflecting the collapse of communism in the Soviet Union, the Komsomol disbanded in 1991.

Both the Pioneers and the Octobrists were preparatory organizations for providing politically directed education and recreation to children ultimately destined for Komsomol membership. The Pioneers were organized into brigades, each attached to a local Komsomol cell.

spite of the fact that it voted to disassociate itself from the Communist Party of the Soviet Union. In August 1991 the Lithuanian legislature voted to remove legal rights from the party and to seize its property.

The political landscape in the early 1990s was complex. Factionalism was predominant, and coalition governments were the norm. The principal political parties after independence were the Lithuanian Reform Movement (Sąjūdis) and the Lithuanian Democratic Labour Party (Lietuvos Demokratinė Darbo Partija; LDDP), which broke away from the Communist Party of Lithuania. The role of national minorities, especially the Poles, further complicated the political arena. By the early 21st century dozens of parties and coalitions had formed. The Homeland Union (Tėvynės Sąjunga; TS), which became one of the country's largest political parties in the early 21st century, was founded in 1993 as a successor to the Lithuanian independence movement.

Other parties include the Labour Party (Darbo Partija; DP), which advocates for workers' rights, and the Lithuanian Social Democratic Party (Lietuvos

Socialdemokratų Partija; LSDP), which supports the nationalization of industry, higher taxes for the wealthy, and increased rights for labour unions. There are other parties representing minority groups, nationalists, conservatives, and other interests.

HEALTH AND WELFARE

Lithuania has significantly improved its social service system since independence. The government provides free medical care to Lithuanian nationals as well as a range of ancillary services, including pension payments and funding for kindergartens and day care.

EDUCATION

A new national educational system was introduced in 1990. Primary and secondary education is free and compulsory beginning at age six. More than nine-tenths of the population age 15 and older are literate. Notable institutions of higher education include Vilnius University (1579), Vytautas Magnus University (founded 1922; reopened 1989) in Kaunas, Vilnius Gediminas Technical University (1956), and the Lithuanian Academy of Music and Theatre (1933), which specializes in music, theatre, and multi-media arts. The Lithuanian Academy of Sciences was founded in 1941.

CHAPTER 14

LITHUANIAN CULTURAL LIFE

In Lithuania there is a high level of interest in various aspects of cultural life. In spite of modern influences, Lithuanian folklore continues to be a significant part of national heritage. Lithuanian songs and a remarkable collection of fairy tales, legends, proverbs, and aphorisms have roots deep in a language and culture that are among the oldest in Europe. In the 20th century, however, war and Soviet occupation stifled the works of many Lithuanian artists, writers, poets, and playwrights.

DAILY LIFE AND SOCIAL CUSTOMS

As a predominantly Roman Catholic country, Lithuania celebrates all the major Christian holidays. The traditional Christmas Eve feast consists of 12 vegetarian dishes served on a straw-covered table, meat being saved for Christmas Day. Cabbages and potatoes form a considerable part of the Lithuanian diet, as do dairy products. Traditional dishes include *cepelinai*, a large, zeppelin-shaped, stuffed potato dumpling; cabbage rolls; cold beet soup; and potato pancakes.

THE ARTS

Lithuanian folk art is mainly embodied in ceramics, leatherwork, wood carving, and textiles; its colouring and its original geometric or floral patterns are characteristic features. Lithuanian drawing, noted for the use of natural colour and a highly refined technique, has won international acclaim. The Vilnius Drawing School, founded in 1866, has had a strong influence on the country's fine arts traditions. The composer and painter Mikalojus Konstantinas Čiurlionis, considered one of Lithuania's most outstanding artists of the early 20th century, was actively involved with the school. Moreover, some of the Lithuanian artists who opposed Soviet ideological constraints produced theatre and art of lasting significance. After the second Soviet occupation in 1944, many Lithuanian artists emigrated and founded art galleries and schools, mainly in other parts of Europe and in North America.

Lithuania's musical traditions did not develop until the late 19th century. From 1918 to 1940 cultural societies, choirs, and orchestras were formed. In 1924 the first all-Lithuanian song festival was held in Kaunas. Romantic songs combined with Lithuanian folk music became a popular style. One of the most well-known composers and the founder of the Kaunas Conservatory (1933), Lithuania's first university-level music school, was Juozas Gruodis. Lithuanians are especially

VINCAS KRĖVĖ-MICKIEVIČIUS

The Lithuanian poet, philologist, and playwright Vincas KreveMickievicius (born October 19, 1882, Subartonys, Russian Lithuania—died July 7, 1954, Broomall, Pennsylvania, U.S.) was known for his mastery of style. His talent gave him a foremost place in Lithuanian literature.

After serving as Lithuanian consul in Azerbaijan, Kreve became professor of Slavonic languages and literature in Kaunas (1922–39) and later in Vilnius. He went into exile in 1944, shortened his name to Vincas Kreve, and from 1947 was professor at the University of Pennsylvania.

Kreve became internationally known by his collection of Lithuanian folk songs (*Dainos*). National feeling suppressed by foreign rule found expression in his plays and won him great popularity among Lithuanians. *Šarūnas, Dainavos kunigaikštis* (1912; "Sharunas, Prince of Dainava"), *Skirgaila* (1925; "Prince Skirgaila"), *Likimo keliais* (1926–29; "Along the Paths of Destiny"), and *Karaliaus Mindaugo mirtis* (1935; "The Death of King Mindaugas") have a romantic view of the past; but he was also a realistic observer with a deep understanding of human nature, as is shown in his village drama *Žentas* (1921; "The Son-in-Law") and in his short stories—particularly those contained in *Sutemose* (1921; "Twilight") or *Po šiaudine pastoge* (1922–23; "Under a Thatched Roof"). He also adapted Lithuanian legends in *Dainavos šalies senu žmoniu padavimai* (1912; "Legends of the Old People of Dainava") and themes from Oriental legends in *Rytu pasakos* (1930; "Tales of the Orient"). Among his last works, *Dangaus ir žemes sūnus* (1949; "The Sons of Heaven and Earth") shows great power of expression in portraying Hebrew life in Herod's time.

proud of their sutartinės, an ancient and unique form of typically two- and three-voiced polyphony notable for its parallel seconds. Song and dance festivals are held every summer throughout the country. Vilnius hosts the National Song and Dance Festival, the International M.K. Čiurlionis Piano and Organ Competition, and the International Balys Dvarionas Competition for Young Pianists and Violinists. Music festivals are also held in Šiauliai, Birštonas, and Panevėžys. Jazz has a strong following, and many jazz clubs can be found in Vilnius.

Until the 18th century most Lithuanian literature was religious in nature. During the 19th century there arose a new movement to create a Lithuanian literary language and foster interest in the early history of the country. The literature of this era sought to rally Lithuanians against the political control of Russia and the cultural influence of Poland. Following independence in 1918, writers began to concentrate on developing national culture and a greater degree of sophistication in literature. Foremost among this group was Vincas Krėvė-Mickievičius, a novelist and dramatist who often used traditional folk songs and legends in his works, and he is regarded by many as one of the greatest Lithuanian writers.

CULTURAL INSTITUTIONS

The Lithuanian National Opera and Ballet (1920) in Vilnius is of international renown. Museums of note include the National Museum of Lithuania in Vilnius, the Trakai Historical Museum (featuring artifacts discovered at the island castle at Trakai), and a war museum in Kaunas dedicated to Vytautas the Great. The Mikalojus Konstantinas Čiurlionis National Art Museum, also in Kaunas, displays the works of the distinguished artist, as well as Lithuanian folk art and other national art. The open-air Rumšiškės Museum of Folk Art, located between Kaunas and Vilnius, includes re-created villages depicting 19th-century Lithuanian life in different regions of the country. Martynas Mažvydas National Library of Lithuania in Vilnius (founded 1919) includes documents dating from the 15th century. Vilnius University's Yiddish Institute (founded 2001) was created to preserve and enrich Yiddish and East European Jewish culture.

SPORTS AND RECREATION

Football (soccer) is Lithuania's most popular sport, and the country boasts several professional leagues. Basketball has grown in popularity, and Lithuania's team has excelled in international competitions. Several of the country's leading players, including Žydrūnas Ilgauskas, Šarunas Marciulionis, and Arvydas Sabonis, have plied their trade in North America's National Basketball Association. Cross-country skiing, ice skating, ice hockey, and ice fishing on

Curonian Lagoon are favourite winter pastimes. Bicycling and canoeing are popular in the summer.

Lithuania's first Olympic appearance was at the 1924 Winter Games in Chamonix, France. After World War II, Lithuanian athletes competed for the Soviet Olympic team. Lithuania was able to again contend as an independent country at the 1992 Olympic Games in Barcelona. Lithuanian discus throwers have been especially successful in Olympic competition, including gold medalists Romas Ubartas (1992) and Virgilijus Alekna (2000, 2004). Lithuania has also fared well in Olympic basketball.

MEDIA AND PUBLISHING

Prior to independence the media were state-owned and controlled by the Communist Party, mainly through state censors. Media censorship was abolished in 1989, and much of the media flourished as the economy became more liberalized. By the 21st century all newspapers were privately owned, though the Lithuanian Telegraph Agency (ELTA), a wire service that serves the local media in Lithuanian and Russian, was state-owned. Several daily newspapers are published in Vilnius, including *Lietuvos Rytas* ("Lithuania's Morning," also published in Russian), *Kurier Wileński* ("Vilnius Courier," published in Polish), and *Lietuvos Aidas* ("Echo of Lithuania," also published in Russian). There are no government-owned newspapers. Both radio and television stations are a mixture of private and state-owned. The languages of broadcast for both media are Lithuanian, Russian, Polish, Belarusian, and Ukrainian, and there are also some Yiddish radio broadcasts.

CHAPTER 15

LITHUANIA: PAST AND PRESENT

Lithuanians are an Indo-European people belonging to the Baltic group. They are the only branch within the group that managed to create a state entity in premodern times. The Prussians, overrun by the Teutonic Order in the 13th century, became extinct by the 18th century. The Latvians to the north were conquered during the first three decades of the 13th century by the Order of the Brothers of the Sword (this order became a branch of the Teutonic Order in 1237). The Lithuanians, protected by a dense primeval forest and extensive marshland, successfully resisted German pressure. Samogitia (Lithuanian: Žemaitija), lying between Prussia and Livonia, two lands already in the hands of the German Crusading knights, was a particular object of German expansion.

The German threat induced the Lithuanian tribes to unite in the middle of the 13th century under Mindaugas. He and his family were baptized in 1251, and two years later he was accepted into the feudal hierarchy of Europe by being crowned king of Lithuania by authority of Pope Innocent IV. Mindaugas, who had reverted to paganism, and two of his sons were assassinated in 1263. The Lithuanians retained their naturalistic pagan religion until the late 14th century.

Traidenis, ruler from 1270 to 1282, was probably the founder of the dynasty named after Gediminas, who began to rule about 1315. Although Lithuanian expansion to the east and south into the area of modern Belarus and Ukraine had begun after the destruction of the Kiev realm, it was Gediminas who systematically carved out the empire that was historic

MINDAUGAS

The Lithuanian ruler Mindaugas (Polish: Mendog, or Mindowe; Russian: Mendovg; died 1263) is considered the founder of the Lithuanian state. He was also the first Lithuanian ruler to become a Christian.

Mindaugas successfully asserted himself over other leading Lithuanian nobles and tribal chiefs, including his brother and his nephews, in 1236. The state thus formed under his leadership included Lithuania proper, Samogitia, and much of Belorussia. In 1251 Mindaugas accepted baptism from the Livonian Knights, thus easing western pressure against his state from the Teutonic and Livonian Knights and from Daniel of Halich-Volynia. In 1253 he received a royal crown from Pope Innocent IV. With the west for a time stabilized, Mindaugas continued his eastern expansion into Russian lands, which he had begun in the 1230s. His efforts led to the incorporation of much Russian territory into Lithuania at the expense of Russia's Mongol subjugators. Indeed, Mindaugas' campaigns in the east checked a Mongol drive toward the Baltic.

Mindaugas turned his attention to the west again in the late 1250s, when the Livonian Knights encroached on Samogitia, causing a local revolt. Mindaugas unofficially supported the Samogitians and reverted to paganism. In 1263 he and two of his sons were murdered by a group of Samogitian rivals.

Lithuania, a wide region inhabited by Lithuanians and East Slavs. As his letters from 1323 indicate, Vilnius was by then the capital. At Gediminas' death in 1341 or 1342, Lithuania's frontiers extended across the upper Dvina in the northeast to the Dnieper in the southeast and the Pripet (Prypyat) Marshes in the south. The Lithuanians were not sufficiently numerous for colonization. Control was maintained through undoubted political talent and a spirit of religious tolerance. The ruling Lithuanian warrior caste intermarried extensively with the ruling princely families of the subject East Slav principalities and accepted Orthodoxy.

Gediminas divided his empire among his seven sons. After a brief period of internecine strife, a diarchy of two remained: Algirdas, with his capital in Vilnius, assumed the title of Great Prince and dealt with eastern affairs; Kęstutis, whose capital was the island castle at Trakai, dealt with the threat from the Teutonic Order. Upon his death in 1377, Algirdas left his eldest son, Jogaila, an expanded empire in the east, which after 1362 included Kiev. Relations between Jogaila and his uncle Kęstutis, however, were inimical. In 1381 Kęstutis drove Jogaila from Vilnius and assumed the title of Great Prince. In the following year fortune changed. Jogaila captured Kęstutis and his eldest son, Vytautas. Kęstutis was imprisoned and killed, but Vytautas escaped and found sanctuary among the Teutonic Order, which hoped to utilize him as its vassal. The German threat had increased significantly. Jogaila had tried to stem the tide in 1382 by granting all of Samogitia up to the Dubysa River to the order. The extended ruling family of Lithuania was split. Those of Jogaila's brothers who ruled in the East Slav regions of the realm counseled alliance with Moscow, including acceptance of Orthodox Christianity. Those in the core lands of the state favoured an alliance with Poland and acceptance of Roman Christianity.

UNION WITH POLAND

Jogaila chose the latter course. On August 14, 1385, he concluded an agreement to join his realm with Poland in return for marriage to the 12-year-old Polish queen Jadwiga and assumption of the Polish throne as king. The agreement was effected early in the following year. In 1387 Jogaila formally introduced Roman Christianity among his Lithuanian-speaking subjects. Newly baptized nobles were granted extensive privileges. Their status was officially patterned on the feudal social structure prevalent in Western Christendom. In 1392 a reconciliation took place between Jogaila and Vytautas, who returned as ruler of Lithuania. The baptism of the Lithuanians removed the basis for the existence of the Teutonic Order, which had officially been founded to defend Christianity. Its stature was considerably reduced after a defeat on July 15, 1410, at Grünwald (Tannenberg) at the

hands of a joint Polish-Lithuanian army. The battle signaled a decisive ebb of the German threat.

The Lithuanian state reached its apogee during the rule of Vytautas, called the Great, who died in 1430. The realm extended from the Baltic Sea south to the shores of the Black Sea and east almost to Mozhaisk, some 100 miles west of Moscow. The Teutonic Order was no longer menacing, but a new threat from the east appeared. In 1480 Ivan III, Grand Prince of Moscow, assumed the title of sovereign of all the Russes. In effect he laid claim to all the lands of the old Kievan state. Most of these, including Kiev itself, were part of the Lithuanian realm.

The struggle with Moscow continued over the next two centuries. Until 1569 the union of Lithuania and Poland remained a loose alliance by virtue of a common ruler. On July 1, 1569, a common Polish-Lithuanian parliament meeting in Lublin transformed the loose personal union of the two states into a Commonwealth of Two Peoples. While Poland and Lithuania would thereafter elect a joint sovereign and have a common parliament, the basic dual state structure was retained. Each continued to be administered separately and had its own law codes and armed forces. The joint commonwealth, however, provided an impetus for cultural Polonization of the Lithuanian nobility. By the end of the 17th century it had virtually become indistinguishable from its Polish counterpart. The peasantry, however, retained the old language.

VYTAUTAS THE GREAT

The Lithuanian state reached its zenith under Vytautas the Great (born 1350, Lithuania—died October 27, 1430, Trakai, Lithuania), who consolidated his country's possessions, helped to build up a national consciousness, and broke the power of the Teutonic Knights. Vytautas the Great (Lithuanian: Vytautus Didysis; Polish: Witold Wielki) also exercised great power over Poland.

Vytautas was the son of Kęstutis, who for years had waged a struggle with his brother Algirdas for control of Lithuania. The conflict between the two branches of the family continued into the next generation, as Vytautas vied with Algirdas' son Jogaila. Both Vytautas and his father were captured by Jogaila in 1382 and Kęstutis was murdered while a prisoner. Vytautas, however, escaped and two years later was able to make peace with Jogaila, who returned to Vytautas the family lands seized earlier. In an effort to consolidate his position and widen his power, Jogaila married the 12-year-old Polish queen Jadwiga and was crowned king of Poland in Kraków on February 15, 1386, as Władysław II Jagiełło.

Vytautas then waged an intermittent struggle for power with Jogaila and on occasion sought further assistance from the Teutonic Order. Vytautas' popularity grew until his cousin was forced to adopt a conciliatory position. Jogaila offered to make Vytautas his vice regent over all of Lithuania. The offer was accepted, and in August 1392 a formal compact was signed. As time was to show, Vytautas by this act became supreme ruler of Lithuania in fact if not in law.

Vytautas began his rule by subduing and banishing rebellious and ineffective nobles and trying to conquer the Mongols in the east. His forces, however, were defeated by the Mongols in the Battle of the Vorskla River in present-day Russia on August 12, 1399.

In this same period, union between Poland and Lithuania was proclaimed in a treaty concluded at Vilnius in January 1401. Under the terms of the treaty, the Lithuanian boyars promised that in the event of Vytautas' death they would recognize Jogaila as grand prince of Lithuania, and the Polish nobility agreed that if Jogaila died they would not elect a new king without consulting Vytautas.

Vytautas and Jogaila then turned their attention westward, and there followed a series of wars with the Teutonic Order, which recognized Švitrigaila (Swidrygiełło), a brother of Jogaila, as grand prince of Lithuania. Vytautas was able to drive Švidrigaila out of the country, but the Teutonic Order was able to retain control of a portion of Lithuania. Early in 1409 Vytautas concluded a treaty with Jogaila for a combined attack on the Order, and on June 24, 1410, the Polish-Lithuanian forces crossed the Prussian frontier. In the Battle of Grunwald (Tannenberg) on July 15, 1410, the Teutonic Knights suffered a blow from which they never recovered. German supremacy in the Baltic area was broken and Poland-Lithuania began to be regarded in the West as a great power.

In 1429 Vytautas revived his claim to the Lithuanian crown, and Jogaila reluctantly consented to his cousin's coronation as king, but before the ceremony could take place Vytautas died.

RUSSIAN RULE

During the 18th century, the Polish-Lithuanian Commonwealth declined as a political power. Attempts at reform triggered foreign intervention. Following three partitions, the old state ceased to exist. During the first two partitions, in 1772 and 1793, Lithuania lost only lands inhabited by East Slavs. The Third Partition (1795) resulted in a division of the land inhabited by ethnic Lithuanians. The bulk of it went to Russia. However, lands southwest of the Nemunas River were annexed by the Kingdom of Prussia. This region was incorporated in the Grand Duchy of Warsaw established by Napoleon in 1807. In 1815, at the Congress of Vienna, the duchy became the Kingdom of Poland and was placed under Russian rule, although as a separate political entity. As a result, this region of Lithuania retained the separate administrative and judicial system introduced under French rule. These changes, including the abolition of serfdom, were significant and made the region distinct from the rest of the Lithuanian lands.

The uprisings of 1830–31 and 1863 in Poland found resonance in the Lithuanian lands. The suppression was particularly harsh after the second revolt. Both insurrections were followed by waves of Russification. The tsarist government treated the Northwest Region—as historic Lithuania, apart from the southeastern lands, was called after 1832—as an integral part of Russia. In 1832 the University of Vilnius, founded in 1579, was closed. In 1840 the Lithuanian legal code, which dated back to the 16th century, was abolished. After the revolt of 1863 the policy of Russification was extended to all areas of public life. Russian was the only language sanctioned for public use, including education. Books and magazines in the Lithuanian language could be printed only in the Cyrillic (Russian) alphabet. Such cultural imperialism triggered an indigenous reaction that fueled a national renaissance. An informal system of Lithuanian "schools of the hearth" in the villages was organized. Books in the Cyrillic alphabet were boycotted, while Lithuanian publications in the Latin script, printed mostly across the German border in neighbouring East Prussia, were smuggled into the country in large numbers.

A liberalization occurred after the Russian Revolution of 1905. The press prohibition had been annulled in 1904, allowing the appearance of the first Lithuanian daily newspaper, *Vilniaus žinios* ("Vilnius News"). On December 4–5, 1905, a congress of some 2,000 delegates was held in Vilnius. The congress demanded an autonomous political entity formed from the ethnic Lithuanian lands. Its frontiers were to be formed in accordance with the freely expressed wish of the inhabitants.

INDEPENDENCE

By late 1915 Lithuania had come under German military occupation. The goal of the German administration was to create a Lithuanian state that would be a satellite of Germany after the final peace treaty. It authorized a gathering in Vilnius, on September 18–22, 1917, of a congress of 214 Lithuanian delegates. The gathering called for an independent Lithuanian state within ethnic frontiers with Vilnius as its capital, and it elected a 20-member Taryba, or council. On February 16, 1918, the Taryba proclaimed an independent Lithuanian state.

The country remained under German occupation, however. The Germans began to withdraw after the armistice of November 11, 1918. The newly independent Lithuanian government was faced with an invasion by the Soviets from the east. On January 5, 1919, Vilnius was occupied by the Red Army, and a communist Lithuanian government was installed. The national government was evacuated to Kaunas. By mid-1919 the tide had turned, and the Russians were successfully pushed back east.

FOREIGN RELATIONS

Lithuania joined the League of Nations on September 22, 1921, as a recognized member of the international community of states. At that time, its frontiers had not been clearly established, and unresolved border questions characterized Lithuania's foreign relations throughout the interwar period. The problem of Vilnius and its surrounding region bedeviled Polish-Lithuanian relations.

Modern Lithuanian nationalism was based on a fusion of ethnicity and historic identity. Vilnius, the capital of the historic state, was a multiethnic city with a heavily Polish cultural veneer. Many in Poland, while not averse to Lithuania's claim, felt that Lithuania itself had historically become a part of a wider Polish cultural realm and sought to resurrect some form of the common political entity that had existed until 1795. On April 20, 1919, the Polish army took Vilnius from the Red Army and prevented the Lithuanians from reoccupying the city. The Western Allied powers then intervened and set up a line of demarcation between the Polish and Lithuanian forces, leaving Vilnius in Polish hands. In 1920 Lithuania concluded a peace treaty with Soviet Russia according to which Vilnius was recognized as Lithuanian. During the Polish-Russian war of 1920, Vilnius was occupied by the Red Army on July 14. The Lithuanians occupied it in the wake of the Soviet retreat a month later. A Polish-Lithuanian armistice signed in Suvalkai on September 5, 1920, left the city in Lithuanian hands. However, two days later, Polish forces overran the area in dispute and set up a government of Central Lithuania. Vilnius remained under Polish control and was formally annexed in 1922. Lithuania, however, refused to recognize the situation and continued to claim Vilnius and its surroundings.

The status of Klaipėda also presented problems. The city, Lithuania's sole potential outlet to the sea, had been part of Prussia and had never belonged to the historic Lithuanian state. Although the city itself was largely German in character, the surrounding countryside was largely populated by Lithuanians. The port was occupied by Allied forces after World War I. The Treaty of Versailles left its status undetermined. In January 1923 Lithuania occupied the territory. The following year an agreement was concluded with the Allied powers according to which Klaipėda became an autonomous part of Lithuania. Although Weimar Germany acceded to Lithuanian control of Klaipėda, the question resurfaced after Hitler's accession to power. Nazi propaganda agitated Germans to rise up against Lithuania.

Border problems figured prominently during the last two years of the independent interwar republic. In the wake of a frontier incident, a Polish ultimatum of March 17, 1938, demanded the establishment of diplomatic relations and normal interstate ties. Lithuania, which had refused to maintain relations with Poland because of the dispute over Vilnius, yielded. On March 21, 1939, Lithuania yielded to another ultimatum and ceded the port to Germany.

DOMESTIC POLICIES

The constitution adopted in 1922 set up a parliamentary democracy. The system proved dysfunctional. Frequent cabinet changes precluded stability. A coup d'état by a group of army officers in December 1926 introduced an authoritarian presidential system with restricted democracy that lasted until the Soviet occupation of 1940. Antanas Smetona, who had been the first president elected by the Taryba in 1918, was reinstated. All political parties were proscribed, except for the ruling Nationalist Union, which supported Smetona. In 1928 a new constitution formalized this state of affairs. On February 12, 1938, a third constitution was adopted, envisaging a gradual return to parliamentary institutions. Although the ban on political parties remained in force, a de facto coalition government representing a wide spectrum of political opinion was appointed. However, by the outbreak of World War II only minimal political change had been achieved.

INDEPENDENCE LOST

A secret protocol to the German-Soviet Nonaggression Pact of August 23, 1939, stipulated that, in the event of a territorial and political rearrangement in the Baltic region, the northern boundary of Lithuania should represent "the boundary of the sphere of influence of Germany and the U.S.S.R." When World War II began, Germany made a concerted effort to induce Lithuania to join in its attack on Poland, making it an ally and protégé. Lithuania opted for neutrality. A secret protocol to the German-Soviet boundary and friendship treaty of September 28, 1939, revised the earlier agreement and

ANTANAS SMETONA

In 1919 Lithuanian statesman and journalist Antanas Smetona (born August 10, 1874, Ukmergė District, Lithuania, Russian Empire—died January 9, 1944, Cleveland, Ohio, U.S.) became the first president of Lithuania. He later returned to power as an authoritarian head of state for the last 13 years of his country's independence.

After the Russian Revolution of 1905 broke out, Smetona, who had recently graduated from law school (1902), became editor of the first Lithuanian daily newspaper, *Vilniaus Žinios*, and of the Democratic Party's organ, *Lietuvos Žkininkas*; he was also elected to the presidium of the Vilnius Diet, which proclaimed Lithuanian autonomy within the Russian Empire (1905). Although the intensity of political activity declined after the revolution was suppressed, Smetona continued his journalistic career, editing the journal *Viltis* (1907–13) and founding *Vairas* (1913), which later became the organ of the Nationalist Party.

During the German military occupation of the country in World War I, Smetona was unanimously elected president (in September 1917) of the Lietuvos Taryba, or Council of Lithuania, and, after the Taryba proclaimed Lithuania's independence (1918), he served as provisional president of the republic (April 1919–June 1920). In 1921 he served as chairman of the Lithuanian delegation at Riga for the settlement of the Latvian–Lithuanian boundary dispute.

After the military coup d'état of December 16–17, 1926, organized by a right-wing Nationalist group and backed by the Christian Democrats, Smetona was again elected president of the Lithuanian Republic. He was reelected in 1931 and in 1938. On June 15, 1940, when Lithuania was occupied by Soviet forces, he fled to Germany and thence, in March 1941, to the United States.

placed most of Lithuania, with the exception of a small portion in the southwest, in the Soviet sphere of influence.

On October 10, 1939, the U.S.S.R. forced Lithuania to accept a treaty of mutual assistance. Lithuania was compelled to admit Soviet garrisons and air bases on its territory. In return Lithuania received Vilnius and surrounding areas that had been occupied by the Red Army during its attack on Poland. The territory formed about one-third of the area that Soviet Russia had recognized as Lithuanian according to the peace treaty of 1920 but that had been under Polish rule since 1920.

On June 15, 1940, the U.S.S.R. confronted Lithuania with an ultimatum demanding the immediate formation of a "friendly" government and the admission of unlimited numbers of Soviet troops to its territory. The same day, the country was occupied. President Smetona fled to Germany, though without resigning. In his absence, the prime minister, Antanas Merkys, in his capacity as acting president, appointed a left-wing journalist, Justas Paleckis, prime minister. Merkys himself resigned, making Paleckis act-ing president as well. The moves clearly violated the constitution. The following month, the new Soviet regime staged elections. On July 21, the newly "elected" people's parliament unanimously requested the incorporation of Lithuania into the Soviet Union. On August 3, 1940, the Supreme Soviet of the U.S.S.R. acceded to this request and declared Lithuania a constituent republic of the Soviet Union.

During the first year of occupation, Sovietization consisted primarily of remolding the old political, social, eco-nomic, and cultural structures into Soviet forms. A land reform was enacted, though its effect was limited, as the land reform of the 1920s had already to a large degree made the country one of agrarian smallholders. A relatively small number of the country's political elite were deported in July 1940, before incor-poration into the U.S.S.R. Large-scale deportations, affecting a wide cross sec-tion of the population, were initiated on the night of June 13–14, 1941. The move-ment was still under way at the time of the German attack a week later. It has been estimated that this wave of depor-tation affected some 35,000 people.

When Germany attacked the U.S.S.R. on June 22, 1941, an insurrection against Soviet rule broke out in Lithuania. On the first day, insurgents gained con-trol of Kaunas, then the capital, and set up a provisional government. Within a week the German army had overrun all of Lithuania. The Lithuanians hoped to reestablish independence in alliance with Germany. However, on July 28, 1941, an Ostland province, consisting of the three Baltic countries and Belorussia (now Belarus), was created. The Lithuanian provisional government refused to serve as administrative agent for the German occupation and disbanded. A German occupation regime was established, but it enjoyed only limited success in fulfilling the demands of the Reich. For three years manpower mobilization efforts were effectively thwarted. Human losses dur-ing the German occupation have been estimated at roughly 250,000. The bulk of these losses came from the Jewish community, which was almost entirely exterminated.

SOVIET REPUBLIC

By the end of 1944 most of Lithuania had been reoccupied by the Red Army. The first postwar decade was a period of extensive repression and Russification. An organized guerrilla resistance, at times involving up to 40,000 fighters, lasted into the early 1950s. Several waves of deportations to Siberia and Central Asia accompanied the collectivization of agriculture: about 70,000 people were deported in late 1947; 70,000 in May 1948; and some 80,000 in 1949. Cultural life stagnated under the imposition of rigid Stalinist norms.

During the thaw in the U.S.S.R. in the late 1950s and early '60s, the ruling

SAMIZDAT

From the 1950s until the early 1990s, a type of literature known as samizdat (from Russian *sam*, "self," and *izdatelstvo*, "publishing") was secretly written, copied, and circulated in the former Soviet Union. It was usually critical of practices of the Soviet government.

Samizdat began appearing following Joseph Stalin's death in 1953, largely as a revolt against official restrictions on the freedom of expression of major dissident Soviet authors. After the ouster of Nikita S. Khrushchev in 1964, samizdat publications expanded their focus beyond freedom of expression to a critique of many aspects of official Soviet policies and activities, including ideologies, culture, law, economic policy, historiography, and treatment of religions and ethnic minorities. Because of the government's strict monopoly on presses, photocopiers, and other such devices, samizdat publications typically took the form of carbon copies of type-written sheets and were passed by hand from reader to reader.

The major genres of samizdat included reports of dissident activities and other news suppressed by official media, protests addressed to the regime, transcripts of political trials, analysis of socioeconomic and cultural themes, and even pornography.

In its earliest days, samizdat was largely a product of the intelligentsia of Moscow and Leningrad. But it soon fomented analogous underground literatures throughout the constituent republics of the Soviet Union and among its many ethnic minorities.

From its inception, the samizdat movement and its contributors were subjected to surveillance and harassment by the KGB, the secret police. The suppression worsened in the early 1970s, at the height of samizdat activity. Culminating in a show trial of Pyotr Yakir and Victor Krasin in August 1973, the government's assault wounded the movement. But it survived, though reduced in numbers and deprived of many of its leaders.

Samizdat began to flourish again in the mid-1980s because of Soviet leader Mikhail Gorbachev's policy of *glasnost* ("openness"). KGB harassment virtually ceased, and as a result a variety of independent journals proliferated, though their readership remained tiny. By the late 1980s, the Soviet government had unofficially accepted samizdat, although it retained its monopoly on printing presses and other media outlets. Samizdat had almost disappeared by the early 1990s following the collapse of the Soviet Union and the emergence of media outlets that were largely independent of government control.

Lithuanian Communist Party, which had been disproportionately composed of immigrant officials, was slowly nativized and transformed into the political machine of the long-term (1936–74) first secretary Antanas Sniečkus. The relative liberalization coincided with the industrialization and urbanization of the country. The possibility of planning socioeconomic change at the local level precluded large-scale immigration of labour from outside the republic.

As a result, Lithuania remained ethnically largely homogeneous, with Lithuanians making up about 80 percent of the population in the early 1990s. The ideological reaction during the 1970s and early '80s failed to stem the development of national consciousness. An extensive dissident movement developed. During the 1970s Lithuania produced more per capita samizdat (unofficial and unsanctioned underground publications) than any other Soviet republic. The most prominent samizdat periodical, *The Chronicle of the Lithuanian Catholic Church*, which first appeared in 1972, outlasted the regime.

INDEPENDENCE RESTORED

The effort during the late 1980s to renovate the U.S.S.R. through *glasnost* ("openness") and *perestroika* ("restructuring") created a new political atmosphere. A mass reform movement, Sąjūdis ("Movement"), emerged in opposition. Elections in early 1990 resulted in a legislature that unanimously declared on March 11 the reestablishment of Lithuania's independence. Soviet reaction initially consisted of a largely ineffectual economic boycott during the spring and summer of 1990. An abortive effort to topple the independent government on January 13, 1991, ended in bloodshed. Political independence and international recognition were secured in the aftermath of the failed coup in Moscow in August 1991.

Lithuania held its first post-Soviet elections in 1992. The former Communist Party, which renamed itself the Lithuanian Democratic Labour Party (LDLP), won 73 of 141 seats. Despite its victory, the LDLP did not seek to reverse policies. Instead, the government liberalized the economy, joined the Council of Europe, became an associate member of the Western European Union, and pursued membership in the EU and the North Atlantic Treaty Organization (NATO).

Internal disagreements, charges of corruption, and economic recession led to a drop in the government's popularity in the mid-1990s. In 1996 the LDLP won only 12 seats and was replaced in government by a coalition between the Christian Democratic Party and the Centre Party. The new government sought to further liberalize the economy and to attract foreign capital. In 1998 Valdas Adamkus, who had been naturalized a U.S. citizen and who sought to curb corruption, was elected president.

Throughout the first half of the 1990s, Lithuania's economy had remained reliant on Russia and was hit by recession. By the late 1990s it had dramatically increased its share of trade with western Europe, and inflation—which had exceeded 1,000 percent in 1991—was reduced to less than 10 percent. Rolandas Paksas, leader of Lithuania's populist Liberal Democratic Party, defeated Adamkus in the 2003 presidential election. Paksas was impeached later that year, however, when the Constitutional Court ruled that he had violated the constitution on at

DALIA GRYBAUSKAITĖ

Lithuanian politician Dalia Grybauskaitė (born March 1, 1956, Vilnyus, U.S.S.R. [now Vilnius, Lithuania]) was elected president of Lithuania in 2009. She was the first woman to hold the post.

Grybauskaitė studied at Zdanov University, Leningrad (now St. Petersburg), and earned a doctorate in economics from the Moscow Academy of Public Sciences in 1988. From 1983 to 1990 she was a lecturer at the Communist Party's training college in Vilnius, and after Lithuania gained full independence in 1991, she held posts in the country's Ministry of International Economic Relations and Ministry of Foreign Affairs. After serving (1996–99) as the plenipotentiary minister at the Lithuanian embassy in the United States, she returned to Vilnius to assume the office of deputy finance minister and became Lithuania's chief negotiator with the IMF and the World Bank.

In 2000 Grybauskaitė was appointed deputy foreign affairs minister and took a leadership role within the delegation responsible for negotiating Lithuania's accession to the EU. From 2001 to 2004 she served as finance minister, and in that post she strongly supported privatization and liberalization efforts, among other reform measures. She also developed a reputation for toughness and blunt talk; numerous media outlets began calling her Lithuania's "Iron Lady," a reference to former British prime minister Margaret Thatcher, for whom Grybauskaitė had publicly expressed admiration. In 2004 Grybauskaitė was tapped to serve in Brussels as the European commissioner responsible for financial programming and budget; she was later selected the 2005 EU Commissioner of the Year. However, after the deepening global economic crisis helped spark violent protests in Vilnius in January 2009, Grybauskaitė left her EU post to run as an independent candidate in Lithuania's presidential election. Touting her extensive experience in finance and economics, she registered an overwhelming victory in May, capturing more than 69 percent of the vote to just under 12 percent for her nearest rival—the largest-ever margin of victory for a Lithuanian presidential candidate.

After taking office in July 2009, Grybauskaitė focused on lifting the country's economic fortunes. To this end, she sought to stimulate exports, cut public expenditures, work to efficiently implement EU aid, and offer tax relief to owners of small businesses. By 2011 the economy was showing some signs of recovery, though it continued to struggle

least three occasions (most notably, in granting citizenship to a Russian-born financial supporter). Moreover, members of Paksas' administration were linked to Russian organized crime. The chairman of the Seimas (legislature) became acting president, and Adamkus won a second term through a special presidential election held in 2004. That same year Lithuania gained full membership in both the EU and NATO, and its economic fortunes turned as European holidaymakers flocked to seaside resorts, including Palanga and Klaipėda.

By May 2008 the country's economy had begun to sour, and the European Commission rejected Lithuania's application to join the euro zone because of the country's high inflation. The ailing economy spurred violent protests in the capital, some of the worst since 1991. Running as an independent with the promise of change, Dalia Grybauskaitė, the EU budget commissioner, won the May 2009 presidential election with about 69 percent of the vote. The first woman in Lithuania to be elected president, Grybauskaitė promised to stimulate exports, implement EU aid, and provide tax breaks to owners of small businesses.

Relations with Russia continued to remain tense into the 21st century. In 2006 Russia ceased supplying Lithuania's main petroleum refinery and further refused to honour Lithuania's request for reparations for the Soviet Union's 50-year occupation of Lithuania. In 2008 Lithuania's parliament banned any public display of Soviet or Nazi symbols.

CHAPTER 16

POLAND: THE LAND AND ITS PEOPLE

The central European country of Poland is located at a geographic crossroads that links the forested lands of northwestern Europe to the sea lanes of the Atlantic Ocean and the fertile plains of the

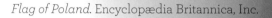

Flag of Poland. Encyclopædia Britannica, Inc.

Eurasian frontier. Irregularly circular in shape, it is bordered to the north by the Baltic Sea, to the northeast by Russia and Lithuania, to the east by Belarus and Ukraine, to the south by Slovakia and the Czech Republic, and to the west by Germany. Poland's capital is Warsaw.

RELIEF

The natural landscape of Poland can be divided broadly into three relief groups: the lowlands, the highlands, and the mountains. The eastern extremes of Poland display characteristics common to eastern Europe, but the rest of the country is linked to western Europe by structure, climate, and the character of its vegetation. The lowland characteristics predominate: the average elevation of the whole country is only 568 feet (173 m) above sea level, while more than three-fourths of the land lies below 650 feet (198 m).

Poland's relief was formed by the actions of Ice Age glaciers, which advanced and receded over the northern part of the country several times during the Pleistocene Epoch (from about 2,600,000 to 11,700 years ago). The great and often monotonous expanses of the Polish lowlands, part of the North European Plain, are composed of geologically

Physical map of Poland. Encyclopædia Britannica, Inc.

recent deposits that lie over a vast structural basin.

In the southern part of the country, by contrast, older and more diverse geologic formations are exposed. The

mountainous arc of the Carpathians, dating from the mountain-building Paleogene and Neogene periods (from about 65 to 2.6 million years ago), dominates the topography. Around the

BALTIC SEA

The Baltic Sea is an arm of the North Sea, and it is Russia's chief outlet to the Atlantic Ocean and the only outlet for Finland, Estonia, Latvia, Lithuania, and Poland. Sweden, Denmark, and Germany also use this waterway as a transportation route. The chief Baltic ports are Copenhagen, Denmark; Stockholm, Sweden; Helsinki, Finland; St. Petersburg, Russia; and Gdańsk, Poland.

The Baltic Sea is roughly finger-shaped, covering 149,000 square miles (386,000 square km) and extending northeastward along the Scandinavian peninsula to very near the Arctic Circle. The water of the Baltic is not very salty because many rivers drain into it. Since it is also shallow, with an average depth of 280 feet (85 m), it is more subject to freezing than is the deeper, saltier ocean. Many of its ports are blocked by ice in winter. In the north, large areas are frozen for three to five months each year.

Because of the relative freshness of the water, ocean fishes are not nearly as plentiful in the Baltic as they are in the North Sea.

Baltic Sea. Encyclopædia Britannica, Inc.

There are also fewer kinds. The Baltic cod are smaller compared with the cod found along the coasts of Norway. The Danish island of Falster has offshore oyster beds, and in summer crayfish and prawns are caught off the coast of southern Sweden. In the warmer waters of the southern Baltic, herring, cod, and a variety of flatfish are caught off the Polish and German coasts.

northern rim of the Carpathians lie a series of structural basins, separating the mountain belt proper from a much older structural mass, or foreland, that appears in the relief patterns of the region as the Bohemian Massif, the Sudeten, and the Little Poland Uplands (Wyżyna Małopolska).

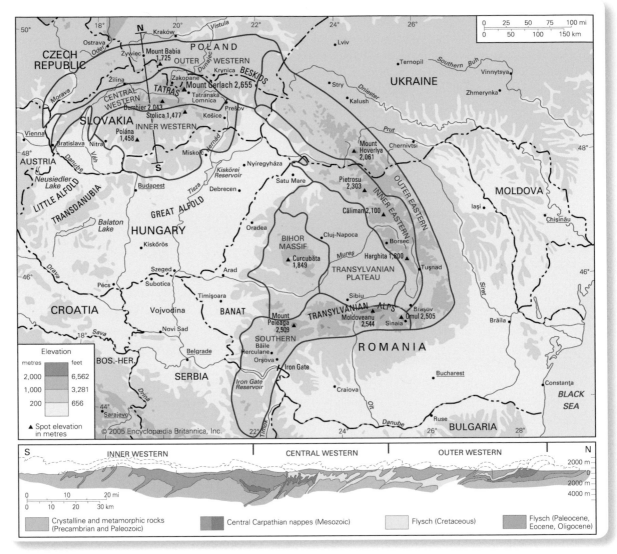

Regional division of the Carpathian Mountains (top) *and a geologic cross section of the Western Carpathians* (bottom). *The location of the cross section is shown by the line N–S on the map.* Encyclopædia Britannica, Inc.

The relief structure can be divided more specifically into a series of east-west–trending zones. To the north lie the swamps and dunes of the Baltic Sea coast; south of these is a belt of morainic terrain with thousands of lakes, the southern boundary of which marks the limit of the last ice sheet. The third zone consists of the central lowlands, whose minimal relief was created by streams issuing from the retreating glaciers. This zone is the Polish heartland, the site of agriculture in places where loess has been deposited over the relatively infertile fluvioglacial deposits. The fourth zone is made up of the older mountains and highlands to the south; though limited in extent, it offers spectacular scenery. Along the southern border of the country are the Sudeten and Carpathian ranges and their foothills.

THE COASTAL PLAIN

The Baltic Coastal Plain stretches across northern Poland from Germany to Russia, forming a low-lying region built of various sediments. It is largely occupied by the ancient province of Pomerania (Pomorze), the name of which means "along the sea." The scarcely indented Baltic coastline was formed by wave action after the retreat of the ice sheet and the raising of sea levels. The Pomeranian (Pomorska) Bay in the west and the Gulf of Gdańsk in the east are the two major inlets. In the southern portion of the former, two islands block off the Szczeciński Lagoon (Zalew Szczeciński), into which the Oder River discharges its waters. In the Gulf of Gdańsk, the Vistula (Wisła) River forms a large delta. Sandbars, on which the winds have created large dunes, line much of the coast, separating the coastal lakes and lagoons from the sea.

The main urban centres are the ports of Szczecin (German: Stettin) on the lower Oder and Gdańsk (German: Danzig) and Gdynia in the east. The central portion of the Baltic Coastal Plain is scantily populated—there are only small fishing ports, of which Kołobrzeg is the most important—and the landscape has a desolate beauty.

THE LAKE REGION AND CENTRAL LOWLANDS

The belt immediately to the south of the coastal plain is a varied landscape with lakes and hills of glacial origin. Wide river valleys divide the region into three parts: the Pomeranian Lakeland (Pojezierze Pomorskie); the Masurian (Mazurskie) Lakeland, east of the lower Vistula; and the Great Poland (Wielkopolskie) Lakeland. The larger settlements and the main communications routes of this zone lie in and along the river valleys; the remainder of the area is mostly wooded and thinly populated. Only the eastern portion of the Great Poland Lakeland has a developed agriculture.

The extensive central lowlands contain isolated relief features shaped by the oldest glaciations, but their character is generally flat and monotonous. The postglacial lakes have long since been filled in, and glacial outwash masks the weakly developed meltwater valley channels. The basins of the main rivers divide the area into the Silesian (Śląska) Lowland, which lies in the upper Oder; the southern Great Poland Lowland, which lies in the middle Warta River basin; and the Mazovian (Mazowiecka) and Podlasian

(Podlaska) lowlands, which lie in the middle Vistula basin. Lower Silesia and Great Poland are important agricultural areas, but many parts of the central lowlands also have large industrial centres. Warsaw, the capital, situated on the middle Vistula, is the most prominent.

THE LITTLE POLAND UPLANDS

South of the central lowlands, the Little Poland Uplands extend from east to west, but they are folded transversely. In the west is the Silesian-Kraków upthrust, with rich deposits of coal. The ancient rocks of the Świętokrzyskie ("Holy Cross") Mountains, which reach a maximum elevation of 2,008 feet (612 m), form a second upthrust. Between these two regions lies the Nida River basin, with an average height of 650 to 1,000 feet (198 to 305 m). East of the Świętokrzyskie Mountains, the uplands are cut by the valley of the Vistula, beyond which lie the Lublin (Lubelska) Uplands. In the south occur patches of loess on which fertile brown- and black-earth soils have developed.

The older geologic regions contain valuable minerals; in the Silesian-Kraków uplands there are coal, iron, zinc, and lead deposits. These mineral resources have made possible the rise of Poland's most important industrial region, and the landscape of Upper Silesia is highly urbanized. Katowice is the largest centre, and the region is closely linked with that around Kraków (Cracow). The Little Poland Uplands protect the Little Poland Lowlands, in which Kraków lies, from the colder air of the north. To the north the Staropolski ("Old Polish") Basin, situated in the foothills of the Świętokrzyskie Mountains, has a long history of industrial production. Kielce is the area's urban centre.

THE SUDETEN

The Sudeten and their foreland, part of the larger Bohemian Massif, have a long and complex geologic history. They owe their present rugged form, however, to earth movements that accompanied the Carpathian uplift, and the highest portion, the Karkonosze ("Giant Mountains"), reaches 5,256 feet (1,602 m) above sea level. The region contains rich mineral deposits, notably coking coal, which has occasioned the growth of an industrial centre around Wałbrzych. The region has many small towns. Resorts and spas are found in more-secluded areas. The foreland of the Sudeten, separated by a large fault from the larger mass, contains many granite quarries.

THE CARPATHIANS

The southernmost, and most scenic, portion of Poland embraces the Carpathian Mountains and their associated chains and basins, created in the Paleogene and Neogene periods. Within the Polish frontiers lie the Oświęcim and Sandomierz basins, a portion of the

Beskid Mountains, the Orawka-Podhale Basin, and the Tatra (Tatry) Mountains. The sub-Carpathian basins contain deposits of salt, sulfur, and natural gas and some petroleum. The region has a large rural population, but there are also many towns of medium size.

The highest peak of the Beskid Mountains, Mount Babia, reaches 5,659 feet (1,725 m); the Tatras, with a maximum elevation of 8,199 feet (2,499 m), are the highest portion of the Polish Carpathians. Zakopane, the largest tourist and resort centre in Poland, lies at

their feet. The Bieszczady Mountains—rolling, carpeted in beech woods, and sparsely inhabited—lie in the extreme southeast.

DRAINAGE AND SOILS

Virtually the entire area of Poland drains to the Baltic Sea, about half via the Vistula River and a third via the Oder River. Polish rivers experience two periods of high water each year. In spring, melted snow swells the lowland rivers. The presence of ice dams (which block

The Vistula, Poland's longest river, flows past the Old Town section of Warsaw. D.C. Williamson, London

the rivers for one to three months) and the fact that the thaw first strikes the upper reaches of the northward-flowing rivers intensify the effect. The summer rains bring a second maximum about the beginning of July.

VISTULA RIVER

The Vistula (Polish: Wisła) is the largest river of Poland and of the drainage basin of the Baltic Sea. With a length of 651 miles (1,047 km) and a drainage basin of some 75,100 square miles (194,500 sq km), it is a waterway of great importance to the countries of eastern Europe; more than 85 percent of the river's drainage basin, however, lies in Polish territory. The Vistula is connected with the Oder drainage area by the Bydgoszcz Canal. Eastward the Narew and Bug rivers and the Dnieper–Bug Canal link it with the vast inland waterway systems of Belarus, Ukraine, and Russia.

The Elbe, Oder, and Vistula river basins and their drainage network. Encyclopædia Britannica, Inc.

The source of the Vistula is found about 15 miles (24 km) south of Bielsko-Biała on the northern slopes of the western Beskid range, in southern Poland, at an elevation of 3,629 feet (1,106 m). It flows generally from south to north through the mountains and foothills of southern

Poland and across the lowland areas of the great North European Plain, ending in a delta estuary that enters the Baltic Sea near the port of Gdańsk. The average elevation of the Vistula basin is 590 feet (180 m)above sea level; the mean river gradient is 0.10 percent, and the mean velocity in the river channel amounts to 2.6 feet (.8 m) per second. In addition to Poland's capital city, Warsaw, a number of large towns and industrial centres lie on the banks of the Vistula. These include Kraków, which was Poland's capital from the 11th century to the close of the 16th, Nowa Huta, Sandomierz, Płock, Torun, Malbork, and Gdańsk. Numerous centres of tourism and recreation as well as many health resorts flank the Vistula valley. Here and there along the river rise the ruins of medieval strongholds, some of which have been restored.

There are some 9,300 Polish lakes with areas of more than 2.5 acres (1 hectare), and their total area is about 1,200 square miles (3,108 sq km), or 1 percent of the national territory. The majority, however, are found in the northern glaciated belt, where they occupy more than 10 percent of the surface area.

Polish soils are varied and without clearly marked regional types. The greatest area is covered by podzol and pseudopodzol types, followed by the less widely distributed brown-earth soils, which are richer in nutrients. In the south are extensive areas of fertile loess-based soils. The rendzinas, formed on limestone rocks, are a unique type. The alluvial soils of the river valleys and the peaty swamp soils found in the lake area and in poorly drained valleys are also distinctive.

CLIMATE

Varying types of air masses collide over Poland, influencing the character of both weather and climate. The major elements involved are oceanic air masses from the west, cold polar air from Scandinavia or Russia, and warmer, subtropical air from the south. A series of barometric depressions moves eastward along the polar front year-round, dividing the subtropical from the colder air and bringing to Poland, as to other parts of northern Europe, cloudy, wet days. In winter, polar-continental air often becomes dominant, bringing crisp, frosty weather, with still colder Arctic air following in its wake. Warm, dry, subtropical-continental air often brings pleasant days in late summer and autumn.

The overall climate of Poland has a transitional—and highly variable—character between maritime and continental types. Six seasons may be clearly distinguished: a snowy winter of one to three months; an early spring of one or two months, with alternating wintry and springlike conditions; a predominantly sunny spring; a warm summer with plenty of rain and sunshine; a sunny, warm autumn; and a foggy, humid period signifying the approach of winter. Sunshine reaches its maximum over the Baltic in summer and the Carpathians in winter, and mean annual temperatures range from 46 °F (8 °C) in the southwestern lowlands to 44 °F (7 °C) in the colder northeast. The climate of the mountains is determined by altitude.

The annual average precipitation is about 24 inches (610 mm), but in the mountains the figure approaches 31 to 47 inches (787 to 1,194 mm), dropping to about 18 inches (457 mm) in the central lowlands. In winter, snow makes up about half the total precipitation in the plains and almost all of it in the mountains.

PLANT AND ANIMAL LIFE

The vegetation of Poland that has developed since the last Ice Age consists of some 2,250 species of seed plants, 630 mosses, 200 liverworts, 1,200 lichens, and 1,500 fungi. Holarctic elements (i.e., those pertaining to the temperate belt of the Northern Hemisphere) are dominant among the seed plants.

The northeastern limits of certain trees—notably beech, fir, and the variety of oak known as pedunculate—run through Polish territory. There are few endemic species; the Polish larch (*Larix polonica*) and the Ojców birch (*Betula oycoviensis*) are two examples. Some relics of tundra vegetation have been preserved in the peat bogs and mountains. More than one-fourth of the country is wooded, with the majority set aside as public property. Poland lies in the zone of mixed forests, but in the southeast a fragment of the forest-steppe vegetation zone intrudes. In the northeast there are portions of the eastern European subtaiga, with spruce as a characteristic component. In the mountains the vegetation, like the climate, is determined by elevation. Fir and beech woods give way to the spruce of the upper woods, which in turn fade into subalpine, alpine, and snow-line vegetation.

Poland's animal life belongs to the European–West Siberian zoogeographic province, itself part of the Palearctic subregion, and is closely linked with the vegetation cover. Among the vertebrate fauna are nearly 400 species, including many types of mammals and more than 200 native birds. Deer and wild pigs roam the woods; elk inhabit the coniferous forests of the northeast; and steppe rodents, such as the brindled gopher, live in the south. Wildcats live in the mountain woods, and the chamois and marmot are found at the highest levels. Brown bears live in the Carpathian Mountains. The European bison, or wisent, which once roamed widely across the continent but became extinct in the wild following World War I, once again roams the great Białowieża Forest in national parks on both sides of the Polish-Belarusian border, having been reintroduced by using zoo-bred animals.

Rapid industrialization following World War II in Poland, as well as in neighbouring Czech Republic, Slovakia, and eastern Germany, severely polluted many areas of the country. By the late 20th century, the Polish Academy of Sciences had described Poland as one of the most polluted countries in the world. Upper Silesia and Kraków, in particular,

BIAŁOWIEŻA FOREST

The Białowieża Forest (also called Belovezhskaya Forest and Belovezh Forest; Belarusian: Byelavyezhskaya Pushcha; Polish: Puszcza Białowieska) is located in western Belarus and eastern Poland. One of the largest surviving areas of primeval mixed forest (pine, beech, oak, alder, and spruce) in Europe, it occupies more than 460 square miles (1,200 sq km). The Białowieża Forest is located near the headwaters of the Narev (Polish: Narew) and Lesnaya (Leśna) rivers, tributaries of the Bug.

The forest has a wide range of flora (some conifers and hardwoods have attained ages of 350 to 600 or more years and reached heights in excess of 150 feet [45 m], with diameters greater than 6 feet [2 m]) and fauna (including elk, deer, lynx, and wild boar) from both western and eastern Europe.

Once the hunting grounds of kings and tsars, the Białowieża is the oldest nature pre-

Bialowieza Forest. Encyclopædia Britannica, Inc.

serve in Europe. Both the Polish and Belarusian portions of the forest have become national parks, and both areas were designated as World Heritage sites (the Polish portion in 1979 and the Belarusian portion in 1992).

had suffered some of the highest levels of atmospheric and groundwater pollution in Europe. Several areas of central Poland, where cement is produced and brown coal (lignite) is burned, also were contaminated by air pollution.

The country's major rivers remain badly polluted by industrial and urban effluents, and Poland's cities and larger towns are major sources of pollution. Much higher levels of respiratory disease, abnormal pregnancy, and infant mortality have been reported in areas of environmental degradation. Pollution has also reduced crop yields and adversely affected tree growth in many

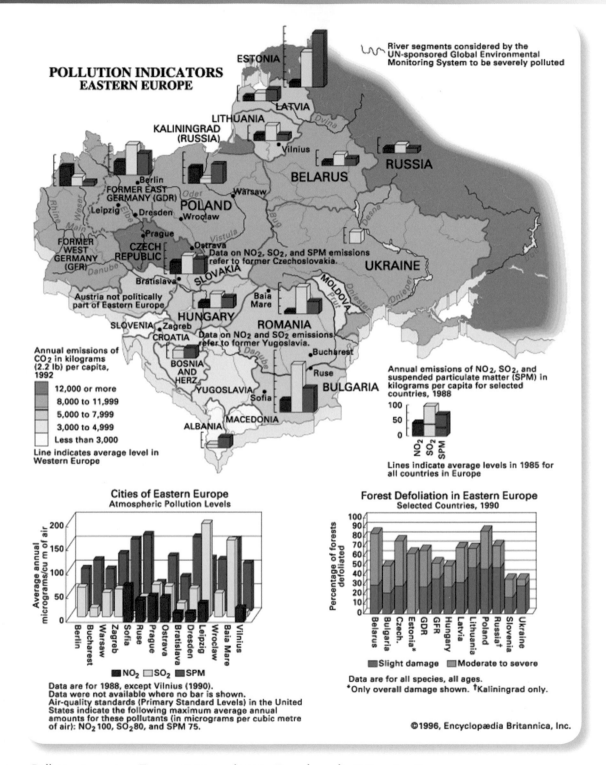

POLLUTION INDICATORS
EASTERN EUROPE

River segments considered by the UN-sponsored Global Environmental Monitoring System to be severely polluted

Data on NO₂, SO₂, and SPM emissions refer to former Czechoslovakia.

Austria not politically part of Eastern Europe

Data on NO₂ and SO₂ emissions refer to former Yugoslavia.

Annual emissions of CO₂ in kilograms (2.2 lb) per capita, 1992

- 12,000 or more
- 8,000 to 11,999
- 5,000 to 7,999
- 3,000 to 4,999
- Less than 3,000

Line indicates average level in Western Europe

Annual emissions of NO₂, SO₂, and suspended particulate matter (SPM) in kilograms per capita for selected countries, 1988

100
50
0
NO₂ SO₂ SPM

Lines indicate average levels in 1985 for all countries in Europe

Cities of Eastern Europe
Atmospheric Pollution Levels

Average annual micrograms/cu m of air

200
150
100
50
0

Berlin, Bucharest, Warsaw, Zagreb, Sofia, Ruse, Prague, Ostrava, Bratislava, Dresden, Leipzig, Wrocław, Baia Mare, Vilnius

■ NO₂ ☐ SO₂ ▨ SPM

Data are for 1988, except Vilnius (1990).
Data were not available where no bar is shown.
Air-quality standards (Primary Standard Levels) in the United States indicate the following maximum average annual amounts for these pollutants (in micrograms per cubic metre of air): NO₂ 100, SO₂ 80, and SPM 75.

Forest Defoliation in Eastern Europe
Selected Countries, 1990

Percentage of forests defoliated

100
90
80
70
60
50
40
30
20
10
0

Belarus, Bulgaria, Czech., Estonia*, GDR, GFR, Hungary, Latvia, Lithuania, Poland, Russia†, Slovenia, Ukraine

■ Slight damage ▨ Moderate to severe

Data are for all species, all ages.
*Only overall damage shown. †Kaliningrad only.

©1996, Encyclopædia Britannica, Inc.

Pollution in eastern Europe, 1980s and 1990s. Encyclopædia Britannica, Inc.

of the forests in the Sudeten and western Carpathians.

The problems of environmental degradation were not officially recognized until the early 1970s and were not addressed until the Solidarity movement began agitating in the early 1980s. Significant reduction in the emission of pollutants occurred, however, as a consequence of the rapid fall in industrial production in the early 1990s, following the abandonment of communism and the introduction of economic reforms. Throughout the decade the government implemented antipollution policies, such as closing the most damaging industrial plants.

ETHNIC GROUPS

Before World War II the Polish lands were noted for the richness and variety of their ethnic communities. The traditional provinces of Silesia and Pomerania were home to a significant minority of Germans. In the southeast, Ukrainian settlements predominated in the regions east of Chełm and in the Carpathian Mountains east of Nowy Sącz. In all the towns and cities, there were large concentrations of Yiddish-speaking Jews. The Polish ethnographic area stretched eastward: in Lithuania, Belarus, and western Ukraine, all of which had a mixed population, Poles predominated not only in the

SILESIA AND POMERANIA

The historic regions of Silesia and Pomerania lie mainly in what is now Poland. Throughout their histories, the two regions have been under the rule of various European powers.

Silesia, located primarily in what is now southwestern Poland, with some parts in areas of Germany and the Czech Republic, was originally a Polish province that became a possession of the Bohemian crown, and thus part of the Holy Roman Empire, in 1335. Because of succession disputes and the region's prosperity, there were at least 16 Silesian principalities by the end of the 15th century. It passed to the Austrian Habsburgs in 1526; it was taken by Prussia in 1742. After World War I it was divided between Poland, Czechoslovakia, and Germany. During World War II Polish Silesia was occupied by Germany and was the site of atrocities against the population by Nazi and, later, Soviet forces. In 1945 the Allied powers assigned virtually all of Silesia to Poland.

Pomerania, located on the Baltic coast between the Oder and Vistula rivers, was originally occupied by Slavs and other peoples before coming under the rule of Polish princes in the 10th century. German immigration into western and central Pomerania began in the late 12th century, and Polish dukes ruled this area under the suzerainty of the Holy Roman Empire until the 17th century. Eastern Pomerania was held by the Knights of the Teutonic Order from 1308 until it was reconquered by Poland in 1454. The elector of Brandenburg acquired the duchies in 1637. Prussia united western and central Pomerania in 1815 as the province of Pommern. Most of the area is now in Poland; its westernmost section is in eastern Germany.

cities but also in numerous rural districts. There were significant Polish minorities in Daugavpils (in Latvia), Minsk (in Belarus), and Kiev (in Ukraine).

The war, however, killed vast numbers of people, precipitated massive migrations, and radically altered borders. As a consequence, the population of Poland became one of the most ethnically homogeneous in the world. In addition, minority ethnic identity was not cultivated publicly until after the collapse of communism in 1989. Virtually all of Poland's people claim Polish nationality, with Polish as their native tongue. Now, in the 21st century, most communities of non-Poles are dispersed but reside in the border provinces, primarily in the south. Ukrainians are scattered in various southwestern and northern districts. Belarusians and Lithuanians live in areas adjoining Belarus and Lithuania, respectively. In Silesia a significant segment of the population tends to declare itself as Silesian or German according to political circumstances. Kashubians live west of Gdańsk near the Baltic Sea. Situated in the southeast are communities of Roma (Gypsy), in Małopolskie województwo (province), and Ruthenians, in Podkarpackie province. The Jewish community, now almost entirely Polonized, has been greatly reduced and can be found in major cities. There are small numbers of Slovaks, Czechs, and Armenians. Conversely, there is a large Polish diaspora, notably in the United States.

LANGUAGES

The country's official language, Polish (together with other Lekhitic languages and Czech, Slovak, and Upper and Lower Sorbian), belongs to the West Slavic branch of Slavic languages. It has several dialects that correspond in the main to the old tribal divisions; the most significant of these (in terms of numbers of speakers) are Great Polish (spoken in the northwest), Little Polish (spoken in the southeast), Mazovian, and Silesian (Śleżanie). Mazovian shares some features with Kashubian, whose remaining speakers number only a few thousand, which is a small percentage of the ethnic Kashubians in the country.

Elsewhere, the Polish language has been influenced by contact with foreign tongues. In Silesia the inimitable regional patois contains a mixture of Polish and German elements. After 1945, as the result of mass education and mass migrations, standard Polish became far more homogeneous, although regional dialects persist. In the western and northern territories, resettled in the second half of the 20th century in large measure by Poles from the Soviet Union, the older generation came to speak a language characteristic of the former eastern provinces. Small numbers of people also speak Belarusian, Ukrainian, and German as well as several varieties of Romany.

Literary Polish developed from the medieval period onward, on the basis of the dialects of Great Poland and Little Poland. By the 19th century Polish was well established both as a literary vehicle and as the dominant language of common speech in Poland, despite attempts of the partitioning powers to Germanize or Russify the population. Indeed, quite the opposite happened, and the Polish language became the main touchstone of national identity.

RELIGION

The overwhelming majority of the Polish population is Roman Catholic, and a large number are practicing Catholics. Though the country claims no official religion, Poland is among the most uniformly Catholic countries in the world, and the Roman Catholic Church in Poland enjoys immense social prestige and political influence.

Following World War II, during the communist era, all religious institutions became subject to the control of the state. In practice the Roman Catholic Church wielded a full measure of independence, partly through the sheer force of the faithful and partly because in all important matters it answered to the pope in Rome and not to the government in Warsaw. Those opposed to communism within Poland were greatly encouraged by the election in 1978 of the archbishop of Kraków, Karol Cardinal Wojtyła, as Pope John Paul II, the first non-Italian pope since the 16th century. The religious minorities, though encouraged by the anti-Roman Catholic policies of the communist state, were barely visible except in local areas. The influence of the Catholic Church became even greater after the fall of communism in Poland in 1989, and this led to its greater involvement in state schools and to the replacement of the country's liberal abortion law, by 1993, with much more restrictive legislation.

The Polish National Catholic Church, a schismatic offshoot of Roman Catholicism, never won popular support, despite strong government advocacy following World War II. Two Protestant strongholds remain in Poland—that of the Polish Lutherans in Masuria and the Evangelicals (Augsburg Confession) in Cieszyn, Silesia. An autocephalous Polish Orthodox church is partly linked with the small Belarusian minority, and a Ukrainian Uniate community survives in southeastern districts. In the last quarter of the 20th century, Charismatics and other renewal movements arrived in Poland.

The constitution of 1997 guarantees religious freedom. Poland has residual communities of Polish Jews, whose synagogues and religious activities were officially sanctioned by the communist government. There are nearly an equal number of Muslims in Poland, located primarily in the east, near Białystok. Small Christian groups representing fundamentalist sects such as the Seventh-day Adventists and the Jehovah's Witnesses operate in a few cities.

SETTLEMENT PATTERNS

Polish society since World War II has been transformed by two interrelated great movements: the growth of a dominant urban industrialized working class and the continuing drift of peasants from the rural areas into towns and cities. Whereas in 1946 there were nearly twice as many people in the countryside as in towns, by the late 1960s the two numbered equally. About three-fifths of the country's population is now urban. So-called peasant workers, who tended to live on the fringes of industrial regions, contrived to benefit from both movements: while one part of the family maintained the farm, other family members earned wages in local factories.

Until the mid-20th century, the pattern of rural settlement differed widely from one part of Poland to another. In the centre and east of the country, many villages were small and irregular in shape, reflecting their origin as self-sufficient clusters of cultivators and pastoralists set in forest clearings. In the mountains, villages stretched along the valleys, in some cases for several miles. In Lower Silesia they were larger and more orderly, associated with the planned settlement of the area by Teutonic people in medieval times. In the north, rural settlement was dominated by large landed estates, which had belonged to the Prussian Junkers. Many houses in the centre, east, and south were wooden. Since the 1950s, however, there have been marked changes. Some attempt has been made to retain traditional building styles in the mountains, but many older single-story houses in all parts of the country have been replaced with two- to three-story cinder-block structures. In addition, many villages have expanded, especially those close to larger cities and in regions popular with tourists.

Warsaw is the largest city in Poland, with a population twice that of Łódź, the next most populous city. About 85 percent of Warsaw's buildings were left in ruins during World War II; much of the city therefore dates from the period since 1950. Many of Warsaw's inhabitants live in large unattractive blocks of flats that were built around the edge of the city in the 1960s and '70s. In the 1990s downtown Warsaw experienced a construction boom as several high-rise hotels and office buildings were added to its skyline at the same time that many single-family houses and villas were erected in the suburbs.

Kraków (the original capital of Poland), Gdańsk, Poznań, and Wrocław (German: Breslau) share many characteristics with Warsaw, all having more or less extensive medieval and early modern cores surrounded by 19th- and, especially, 20th-century suburbs containing a mixture of manufacturing complexes and poor-quality apartment-style housing, as well as newer (post-1990) subdivisions of single-family dwellings. In contrast, Łódź, Poland's second largest city, dates from the 19th century, when it grew rapidly to become one of the most important centres of the textile industry in the Russian

WARSAW

The capital of Poland is Warsaw (Polish: Warszawa). Located in the east-central part of the country, the city lies on the Vistula (Wisła) River, which divides Warsaw into right- and left-bank portions.

Founded *c.* 1300, Warsaw flourished as a trade centre, came under Polish control in 1526, and became the capital in 1596. The city suffered damage during the Swedish and Prussian occupation of 1655–56. During the late 18th century it expanded rapidly but was again assaulted in 1794 when the Russian army massacred the population of the right-bank suburb of Praga. In 1807 it was made the capital of the Duchy of Warsaw by Napoleon. Taken by the Russians in 1813, it was the centre of Polish insurrections in 1830–31 and

Palace of Culture and Science, Warsaw. © Digital Vision/Getty Images

1860. It was occupied by the Germans in World War I and again in World War II, when its large Jewish population revolted in the Warsaw Ghetto Uprising (1943). After the Polish Home Army launched the failed Warsaw Uprising in 1944, Adolf Hitler ordered the city to be razed; the left-bank suburbs, controlled by the Germans, were emptied of their remaining population; and the buildings were systematically reduced to rubble by fire and dynamite. In 1945 the people of Warsaw, the Varsovians, returned, and the city resumed its role as the capital of Poland and the country's centre of social, political, economic, scientific, and cultural life. Warsaw's historically multinational population was transformed as a result of World War II, however, and today the city is composed almost entirely of Poles. The overwhelming majority of the people are Roman Catholic.

Warsaw possesses a wide variety of architectural monuments, whether as replicas or originals. In the Old Town, which was designated by UNESCO as a World Heritage site in 1980, the Gothic St. John's Cathedral and the red-brick fortifications known as the Barbican remain from the medieval period. The houses of the Old Town Market Square have been rebuilt in the splendour of their 15th-century style. There are many Baroque churches of the Counter-Reformation period, including the Church of the Holy Cross, which contains the heart of the Polish French composer Frédéric Chopin. The magnificently reconstructed Royal Castle, decorated in late

18th-century style, is on Zamkowy Square. Belweder (Belvedere) Palace, a former presidential residence used now for ceremonial occasions. Remnants of the tsarist era are evident in the Church of St. Alexander in the middle of Trzech Krzyży Square and in the vast Alexander Citadel on the riverside, north of the New Town. The massive Palace of Culture and Science (1949), built by the Soviets south of the Old Town, still dominates the skyline. Warsaw's cultural attractions include the National Museum, the Zachęta National Gallery of Art, the National Philharmonic Orchestra, and National Opera. The city is also home to the headquarters of the Polish Academy of Sciences, the Technical University of Warsaw, the University of Warsaw, and the National Library.

With the demise of the communist government in Poland in 1989, Warsaw underwent a rapid transition from command to market economy. Closed since World War II, the Warsaw Stock Exchange reopened in 1991 and became an important market in central Europe. The role of services, notably banking and insurance, has grown. There are increasing numbers of new private-sector firms and foreign companies in the city as well. An economic and construction boom, which transformed the city's skyline with new office towers and hotels, continued into the early 21st century.

Empire. The other major urban area is that of southern Upper Silesia, a conurbation of mining and industrial settlements stretching some 30 miles (48 km) from Dąbrowa Górnicza to Gliwice.

DEMOGRAPHIC TRENDS

The population of Poland was transformed during and immediately after World War II. Nearly 35 million people lived within the Polish frontiers in 1939, but by 1946 only about 24 million resided within the country's new borders. The decrease of some 11 million can be accounted for mainly by war losses but also in part by changes in frontiers.

Polish war losses are the subject of some controversy. The official figure, issued in 1947, was 6,028,000 (some 3,000,000 of them Polish Jews), although it referred exclusively to losses within the postwar frontiers. As a result of the changes in frontiers, millions of Germans were forcibly expelled from 1946 to 1947. On the other hand, millions of Poles were transferred from former Polish homelands that were incorporated into the Soviet Union during the same period. An estimated 500,000 Ukrainians and Belarusians also were transferred into the Soviet Union. At the same time, there were vast internal movements into the new northern and western territories annexed from Germany.

Population losses and movements on this scale introduced long-term distortions into demographic structures and trends. At the end of the war, there were huge deficiencies in certain categories, especially males, urban dwellers, and the educated as a whole. However, the immediate postwar generation had an unprecedented birth rate, and the population grew rapidly again, especially in the northern and western portions of the country, returning to its prewar level in 1977. The birth rate fell sharply after the early 1980s, and population growth slowed, though the death rate approximated the world average. By the early 21st century, the natural increase rate (balance of births against deaths) was virtually nil.

Emigration was a permanent feature of Polish life for most of the 19th and 20th centuries, and roughly one Pole in three lives abroad. Wave after wave of political émigrés has left Poland since the mid-18th century. By far the greatest numbers of people left, however, for economic reasons. Starting in the mid-19th century, Polish emigrants moved into the new industrial areas of Europe and later to the United States and Canada.

CHAPTER 17

THE POLISH ECONOMY

Before World War II, Poland was a free-market economy based largely upon agriculture but with a few important centres of manufacturing and mining. After the initiation of communist rule in the 1940s, the country developed an increasingly industrial, state-run command economy based on the Soviet model. It operated within the rigid framework of Comecon (Council for Mutual Economic Assistance), an organization of Eastern-bloc countries dominated by the Soviet Union.

From the mid-1970s the Polish economy struggled with limited growth, largely as a result of an antiquated industrial infrastructure, government subsidies that masked inefficient production, and wages that were artificially high relative to productivity. In the late 1980s a swelling government deficit and hyperinflation brought about economic crisis. With the fall of communism and the demise of Comecon, the Polish economy became increasingly involved in the market-oriented global economy, for which it was ill-suited. To try to achieve economic stability, the postcommunist government introduced an approach known as "shock therapy," which sought both to control inflation and to expedite Poland's transition to a market economy. As part of that plan, the government froze wages, removed price controls, phased out subsidies to state-owned enterprises, and permitted large-scale private enterprise.

As a result, in the early 1990s industrial output and gross domestic product (GDP) dropped significantly (agricultural production also fell, though largely owing to drought).

COMECON

Comecon is the byname of the Council for Mutual Economic Assistance (CMEA), also called (from 1991) the Organization for International Economic Cooperation. The organization was established in January 1949 to facilitate and coordinate the economic development of the eastern European countries belonging to the Soviet bloc. Comecon's original members were the Soviet Union, Bulgaria, Czechoslovakia, Hungary, Poland, and Romania. Albania joined in February 1949 but ceased taking an active part at the end of 1961. The German Democratic Republic became a member in September 1950 and the Mongolian People's Republic in June 1962. In 1964 an agreement was concluded enabling Yugoslavia to participate on equal terms with Comecon members in the areas of trade, finance, currency, and industry. Cuba, in 1972, became the 9th full member and Vietnam, in 1978, became the 10th. Headquarters were established in Moscow. After the democratic revolutions in eastern Europe in 1989, the organization largely lost its purpose and power, and changes in policies and name in 1990–91 reflected the disintegration.

Comecon was formed under the aegis of the Soviet Union in 1949 in response to the formation of the Committee of European Economic Cooperation in western Europe in 1948. Between 1949 and 1953, however, Comecon's activities were restricted chiefly to the registration of bilateral trade and credit agreements among member countries. After 1953 the Soviet Union and Comecon began to promote industrial specialization among the member countries and thus reduce "parallelism" (redundant industrial production) in the economies of eastern Europe. In the late 1950s, after the formation of the European Economic Community in western Europe, Comecon undertook more systematic and intense efforts along these lines, though with only limited success.

The economic integration envisaged by Comecon in the early 1960s met with opposition and problems. A major difficulty was posed by the incompatibility of the price systems used in the various member countries. The prices of most goods and commodities were set by individual governments and had little to do with the goods' actual market values, thus making it difficult for the member states to conduct trade with each other on the basis of relative prices. Instead, trade was conducted mainly on a barter basis through bilateral agreements between governments.

Comecon's successes did include the organization of eastern Europe's railroad grid and of its electric-power grid; the creation of the International Bank for Economic Cooperation (1963) to finance investment projects jointly undertaken by two or more members; and the construction of the "Friendship" oil pipeline, which made oil from the Soviet Union's Volga region available to the countries of eastern Europe.

After the collapse of communist governments across eastern Europe in 1989–90, those countries began a pronounced shift to private enterprise and market-type systems of pricing. By January 1, 1991, the members had begun to make trade payments in hard, convertible currencies. Under agreements made early in 1991, Comecon was renamed the Organization for International Economic Cooperation, each nation was deemed free to seek its own trade outlets, and members were reduced to a weak pledge to "coordinate" policies on quotas, tariffs, international payments, and relations with other international bodies.

Unemployment grew, affecting as many as one in seven Poles. Inflation, however, began to drop, from 250 percent in 1990 to 10 percent in 2000. Production and GDP also recorded dramatic turnarounds, with an average annual GDP growth of about 4 percent from 1990 to 2000. Poland's balance of payments improved (partly as the result of debt forgiveness), and the country developed one of the leading economies of the former Eastern bloc, as well as one of the fastest growing in Europe. Unemployment, which had been high at the beginning of the decade, righted itself in the late 1990s, falling to levels similar to those in western Europe in 1997–98 (i.e., to about 10 percent). The percentage of unemployed persons, however, rose once again in the early 21st century, climbing above 18 percent in 2003, when a downturn in the Polish economy was accelerated by a worldwide economic slowdown.

Privatization of some of Poland's large industries proved to be a slow process. Under communism the principal branches of industry, services, and trade were directly owned by the state. There was, however, a surprisingly large sector of legal self-employment, and small-scale private businesses—including workshops, services, and restaurants—proliferated. Moreover, some three-fourths of Poland's farmland remained privately owned. A government collectivization campaign begun in 1949 was abandoned in 1956. After the fall of communism, both industry and agriculture became increasingly privatized. By the early 1990s, more than half the Polish economy was in private ownership, while more than four-fifths of Polish shops were privately owned.

The privatization of larger enterprises was more complicated. A number of these were transformed into joint-stock and limited-liability companies. To distribute ownership in them, the Mass Privatization Program was introduced in 1994, which created 15 national investment funds (NIFs) to serve as joint-stock companies for more than 500 large and medium-size firms that were privatized. Poles were able to purchase shares in these funds at a nominal price. Listed on the Warsaw Stock Exchange, the NIFs comprised a broad range of enterprises—not just individual companies or groups of companies—and this enabled citizens to possess a diversified interest in key Polish industries. By 2001 more than 6,800 state-owned enterprises had been involved in the privatization process, and the private sector accounted for more than 70 percent of GDP.

Development under the communist government stressed the classless and proletarian nature of society; however, the party elite enjoyed a range of privileges unavailable to ordinary workers. In postcommunist Poland, as private businesses proliferated, a small number of people became wealthy, and a middle class composed of entrepreneurs and urban professionals emerged. However, many people, in particular those on fixed incomes, suffered sharp declines in their standard of living. Crime, drug use, and corruption also increased, but such problems are not uncommon elsewhere in Europe. Also, greater wealth was found in western provinces near Germany than in eastern districts near Belarus and Ukraine.

As it made the transition to private ownership and the market economy, Poland became increasingly involved with international economic and political organizations. In 1991 it joined the Council of Europe; in 1995 it became a member of the World Trade Organization; and in 1996 it joined the Organisation for Economic Co-operation and Development. It gained full membership in the North Atlantic Treaty Organization (NATO) in 1999, along with Hungary and the Czech Republic. An associate member of the European Union (EU) since 1994, Poland ascended to full membership in 2004.

AGRICULTURE, FORESTRY, AND FISHING

Polish agriculture was unique in the Soviet bloc in that private farms accounted for most of total output. Most of those private farms continue to be smaller than 12 acres (5 ha). In postcommunist Poland farm incomes declined rapidly in real terms as the prices of industrial products rose, and imported processed foods from western Europe competed strongly with lower-quality Polish products. Many state farms collapsed after 1989, as did the system of state purchase upon which much of the private sector had relied. Throughout the 1990s the percentage of people employed in agriculture declined each year, owing in part to the liquidation of state farms, the aging of agricultural workers, and the drought of the early 1990s.

Nevertheless, Poland remains one of the world's leading producers of rye and potatoes. Other principal crops include wheat and sugar beets. Poland's largest fertile areas are Lower Silesia, the Little Poland Lowlands, the Kujawy, the Vistula delta, and the Lublin area. Soil quality varies, and the soil is somewhat poorer in large parts of central and northern Poland. Most farming is mixed, and beef cattle, dairy cows, and pigs are raised throughout the country. As Poland became increasingly integrated into the global economy during the mid-1990s, about half its agricultural exports went to the EU.

Although timberland and fisheries still struggle with a legacy of environmental damage, improvements in natural resources could be seen throughout the 1990s. In 2000 almost one-third of Polish tree stands still had defoliation of more than 25 percent, exceeding the levels for many of Poland's European neighbours. Some four-fifths of the country's wooded land is occupied by coniferous trees, with pine, larch, and spruce the most economically important. About 918,000 cubic feet (26,000 cubic metres) of roundwood was farmed in 2001. The fishing industry in Poland is small, and the total fish catch is between 200,000 and 300,000 metric tons per year.

RESOURCES AND POWER

Poland is relatively well endowed with natural resources. Its principal mineral asset is bituminous coal, although brown coal is mined as well. Most of the bituminous output is derived from the rich Upper Silesian coalfield. During the late 20th century, however, extraction costs in many mines began to exceed profits. Falling prices and the challenges of privatization have slowed production levels. Other fuel resources include small amounts of petroleum and moderately large deposits of natural gas.

Sulfur is Poland's second most important mineral, and the republic ranks among the world leaders in both reserves and production. Other important nonmetallic minerals include barite, salt, kaolin, limestone, chalk, gypsum, and marble. The historic salt mine in Wieliczka, near Kraków, has been in continuous use since the 13th century; in 1978 it was among the first places to be named a UNESCO World Heritage site. Poland also has important deposits of metallic minerals such as zinc and is a major world producer of copper and silver.

Nearly all of Poland's energy is provided by thermal plants fired by bituminous coal and lignite, though in 1998 the government declared its intention to rely more on imported natural gas. Natural gas has largely replaced manufactured gas. Poland imports almost all of its petroleum and petroleum products. In 2000 mineral fuels and lubricants constituted about one-tenth of all imports. On the other hand, about one-fifteenth of electricity generated in Poland was exported. The bulk of the country's hydroelectricity comes from the Carpathians, the Sudeten region, and the Brda and Vistula rivers.

MANUFACTURING

During the period of communist rule, remarkable advances in industrial production were overshadowed to some extent by shortcomings in quality and by problems of organization. Moreover, industrial production in Poland—governed almost solely by quantitative requirements and dependent on inexpensive raw materials provided through Comecon—was largely inefficient and poorly prepared to compete in the global marketplace. Industrial output fell dramatically after the demise of communism, especially during the first years of shock therapy. There were declines of one-third or more in almost all areas of manufacturing and mining following the freeing of prices and the collapse of Comecon.

As Polish industry began to downsize, however, production improved, and by the mid-1990s manufacturing accounted for about two-fifths of GDP. As other sectors grew more quickly, manufacturing totaled about one-fifth of GDP by the end of the decade. The principal branches of the manufacturing sector are machinery and transport equipment, food products, metals and metal products, chemicals, beverages, tobacco, and textiles and clothing.

FINANCE

During the communist era, all financial institutions were owned by the state beginning in 1944–45 and formed an integral part of centralized economic planning after 1949. The National Bank of Poland (Narodowy Bank Polski) acted as the main agent of the government's financial policy, managing everything from the currency and money supply to wages and prices, credit, investment, and the detailed business of all state enterprises. In the late 1980s and early '90s, the banking industry was reorganized. The National Bank became an independent central bank, with responsibility for regulating the banking sector and the currency. By 2000 there were about 75 private banks, though the state retained the controlling interest in about one-tenth of them.

Until 1990, internal monetary operations were conducted in inconvertible local currency, while external operations were conducted either in foreign currency, especially U.S. dollars, or, for the Soviet bloc, in special units of account such as convertible rubles. Exchange rates against foreign hard currency were flexible according to the needs of the state bank. In 1990, as part of a government program to move the Polish economy toward a free-market system, the exchange rate of the złoty, Poland's currency, was allowed to be set freely on the international currency markets. In 1995 a new, devalued złoty was introduced; it equaled 10,000 of the old złotys.

After joining the EU in 2004, Poland prepared to also enter the EU's economic zone and to adopt the euro as its currency.

Poland established a stock exchange in 1991 in Warsaw, and, by the end of 2001, some 230 companies were listed on it. A derivatives market was begun in 1998. At the turn of the century, more than 50 insurance companies were in operation, the largest of which was Polish National Insurance (Powszechny Zakład Ubezpieczeń). In the first decade of the postcommunist era, Poland received more foreign direct investment than any other former socialist country of Europe, rising from $89 million in 1990 to $10.6 billion in 2000

TRADE

The fall of communism greatly affected Poland's trade, which prior to the demise of the Soviet bloc was conducted within Comecon, including the export of coal and machinery to the Soviet Union and eastern Europe. In 1990, however, Germany edged out the Soviet Union as Poland's primary trading partner, and by 2001 Germany accounted for one-fourth of Poland's imports and one-third of its exports. Italy and France are also important to Polish trade. Machinery, metals, textiles and clothing, coal, and food account for the bulk of exports, and machinery, chemicals, and fuels are the major imports. Germany is the largest market for almost all categories of exports, while Russia remains by far the most important source of energy imports, and Germany and Italy serve as the chief sources of foreign machinery and chemicals.

SERVICES

The service industry greatly expanded in the final decade of the 20th century, at a rate of about 4 percent of GDP per year. Growth was pronounced in the sectors of financial services, retail, and travel and leisure. By the turn of the 21st century, the service industry accounted for about two-thirds of the country's GDP and employed just less than one-half of the Polish workforce. In 2005 tourism contributed about $6 billion to the Polish economy, with most foreign tourists arriving from Germany and the Czech Republic.

LABOUR AND TAXATION

Under the communist system, unions, organized by individual industries, had to be approved by the state and party. Inasmuch as the government was a monopoly employer in all important branches of industry and because the trade union organization was run by the party, it can be argued that the trade unions were employer unions. Links between employees in different trades or different enterprises were not possible, and the rights to organize freely and strike were denied until the advent of the Independent Self-Governing Trade Union Solidarity (Niezależny Samorząd Związków Zawodowych Solidarność),

better known simply as Solidarity. Founded in September 1980, shortly after widespread strikes organized by the Interfactory Strike Committee, Solidarity broke the monopoly of the official party unions, quickly gained mass support (even among party members), and extended its activities far beyond narrow syndicalist concerns. Widespread labour unrest during 1981 resulted in a government declaration of martial law in December and the arrest and detention of Solidarity leader Lech Wałęsa and others. Solidarity and its satellite organizations, such as Rural Solidarity (Wiejska Solidarność), were officially suppressed, and the leaders of the independent labour movement were denounced as "criminals." The party ordered its managers and ministers to create new trade unions affiliated with the government-sponsored All Poland Trade Unions Alliance (Ogólnopolskie Porozumienie Związków Zawodowych; OPZZ) that would operate along the old lines of party control. Much of the membership of the re-created unions consisted of former Solidarity sympathizers, however, and the new unions were not entirely uncritical of party policy. In addition, despite its illegal status, Solidarity continued to have influence as an underground organization.

In 1988 renewed labour unrest and nationwide strikes forced negotiations between the government and Solidarity (held in early 1989) that resulted in the legalization of Solidarity and in Poland's first free elections since World War

II. From the 1990s both Solidarity and OPZZ were directly involved in politics, becoming core members of major political alliances, the Solidarity Electoral Action (Akcja Wyborcza Solidarność; AWS) and the Democratic Left Alliance (Sojusz Lewicy Demokratycznej; SLD), respectively. Following the political legitimization of Solidarity, Wałęsa, who had received the Nobel Prize for Peace in 1983, became Poland's first directly elected president (1990–95).

Poland overhauled its system of taxation in the early 1990s, primarily via legislation passed in January 1993 that replaced a turnover tax with a type of value-added tax (VAT). Under that tax, fees accrued for the final purchaser with each transaction during a product's development. Small businesses and some taxpayers were exempt from paying this VAT, and it was not applied to certain foodstuffs, medicines, and exports. Also in 1993, an excise duty was introduced, with higher rates applied to alcoholic beverages, tobacco products, and automobiles. In 1994 Poland unveiled three levels of personal income tax (21 percent, 33 percent, and 45 percent; in 2000 reduced to 19 percent, 30 percent, and 40 percent), attempting to offset the new burden with a simultaneous program of investment tax relief. Moreover, the extant corporate tax rate of 40 percent was reaffirmed (but reduced to 19 percent in 2003), and an import tax on foreign goods was initiated. Property tax laws in Poland allow tax breaks for owners of farms or forested lands.

TRANSPORTATION AND TELECOMMUNICATIONS

The communications system in Poland developed in the 19th and early 20th centuries, when the country was divided between Russia, Germany, and Austria. The three areas thus developed in different economic and political conditions.

RAILWAYS

The main railway lines were centred on the capitals of the three empires. The density of the railway networks in the three sectors was uneven. In 1918 independent Poland took over the railroad system and redesigned and rebuilt it according to the standard European gauge. Among the most important railway lines built after that date were those linking Warsaw with Poznań and Kraków and a coal trunk line linking Upper Silesia with the newly built seaport of Gdynia.

After the devastation of World War II, the railway system was reconstructed once again, and the most heavily used lines were converted to electric power. Because of the location of the country, Polish lines were important in the carriage of transit freight among the socialist countries of eastern Europe, notably between the Soviet Union and East Germany and between Czechoslovakia and Poland's ports.

Demand for rail transport fell sharply, however, after the communist era, for both freight and passengers. In the last decade of the 20th century, there was a 41 percent drop in railway tonnage and a 58 percent decrease in passenger trips by rail. The railways, administered by the Polish State Railways (Polskie Koleje Państwowe), began the process of privatization in the early 21st century. Light rail is available to commuters in more than a dozen cities.

HIGHWAYS

The highway system originally showed disproportions similar to those of the railways; that is, the densest network was on land belonging to Germany and the least dense on land belonging to Russia. An attempt to remedy this situation was made between 1918 and 1938 and again, though more intensively, after 1945. Modern multilane highways designed for high traffic volumes have been built in Warsaw, and projects have been undertaken to link Warsaw to provincial centres, but the road system in general is of low quality. About two-thirds of its 263,000 miles (424,000 km) is paved. In the 1990s the government began construction of limited-access highways built to European standards.

WATERWAYS

The middle course of the main Polish river, the Vistula, contains many navigational hazards, and the river is thus a less-important waterway than the smaller Oder. The modern Gliwice Canal links the Oder to the Upper Silesian industrial region and carries coal to the port of Szczecin. The Oder basin is also linked to the lower Vistula by the Bydgoszcz Canal. Inland navigation is of little importance in Poland, however, with less than 1 percent of Polish freight being carried on rivers and canals. On the other

SZCZECIN

Szczecin (German: Stettin) is a port city in northwestern Poland located on the western bank of the Oder River near its mouth, 40 miles (65 km) from the Baltic Sea. Shipbuilding and shipping are the main occupations. Evidence suggests that the area was first inhabited by seafaring people 2,500 years ago.

In the 8th and 9th centuries Szczecin was a Slavic fishing and commercial settlement in Western Pomerania (Pomorze Zachodnie). During the 10th century it was annexed to Poland by Mieszko I. It was granted municipal autonomy in 1243 and remained capital of the dukedom of Western Pomerania. It grew and prospered, joining the Hanseatic League in 1360. In 1637 it passed to the Brandenburg Electorate, which controlled it until 1648, when it was seized by the Swedes. In 1720 it passed to Prussia and remained under German control until its transfer to Poland after World War II.

Modern development of the port of Szczecin began in 1826 with regular navigation of the Oder. The port grew steadily until World War II, mainly through its proximity to Berlin, 90 miles (145 km) to the southwest. In 1926–27 the channel through the Szczecinski Lagoon to the outport of Świnoujście (Swinemünde) was deepened. During World War II the port was completely destroyed and the city itself was greatly depopulated. Under Polish administration the port and city were rebuilt.

Szczecin is, with Świnoujście, now Poland's largest port complex. It is an important port for cargo shipped down the Oder from the Czech Republic, Hungary, and Germany; coal is the major export. Other industries, in addition to shipbuilding, include food processing, metalworking, fertilizer production, and synthetic-textile-machinery manufacturing. Power for these industries and for the northwest of Poland is supplied by the Dolna Odra power plant.

Szczecin is a cultural centre of western Poland, having four institutions of higher education, several theatres, a philharmonic orchestra, libraries, and the National Museum. It is a picturesque city containing many monuments, parks, and small lakes. The Castle of the Dukes of Pomerania, built in the Renaissance style, was reconstructed after incurring heavy damage during World War II. It features five main wings and two towers. The Tower of the Seven Cloaks, a remnant of Szczecin's medieval town walls, can be viewed from the castle balcony.

hand, shipping is well developed, and there are three large seaports—Szczecin (the largest), Gdynia, and Gdańsk—as well as smaller fishing and coastal navigation ports.

AIR TRANSPORT

Passenger air traffic has more than doubled since the collapse of Polish communism. Domestic and international air transport is provided by LOT (from Polskie Linie Lotnicze), a state-owned enterprise that completed negotiations for partial privatization in 1999. There are numerous international routes centred on the airport at Warsaw. Other airports are located in Kraków, Gdańsk, Wrocław, Katowice, Poznań, and Szczecin.

TELECOMMUNICATIONS

At the start of the 21st century, Poland had 11.4 million main telephone lines and more than 10 million cellular telephone users. In online communications the number of Internet users (3.8 million) slightly exceeded the number of personal computers (3.3 million), reflecting the presence of multiple users per terminal and of public computer stations. Televisions and radios were ubiquitous in Poland, with 15 and 20 million units, respectively.

CHAPTER 18

POLISH GOVERNMENT AND SOCIETY

The constitution of Poland's postwar socialist state, the Polish People's Republic, took effect in 1952 but was amended numerous times, most significantly in early 1989, when constitutional reforms worked out between the government and Solidarity were passed by the Sejm (legislature). Among the changes were the replacement of the Council of State by the office of president (a position that had been eliminated in 1952) and the reinstatement of the Senate, which had been abolished in 1946 in an allegedly rigged national referendum. The existing Sejm, with 460 members, became the lower house of the new legislature, and the Senate, or the upper house, was assigned 100 members. Additional reforms passed later in 1989 by the legislature included the guarantee of free formation of political parties and the return of the state's official name to the Republic of Poland.

The new constitution of 1997, which replaced a 1992 interim constitution, was adopted in April by the National Assembly (Zgromadzenie Narodowe; as the Sejm and the Senate are referred to when they meet in a joint session to debate constitutional issues), approved in a national referendum in May, and promulgated in October. The constitution confirmed the mixed presidential-parliamentary form of government that had been established during the period 1989–92. Under its provisions the president is directly elected to not more than two five-year terms. The president serves as commander in chief of the armed forces, has the power (albeit restricted) to declare martial law or a state of emergency, and can veto an act of the Sejm (which in turn can override that veto with a three-fifths majority vote).

The president nominates the prime minister and, on the prime minister's recommendation, the cabinet, subject to the Sejm's approval, but the president cannot dismiss the government. Deputies in the Sejm and senators are popularly elected to four-year terms. Laws must be adopted by both houses. The Senate has the right to amend or reject a law passed by the Sejm. The Sejm may override the Senate's decision with a majority vote. The Sejm appoints the members of the Constitutional Tribunal, the commissioner for civil rights protection (the ombudsman), the chairman of the Supreme Chamber of Control (the state audit commission), and the president of the Bank of Poland. The main executive power is vested in the prime minister and the Council of Ministers, who are responsible to the Sejm. The government can be terminated by the Sejm only by a constructive vote of no confidence. The prime minister has a role comparable to that of a chancellor in the German political system.

LOCAL GOVERNMENT

Local government in Poland is organized on three levels. The largest units, at the regional level, are the *wojewódz-twa* (provinces), which were consolidated and reduced in number from 49 to 16 in 1999. At the next level are some 300 *powiaty* (counties or districts), followed by about 2,500 *gminy* (towns and rural communes). The last are the fundamental

territorial units within Poland. The status of the capital city of Warsaw is regulated by a special legislation. Both *powiaty* and *gminy* are governed by councils, elected to four-year terms. These councils in turn elect the heads of local administration. The representatives to the *sejmiki wojew-ódzkie* (provincial legislature) also are elected to four-year terms. The head of provincial administration, the *wojewoda*, is nominated by the prime minister.

JUSTICE

The constitution guarantees the independence of the judiciary. The supreme representative of the judiciary is the National Judiciary Council. Poland has a Supreme Court and other special judicial bodies (including the High Administrative Court, military courts, and industrial tribunals) as well as general courts, comprising appellate, provincial, and district courts. General courts deal with criminal, civil, and family matters; commercial courts deal with civil law disputes between businesses. The Constitutional Tribunal provides judicial review of legislation. The Tribunal of State reviews violations of the constitution and other laws by the top state officials.

POLITICAL PROCESS

Beginning in 1948, Poland was governed by the Polish United Workers' Party (PUWP; Polska Zjednoczona Partia Robotnicza), the country's communist party, which was modeled on the Communist Party of the Soviet Union. The postwar government was run as a dual system in which state organs were controlled by parallel organs of the PUWP. The executive branch of government, therefore, was in effect the PUWP, with the party's first secretary acting as the de facto head of state and the most powerful authority. The party's Political Bureau, or Politburo, operated as the central administration, and the party ensured its control over all offices and appointments by use of the *nomenklatura*, a list of politically reliable people.

Two other parties, the United Peasant Party (Zjednoczone Stronnictwo Ludowe; ZSL) and the Democratic Party (Stronnictwo Demokratyczne; SD), were permitted to exist but only as entirely subservient allies of the PUWP. However, in 1989 economic and political problems obliged the government to recognize the independent trade union Solidarity (which had been banned not long after it came into being in 1980) and allow it to contest at least some seats in a general election. The PUWP and its allies were guaranteed 65 percent of the seats in the Sejm, but Solidarity won all the rest and all but one of those in the Senate, going on to form Poland's first postcommunist government with the support of the SD and the ZSL, which broke their alliance with the PUWP. In 1990 the PUWP voted to disband and reform as the Social Democracy of the Republic of Poland (Socjaldemokracja

Rzeczypospolitej Polskiej; SdRP). In the same year, Lech Wałęsa, the leader of Solidarity, was elected president.

Thereafter, however, as Poles experienced the costs of economic reform, support for Solidarity waned, and the party split into several smaller groups. In the first completely free elections, in 1991, no party obtained more than one-eighth of the vote, which led to a succession of short-lived coalition governments. In the 1993 legislative election the Polish Peasant Party (Polskie Stronnictwo Ludowe, or PSL, as the ZSL was renamed) and the Democratic Left Alliance (Sojusz Lewicy Demokratycznej; SLD), a coalition comprising the SdRP and All Poland Trade Unions Alliance (Ogólnopolskie Porozumienie Związków Zawodowych; OPZZ), won a majority of seats and formed a coalition government. In the presidential election of 1995, Wałęsa was defeated by a former communist, Aleksander Kwaśniewski, who was reelected in 2000. Nevertheless, there was no fundamental change in economic and political policy: all postcommunist governments gave high priority to the integration of Poland into the EU and NATO.

Before the 1997 parliamentary election, the fragmented political right united under the banner of the Solidarity Electoral Action (Akcja Wyborcza Solidarność; AWS), which was later reorganized as the Solidarity Electoral Action of the Right (AWSP). In the decade following, other leading political parties were the SLD, the PSL, the leftist Union of Labour (Unia Pracy; UP), the liberal-democratic Freedom Union (Unia Wolności; UW), and the centre-right Law and Justice (Prawo i Sprawiedliwość; PiS) and Civic Platform (Platforma Obywatelska; PO) parties. Poland grants universal suffrage at age 18.

SECURITY

Poland's armed forces consist of three services—the army, the air force, and the navy. They are divided into the four military districts of Warsaw, Pomerania, Kraków, and Silesia. Under the communist

WARSAW PACT

The Warsaw Pact was the informal name of the Warsaw Treaty of Friendship, Cooperation, and Mutual Assistance (May 14, 1955–July 1, 1991). The treaty established a mutual-defense organization (Warsaw Treaty Organization) composed originally of the Soviet Union and Albania, Bulgaria, Czechoslovakia, East Germany, Hungary, Poland, and Romania. (Albania withdrew in 1968, and East Germany did so in 1990.) The treaty (which was renewed on April 26, 1985) provided for a unified military command and for the maintenance of Soviet military units on the territories of the other participating states.

The immediate occasion for the Warsaw Pact was the Paris agreement among the Western powers admitting West Germany to the North Atlantic Treaty Organization. The Warsaw Pact was, however, the first step in a more systematic plan to strengthen the Soviet hold over its satellites, a program undertaken by the Soviet leaders Nikita Khrushchev and Nikolay Bulganin after their assumption of power early in 1955. The treaty also served as a lever to enhance the bargaining position of the Soviet Union in international diplomacy, an inference that may be drawn by the concluding article of the treaty, which stipulated that the Warsaw agreement would lapse when a general East-West collective-security pact should come into force.

The Warsaw Pact, particularly its provision for the garrisoning of Soviet troops in satellite territory, became a target of nationalist hostility in Poland and Hungary during the uprisings in those two countries in 1956. The Soviet Union invoked the treaty when it decided to move Warsaw Pact troops into Czechoslovakia in August 1968 to bring the Czechoslovak regime back into the fold after it had begun lifting restraints on freedom of expression and had sought closer relations with the West. (Only Albania and Romania refused to join in the Czechoslovak repression.)

After the democratic revolutions of 1989 in eastern Europe, the Warsaw Pact became moribund and was formally declared "nonexistent" on July 1, 1991, at a final summit meeting of Warsaw Pact leaders in Prague, Czech. Deployed Soviet troops were gradually withdrawn from the former satellite countries, now politically independent countries; and the decades-long confrontation between eastern and western Europe was formally rejected by members of the Warsaw Pact.

government the armed forces were highly politicized. The military command was controlled by the party's Main Political Administration, which also oversaw the political indoctrination and supervision of all units. Most officers were party members. Senior officers normally graduated from Soviet academies. One of the founding members of the Warsaw Pact, a mutual-defense organization dominated by the Soviet Union, Poland supplied the second largest contingent to its forces. After the organization dissolved in 1991, Poland's forces were depoliticized in preparation for joining NATO. Poland, along with the Czech Republic and Hungary, joined NATO on March 12, 1999. That year compulsory military service was reduced from 18 months to 12 months; beginning in 1988, conscientious objectors were allowed to perform a civilian alternative to conscription.

The regular defense of Poland's frontiers is provided by the border guard. The Office of the Protection of the State (UOP), established in 1990, was charged with the country's intelligence services. In 2002 it was replaced by the Internal Security Agency (ABW). Normal civilian police services are under the authority of the Ministry of Internal Affairs. Under the communist government, police services were undertaken by the Citizens' Militia— of which the Motorized Detachments of the Citizens' Militia (ZOMO) acted as a mobile paramilitary riot squad—and the Security Service (SB), a secret political police force. In the early 1980s ZOMO played a key role in enforcing martial law and controlling demonstrations. The paramilitary nature of the Policja ("Police"), as they became known after 1990, has diminished.

HEALTH AND WELFARE

Health care in Poland has been handled largely by the Ministry of Health and Social Welfare, which oversees the health departments of the regional governments. Facilities include clinics; hospitals; sanatoriums, rest homes, and spas; and ambulance services. Private medical and dental practices proliferated after the fall of communism, and the pharmaceutical industry also was privatized. In general, the health care system was in a state of transition during the 1990s, and medical services were seriously strained during periods of general economic crisis. In 1999 the government launched a major reform of the universal health care system.

Under communism, social insurance for health services provided for free treatment for all workers and the members of their families, as well as for pensioners, invalids, students, and others. In addition, there was a social service whose purpose was to ensure a suitable means of support for the elderly and invalids. Services for the unemployed were established as a part of the 1989–90 economic reforms. During the mid-1990s, however, a number of laws were enacted that reduced the formerly comprehensive coverage of the unemployment program. In 1990–2000 the incidence of many diseases, including measles, mumps, venereal disease, and salmonella infections, fell precipitously, but other diseases, such as influenza and mental and behavioral disorders, rose during this period.

HOUSING

As a result of the program of urbanization that began in the 1940s, Polish cities became overwhelmed by migrant workers from the countryside, and the demand for housing vastly exceeded supply. In urban areas, various cooperative housing schemes were put into operation by the local government authorities, but the standard apartment was inadequate for many families. As a result of the low priority placed on the creation of housing during communist rule, housing shortages were extreme in the 1980s and '90s. In postcommunist Poland private ownership of housing increased significantly. In 2001 some 106,000 dwellings were completed, slightly more than were built in the five-year period from 1991 to 1995 (101,000).

EDUCATION

Schools of all types and on all levels are free; the system of schooling is standard; and attendance from age 7 to 18 is compulsory. The system, reformed in 1999, contains nursery, primary (six grades), and secondary schools. There are two levels of secondary schools, the *gimnazjum* (grades 7 through 9) and the *liceum* (two to four additional years). Several types of the upper-level secondary schools offer vocational training, technical training, and general college-preparatory education. In general, all schools are subject to the Ministry of National Education, but medical schools and colleges are subject to the Ministry of Health and Social Welfare, army colleges to the Ministry of National Defense, and higher schools of art to the Ministry of Culture and Arts. A substantial number of private schools of all levels (including colleges) emerged in the 1980s and '90s.

Prominent universities include the University of Warsaw (founded 1818), the Jagiellonian University (1364) in Kraków, Adam Mickiewicz University (1919) in Poznań, and the Catholic University of Lublin (1918; from 1945 to 1989 the only private university in the Soviet bloc). The highest academic institution is the Polish Academy of Sciences, which has numerous research institutes and represents Polish learning abroad.

CHAPTER 19

POLISH CULTURAL LIFE

The culture of Poland has been nurtured by a great variety of folk traditions, with influences and borrowings from France, Scandinavia, Russia, and, more recently, the United States. Poland's strong connections to the Roman Catholic Church, dating to the 10th century, brought it into close orbit with western Europe. This gave Poland access to cultural developments that had a lesser impact on some of its neighbours. Unlike Russia, Poland was deeply immersed in all the great movements of Western culture—such as humanism, the Renaissance, the Reformation, the Enlightenment, and Romanticism—and its cultural identity was already strong before the series of partitions of Polish territory began in 1772. Because of its loss of political independence, Poland in the 19th and 20th centuries was characterized by an unrelenting struggle to preserve its national culture and values from foreign impositions and government policy.

The Roman Catholic Church in Poland has played a social and cultural role far beyond the religious sphere. After World War II and the arrival of state socialism, catechism lessons—conducted with great zeal in the parishes—exposed children to a nonofficial view of the world. Church-sponsored societies, such as the Catholic Intellectual Clubs, provided adults with a unique forum for free public discussion. Parish halls provided shelter for a wide variety of uncensored exhibitions, plays, films, and meetings. And the work and example of Pope John Paul II lent support to the popular movement that resulted in

Poland's transition from communist satellite to independent, democratic nation in the last years of the 20th century.

DAILY LIFE AND SOCIAL CUSTOMS

Because of rapid industrialization and urbanization, as well as a certain distrust of rural conservatism during the years of communist rule, Poland's traditional folk culture has been seriously undermined since World War II. Regional dress, regional dialects and forms of speech, peasant arts and crafts, and religious and folk festivals have all been swamped by mass culture from the cities and the media. In an effort to compensate, the Roman Catholic Church has tried to preserve the religious elements of folk culture, notably in the large annual pilgrimages to shrines such as Częstochowa, Kalwaria Zebrzydowska (a UNESCO World Heritage site), Lanckorona, and Piekary Śląskie. Similarly, the communist authorities supported folk music and folk dancing. The colourful and stylized repertoire of the State Folk Ensemble, Mazowsze, for example, won international acclaim. Several regional communities, including the Górale ("Highlanders") of Podhale, the Kurpie in the northeast, and the inhabitants of Łowicz, near Warsaw, have created an authentic blend of the old and the new culture.

Classical music festivals also are quite popular, particularly those commemorating Romantic pianist and composer Frédéric Chopin (Fryderyk Franciszek Szopen), though the music of Beethoven is celebrated in Kraków in spring and that of Mozart in Warsaw in summer. Traditional Polish cuisine includes hearty dishes such as duck soup (*czarnina*), red beet soup (*barszcz*), dumplings (pierogi), smoked salmon and eel, sausages and sauerkraut, and pork and poultry dishes, the latter often served with a sweet sauce. The products of both gardens and forests, such as horseradish, currants, cabbages, gooseberries, and mushrooms, figure in many Polish dishes, such as *bigos*, which makes use of cabbage and freshly harvested mushrooms, and the traditional soup called *grzybowa*. *Pączki* are fruit-filled deep-fried pastries served on the Christian feast days prior to the Lenten season of fasting.

The national flag of Poland, which was adopted in 1919, comprises a white horizontal band above a red horizontal band. The Polish coat of arms features a white eagle on a red background. The national anthem is "Jeszcze Polska nie zginęła" ("Poland Has Not Yet Perished"). Major holidays either are Christian in nature (Easter, Christmas, Feast of the Assumption, Corpus Christi, and All Saints' Day) or commemorate nation building, such as Constitution Day on May 3 and Independence Day on November 11. Traditional holidays include Topienie Marzanny (March 23), when children throw dolls symbolizing winter into newly flowing rivers.

THE ARTS

The Polish arts have been influenced by several factors throughout history. Folk traditions, nationalism, religion, and other cultures have all left their marks on popular forms of Polish cultural expression.

LITERATURE

Polish literature developed long ago into the main vehicle of national expression. For many Poles, literature and religion stand as the twin pillars of their heritage. Literature provides one of their most cherished links with Western civilization and is one of the main safeguards of their national identity. The close relationship between local political events and literary trends, however, together with a necessary resort to elaborate allegories, allusions, and symbols during the communist period, rendered many excellent Polish works inaccessible to the foreign public.

The first half of the 19th century produced the three most renowned Polish poets: Adam Mickiewicz, Juliusz Słowacki, and Zygmunt Krasiński. During the second half of the 19th century and the beginning of the 20th century, great Polish prose writers—including Bolesław Prus, Eliza Orzeszkowa, Stefan Żeromski, and the Nobel Prize winners Henryk Sienkiewicz (1905) and Władysław Reymont (1924)—were active, some of whom were part of the Young Poland movement. To this number should be added the outstanding

WISŁAWA SZYMBORSKA

The Polish poet Wisława Szymborska (born July 2, 1923, Bnin [now part of Kórnik], Poland—died February 1, 2012, Kraków) was known for her intelligent and empathic explorations of philosophical, moral, and ethical issues. She won the Nobel Prize for Literature in 1996.

Szymborska's father was the steward on a count's family estate. When she was eight, the family moved to Kraków, and she attended high school there. Between 1945 and 1948 she studied literature and sociology at Kraków's Jagiellonian University. Her first published poem, "Szukam słowa" ("I Seek the Word"), appeared in a Kraków newspaper in March 1945. *Dlatego żyjemy* (1952; "That's Why We Are Alive"), her first volume of poetry, was an attempt to conform to Socialist Realism, the officially approved literary style of Poland's communist regime. In 1953 she joined the editorial staff of *Życie Literackie* ("Literary Life"), a weekly magazine of intellectual interests, and remained there until 1981. During this period she gained a reputation not only as a poet but also as a book reviewer and translator of French poetry. In the 1980s she wrote for the underground press under the pseudonym Stanczykówna and also wrote for a magazine in Paris.

Between 1952 and 1993 Szymborska published more than a dozen volumes of poetry. She later disowned the first two volumes, which contain poems in the style of Socialist Realism, as not indicative of her true poetic intentions. Her third volume, *Wołanie do Yeti* (1957; "Calling Out to Yeti"), marked a clear shift to a more personal style of poetry and expressed her dissatisfaction with communism (Stalinism in particular). Subsequent volumes, such as *Sól* (1962; "Salt"), *Sto pociech* (1967; "No End of Fun"), and *Wszelki wypadek* (1972; "Could Have"), contain poems noteworthy for their precise, concrete language and ironic detachment. Selections of her poems were translated into English and published in such collections as *Sounds, Feelings, Thoughts: Seventy Poems* (1981), *People on a Bridge: Poems* (1990), *View with a Grain of Sand* (1995), *Monologue of a Dog* (2005), and *Here* (2010).

novelist Joseph Conrad (Józef Teodor Konrad Korzeniowski), whose mature writings were in English but who brought a distinctly non-English tragic sensibility into English literature. The underground literature that began during World War II but was not appreciated until the 1950s and '60s is exemplified by the reception accorded Bruno Schulz, a short-story writer killed by the Nazis in 1942. Important poets of the postwar period included Zbigniew Herbert, Tadeusz Różewicz, and the Nobel Prize winners Czesław Miłosz (1980) and Wisława Szymborska (1996). In the latter part of the 20th century, playwrights Witold Gombrowicz and Sławomir Mrożek, science-fiction author Stanisław Lem, and reporter and essayist Ryszard Kapuściński earned international reputations, as did the expatriate novelist Jerzy Kosinski, and the expatriate *Nowa fala* (New Wave) poet Adam Zagajewski gained notice. Written at the margins of Europe during most of the 20th century, Polish literature has been recognized as an exceptionally vital force not only in the cultural life of its nation but also in world letters generally.

MUSIC

Polish music, like Polish literature, has a continuous tradition reaching back to the Middle Ages. As the least overtly political of the arts, it suffered less from official constraints. The native characteristics of this music founded on the inimitable rhythms and melodies of folk music—the *krakowiak*, mazurka, and polonaise—developed early, and a distinctive school of Polish church music had become well established by the Renaissance. The first major Polish opera, *Cud mniemany, czyli Krakowiacy i Górale* ("The Pretended Miracle, or Krakovians and Highlanders") by Jan Stefani and Wojciech Bogusławski, was staged in 1794. In the 19th century Stanisław Moniuszko wrote a series of popular operas, including *Halka, Straszny dwór* ("The Haunted Manor"), and *Hrabina* ("The Countess").

Frédéric Chopin is considered to have created the quintessence of Polishness in music. In addition to his renown as one of the supreme master composers, he was the first of a constant stream of instrumentalists from Polish lands who have won international acclaim. Pianists such as

FRÉDÉRIC CHOPIN

Perhaps the greatest of all composers for the piano was Frédéric Chopin (born March 1, 1810, Zelazowa Wola, Duchy of Warsaw [now in Poland]—died October 17, 1849, Paris, France). Called a "musical genius" when he was a teenager, Chopin composed a remarkable variety of brilliant pieces—warlike polonaises, elegant waltzes, romantic nocturnes, and poetic ballades and études.

Chopin was born in a village near Warsaw, Poland. His father, Nicholas, was a Frenchman who had lived in Poland for many years. His Polish mother was of noble birth. Several months after Frédéric's birth the family moved to Warsaw.

Even as a small child, Chopin loved piano music. He began to take piano lessons when he was 6 years old. He started to compose music even before he knew how to write down his ideas. At the age of 8 he performed in a public charity concert. Chopin's first published musical work, a rondo, appeared when he was 15 years old. When Chopin graduated from the lyceum, at 17, he was recognized as the leading pianist of Warsaw and a talented composer.

After Chopin gave two successful concerts in Vienna when he was 19, he began writing works designed for his original piano style. At the same time as his return to Vienna in 1830, Poland revolted against its Russian rulers. The uprising failed, and as a result the Russian czar put Warsaw under harsh military rule. Chopin decided to go to Paris, which was the center of the romantic movement in the arts. Except for occasional trips, Chopin spent the rest of his life in Paris. He gave lessons and concerts, and publishers paid well for his compositions.

The French loved him for his genius and his charm. Poets, musicians, wealthy Parisians, and Polish exiles were his friends. An important influence was a romantic friendship with Baroness Dudevant, better known as the novelist George Sand. Chopin died of tuberculosis at age 39.

Chopin wrote few concertos and sonatas. Instead he perfected freer musical forms. Among his compositions are some 50 mazurkas, 26 preludes, 24 études, 19 nocturnes, 15 waltzes, 11 polonaises, 4 ballades, and 3 sonatas. For his polonaises and mazurkas he used the rhythms and spirit of Polish folk dances.

Ignacy Paderewski and Artur Rubinstein and violinists such as Henryk Szeryng attest to the vitality of Polish musical life. Contemporary Polish composition has been dominated by Karol Szymanowski, Witold Lutosławski, Henryk Górecki, and Krzysztof Penderecki. All branches of classical music—opera, symphony, chamber, and choral—are well represented in Poland, and several orchestras and choirs appear regularly on the international circuit. Popular music in Poland derives largely from Western styles, although Polish jazz, officially suppressed during the first two decades of communist rule, has earned a reputation for experiment and excellence, in part owing to the pioneering work of musicians such as Michał Urbaniak, Tomasz Stanko, and Leszek Możdżer. Well-attended festivals such as the Warsaw Jazz Jamboree and Jazz on the Oder draw performers and spectators from around the world.

VISUAL ARTS

Many fine examples of medieval Romanesque and Gothic architecture, both secular and religious, have been preserved, together with outstanding sculptures, among which the wooden altar of Veit Stoss (Wit Stwosz), in St. Mary's Church (Kościół Mariacki) in Kraków, is the most famous. The vast red-brick castle of Malbork (Marienburg), once the headquarters of the Teutonic Knights, is among the most impressive in Europe; the well-restored castle was named a World Heritage site by UNESCO in 1997. The architecture and sculpture of the Renaissance and Baroque periods were formed under Italian influence but nevertheless developed individual Polish forms, as seen in the town hall of Poznań or the decorated granaries at Kazimierz Dolny. Zamość, a model Renaissance city built in the 1580s, has survived virtually intact. Like the medieval town of Toruń, it was designated a World Heritage site. The best-preserved urban architecture of the

MAGDALENA ABAKANOWICZ

The Polish artist Magdalena Abakanowicz (born June 20, 1930, Falenty, Poland) earned international acclaim for her massive series of sculptures. Her artwork has appeared in more than 100 group and solo exhibitions. She also has served as an instructor of her craft: from 1965, she taught at the Academy of Fine Arts in Poznań, Poland, becoming a professor in 1979.

A descendant of Polish nobility, Abakanowicz studied at the School of Fine Arts in Sopot, Poland (1949), and graduated from the Academy of Fine Arts in Warsaw (1954). She began working as an independent artist in 1956 and initially earned success for large, three-dimensional woven sculptures known as *Abakans*, a derivation of her family name. These monumental, often garmentlike, pieces are ambiguous and compelling. Although initially Abakanowicz was best known for her work with textiles, she also exhibited paintings and drawings. Her later work, generally made of hard surfaces—though several contained fibres, rope, or textiles—characteristically employed groupings of repeated forms often based on the human body (described by one critic as "headless human husks") or on animals or trees. These forms are similar in appearance and gesture to one another, but each has its individuality. Works such as *Heads* (1975), *Backs* (1976–82), and *Embryology* (1978–81) were composed of multiple forms, primarily made of organic materials such as burlap, rope, and canvas. Much of her later work was done in bronze, stone, or concrete: *Katarsis* (1985; 33 cast bronze sculptures); *Becalmed Beings* (1993; 40 cast bronze figures); and *Space of Stone* (2003; 22 granite blocks). Many are large permanent outdoor installations. These are scattered throughout the world in places such as Jerusalem; Seoul; Minneapolis, Minnesota; Kansas City, Missouri; Dallas, Texas; Washington, D.C.; Lisbon; Paris; and New York City.

late Middle Ages and Renaissance is that of the Old Town and the Wawel Castle in Kraków. The classicism of the end of the 18th century and the beginning of the 19th century left its most valuable monuments in some of the great palaces, such as that of the Radziwiłłs at Nieborów or at Łazienki in Warsaw. Moreover, there are many examples of imperial German and Russian architecture from the 19th century, notably Lublin Castle.

Polish painting attained its greatest development in the second half of the 19th century, encompassing western European styles but again with specific national characteristics. Henryk Siemiradzki, Jan Matejko (the creator of monumental romantic historical canvases), and a number of landscape and genre painters achieved the widest fame. Great sensitivity was shown in portraits by Stanisław Wyspiański, a painter who was active in drama and design. With her woven sculptures, Magdalena Abakanowicz brought fibre arts to the forefront in the late 20th century.

THEATRE AND MOTION PICTURES

The Polish national theatre, as distinct from the performance of earlier religious, court, and foreign plays that had circulated since the Middle Ages, dates from the end of the 18th century. The great pioneer was Wojciech Bogusławski, an actor, director, and playwright. Political conditions during the period of partition (1772–1918) inhibited theatrical development, however, and most of the Romantic masterworks of Mickiewicz or Słowacki, who wrote drama in addition to poetry, were never staged during their lifetimes. The comedian and satirist Aleksander Fredro earned a less-exalted but no-less-lasting reputation. Kraków, in Austrian Galicia, became a centre of lively theatre at the turn of the century. Between World Wars I and II, Juliusz Osterwa in Warsaw and Leon Schiller in Lwów (now Lviv, Ukraine), Warsaw, and Łódź (after 1945) launched the experimental tradition. After 1956, once the era of Socialist Realism had passed, the avant-garde came into its own. The Theatre of the Absurd was explored alongside the revival of the classical repertoire. During the 1960s the Laboratory Theatre of Jerzy Grotowski (whose theories and methods emphasized the nonverbal aspects of theatre) gained international acclaim, and his work had a broad impact, especially in the United States. Henryk Tomaszewski's Pantomime Theatre experienced parallel success. Tadeusz Kantor, a painter, designer, and director, also has been an important influence.

The origins of Polish cinema date to 1909. The communist government supported war films and themes connected with the Nazi occupation but allowed and subsidized projects on a wide range of contemporary issues. Many artists critical of the communist regime expressed themselves in innovative documentary films. Historical epics have also enjoyed great popularity. During the late 1950s

ANDRZEJ WAJDA

The filmmaker Andrzej Wajda (born March 6, 1926, Suwałki, Poland) was a leading director in the "Polish film school," a group of highly talented individuals whose films brought international recognition to the Polish cinema during the 1950s. His contributions to the development of the Polish motion-picture industry have been enormous.

Wajda became interested in the visual arts when working as assistant to a restorer of old church paintings in Radom. He studied painting at the Academy of Fine Arts in Kraków, then film directing at the Leon Schiller State Theatre and Film School at Łódź. His first three films, *Pokolenie* (1954; *A Generation*), *Kanał* (1957; *Canal*), and *Popiół i diament* (1958; *Ashes and Diamonds*), won prizes at international film festivals. They constituted a trilogy that dealt in symbolic imagery with sweeping social and political changes in Poland during the German occupation, the Warsaw uprising of 1944, and the immediate postwar years. The actor Zbigniew Cybulski became famous for his portrayal of the hero, a boy growing into manhood whose idealism survives the humiliation and defeat of the occupation and the deaths of friends and the girl he loves.

Wajda became increasingly concerned with the problems of youth in the contemporary world and with the conflicts inherent in the human situation in later films such as *Lotna* (1959), *Wszystko na sprzedaż* (1968; *Everything for Sale*), *Ziemia obiecana* (1974; *The Promised Land*), *Czlowiek z marmuru* (1977; *Man of Marble*), *Bez znieczulenia* (1978; *Without Anesthetic, or Rough Treatment*), *Panny z Wilka* (1979; *The Young Girls of Wilko*), *Czlowiek z zelaza* (1981; *Man of Iron*), and *Danton* (1983). The highly acclaimed *Korczak* (1990) is a true story of the final days of Henryk Goldszmit (better known by his pen name Janusz Korczak), a Jewish doctor, writer, and child advocate who refused to escape Nazi-occupied Poland during World War II in order to maintain his orphanage. Other films include *Nastasja* (1994); *Pan Tadeusz* (1999), which is based on Adam Mickiewicz's epic poem of the same name; *Zemsta* (2002; *The Revenge*), which starred Roman Polanski; *Katyn* (2007), about the Katyn Massacre in 1940; and *Tatarak* (2009; *Sweet Rush*), a meditation on death that combined elements of fact and fiction. Wajda received an honorary Academy Award in 2000.

Polish films began to attract worldwide attention. Just as the State Film School at Łódź earned high standing in the filmmaking profession, so did the work of individual directors who broke free of official preferences. Undoubtedly, the leading figure was Andrzej Wajda, whose films and theatre productions set precedents for independence and excellence in exploring the conflicts in Polish society. Roman Polanski, who worked internationally, won an Academy Award for his direction of *The Pianist* (2002). Krzysztof Kieślowski, known for his trilogy of films, *Trzy kolory* ("Three Colours"), also worked outside Poland.

Among other distinguished directors are Andrzej Munk, Aleksander Ford, Tadeusz Konwicki, Wojciech Has, Jerzy Kawalerowicz, Krzysztof Zanussi, and Agnieszka Holland.

CULTURAL INSTITUTIONS

Poles have made great efforts to preserve and cherish the records and artifacts of the past. Archives and museums of art, ethnography, archaeology, and natural history can be found in many Polish cities. The Czartoryski Museum in Kraków dates to the beginning of the 19th century, the Archaeological Museum in Poznań to 1857, and the National Museum in Warsaw to 1862. After World War II, official policy concentrated on the creation of new regional museums in cities recovered from German occupation, on museums connected with the history of the communist movement, on former private palaces and collections acquired by the state, and on sites connected with Nazi war crimes, such as the concentration and extermination camps at Oświęcim (Auschwitz) or Majdanek. The government also supported traditional museums and galleries of modern art (e.g., the Zachęta State Art Gallery in Warsaw, established 1900). The Roman Catholic Church is active in preserving and exhibiting the art treasures and records connected with Poland's religious heritage. The Churches of Peace in Jawor and Swidnica, which have been designated UNESCO World Heritage sites, were built for Protestants in Silesia in the 17th century.

SPORTS AND RECREATION

Team sports and spectator sports thrive in Poland. Professional football (soccer) teams attract large crowds in the towns, and local authorities provide facilities for athletics (track and field) and swimming. Skiing and mountaineering in the Tatras and sailing on the Baltic or the Masurian Lakes are popular. In addition, many Poles enjoy cycling, horseback riding, and spelunking. There are a large number of recreation clubs devoted to football, volleyball, table tennis, athletics, basketball, and martial arts.

Since 1924 Poland has participated in all Summer and Winter Olympic Games, with the exception of the 1984 Games in Los Angeles, boycotted by the communist regime along with other Soviet-bloc governments. Among Poland's most accomplished Olympians were Irena Kirszenstein-Szewińska, who participated in the Olympic Games from 1964 to 1980 and won seven medals (three gold) in track and field; Józef Szmidt, a triple jumper who dominated the event for six years and won two gold medals; and Robert Korzeniowski, who at the 2000 Olympic Games in Sydney, Australia, became the first man to win both race-walking events. The Polish national football team won the Olympic gold medal in 1972 and earned third place at the 1974 World Cup. In 1982 the team, led by star forward Zbigniew Boniek, again reached the World Cup semifinals.

MEDIA AND PUBLISHING

Under the communist government, the Main Office for the Control of the Press, Publications, and Public Performances (GUKPIW), headquartered in Warsaw, controlled the media, publishing, films, theatres, exhibitions, advertising, and related activities. The bureau maintained an office in all television and radio stations, press and publishing houses, film and theatre studios, and printing establishments throughout the country. Authorization was required even for such printed items as wedding invitations, obituary notices, and stationery. The government closely controlled access to photocopiers and printing machines, and all purchases of paper in bulk required a permit. Censorship of foreign mail was routine. No sphere of information was immune, however distant from immediate political concerns; censors attempted not only to suppress material but also to mold all information at its source.

The Polish press included the official organs of the party and state, such as *Trybuna Ludu* ("People's Tribune"), the organ of the PUWP, and a variety of less closely controlled semiparty newspapers and journals, such as *Życie Warszawy* ("Warsaw Life"), *Polityka* ("Politics"; a lively weekly), and *Twórczość* ("Creativity"; an intellectual monthly). Despite the official controls, speech was not generally suppressed in Poland, and the highly literate Poles became masters at writing and reading "between the lines." Moreover, alternative perspectives were offered in the respected independent Kraków publication *Tygodnik Powszechny* ("Universal Weekly"), in the Roman Catholic journals *Znak* ("The Sign") and *Więź* ("The Link"), and in the underground "free sector." The latter developed in the 1970s and 1980s into a vast network, publishing everything from books banned by the regime to academic journals and local newssheets.

Restrictions on the media eased in 1989, and Solidarity supporters began publishing numerous journals and newspapers, including the daily newspaper *Gazeta Wyborcza* ("Voters Daily"; Eng. ed. *Gazeta International*). In 1990 the state abandoned censorship of the press, and this led to the appearance of a wide range of new publications. Though in the 1990s the number of newspaper titles was reduced by half, the number of books and magazines doubled. The private sector in both broadcast and print media has grown rapidly, in great part owing to foreign investments. It includes television and radio stations, national and regional newspapers and magazines, and publishing houses. Many communities publish local newsletters and bulletins. *Rzeczpospolita* ("The Commonwealth") is a semiofficial newspaper of record.

CHAPTER 20

BEGINNINGS OF THE POLISH STATE TO THE JAGIELLONIANS

The terms "Poland" and "Poles" appear for the first time in medieval chronicles of the late 10th century. The land that the Poles, a West Slavic people, came to inhabit was covered by forests with small areas under cultivation where clans grouped themselves into numerous tribes. The dukes (*dux*) were originally the commanders of an armed retinue (*drużyna*) with which they broke the authority of the chieftains of the clans, thus transforming the original tribal organization into a territorial unit. Two tribes, the Polanie—based around the fortified settlement (*castrum*) of Gniezno—and the Wiślanie—who lived near Kraków—expanded to bring other tribes under their control.

THE PIAST MONARCHY

Exposed to some missionary activities linked with St. Methodius, the state of Wiślanie fell under the rule of Great Moravia—which was destroyed by the Magyar invasion of the early 10th century—and came eventually under the rule of Mieszko I, the first ruler of the Polanie to be mentioned in written records. He is regarded as the founder of the Piast dynasty, the beginnings of which are clouded in legend, though the names of three of his predecessors are known.

THE EARLY STATE

Creating what a contemporary Spanish-Jewish traveler, Ibrāhīm ibn Ya'ḳūb, described as the most powerful of the existing Slav states, Mieszko accepted Roman Catholicism via Bohemia in 966. A missionary bishopric directly dependent on the papacy was established in Poznań. This was the true beginning of Polish history, for Christianity was a carrier of Western civilization with which Poland was henceforth associated.

Facing the crucial problem of Poland's relationship to the two pillars of medieval Christendom, the Germanic Holy Roman Empire and the papacy, Mieszko battled the expansive tendencies of the former—a record that dates from 963 refers to a struggle with the German dukes—while he sought reliance on Rome, to which he subordinated his state in a curious document, the *Dagome iudex* (c. 991). Poland alternately competed and cooperated with neighbouring Bohemia and Hungary as well as with the principality of Kievan Rus. At Mieszko's death the Polish state stretched from the Baltic Sea to the Carpathian Mountains, resembling in shape post-World War II Poland.

Because the principle of primogeniture was unknown in the country, every succession led to internal strife. Mieszko's successor was Bolesław I (the Brave). Commanding a huge military force, he sought hegemony in east-central Europe. In 1000 he received the Holy Roman Emperor Otto III, who dreamed of restoring a universal Roman empire and who recognized the sovereign status of the Polish duke. Moreover, Otto agreed to an independent Polish ecclesiastical organization that added an archbishopric in Gniezno and bishoprics in Kraków,

Wrocław, and Kołobrzeg to the already extant bishopric in Poznań. Given the role of the church in medieval statehood, this was a great achievement. Paying their respects to St. Adalbert (Vojtěch)—the former bishop of Prague slain by the pagan Prussians and later elevated to sainthood—the two rulers sought to coordinate their missionary activities in the pagan Slav lands between the Elbe and Oder rivers. This area, home of the so-called Polabian Slavs, formed a kind of buffer between the two states and was the object of their respective expansion.

The successors of Otto pursued German objectives rather than imperial mirages and struggled with Bolesław, who briefly occupied Bohemia and intervened in Kievan Rus. Polish-German strife continued intermittently until 1018. In 1025 Bolesław assumed the royal crown, which made him the equal of the other monarchs of Europe.

COLLAPSE AND RESTORATION

The virtual collapse of the state under Bolesław's son Mieszko II, who was even obliged to renounce his kingly status, showed how much the political fortunes of a state were bound to the personality of its ruler. Mieszko's successor, Casimir I, had to flee the country, which was torn by internal strife. A pagan reaction against Christianity combined with revolt against fiscal and administrative burdens to bring about a popular uprising. Casimir had to be restored by the emperor, Conrad II, who wished to

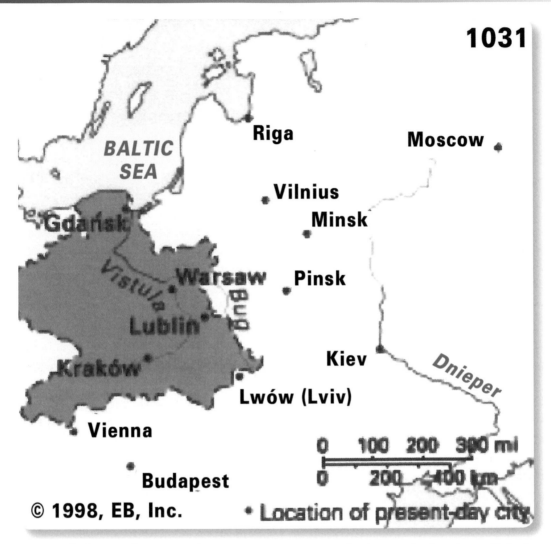

preserve a balance of power in the region. Known later as "the Restorer," Casimir eventually succeeded in bringing under his sway most of the Polish lands, reviving the ecclesiastical organization, and making Kraków his capital instead of Gniezno or Poznań, which had been devastated by the Czechs.

Casimir's son and successor, Bolesław II (the Bold), sought to revive the great power designs of the first Bolesław. Skillfully exploiting the great Investiture Controversy between the empire and the papacy that affected most of Europe, Bolesław II sided with Rome and gained the royal crown in 1076. Bolesław was later drawn into a conflict with Stanislaus (Stanisław), the bishop of Kraków, whom the king ordered killed in 1079 under circumstances still debated by historians.

INVESTITURE CONTROVERSY

The struggle between the papacy and the secular rulers of Europe over the latter's presentation of the symbols of office to churchmen was known as the Investiture Controversy. Pope Gregory VII condemned lay investiture in 1078 as an unjustified assertion of secular authority over the church; the issue was pivotal in his dispute with King Henry IV and in the larger struggle over Henry's refusal to obey papal commands. Henry successfully drove Gregory from Rome and installed an antipope, but it would be Gregory's rejection of lay investiture that would ultimately prevail. Henry I of England renounced lay investiture in 1106 in return for the guarantee that homage would be paid to the king before consecration.

The Concordat of Worms, reached in 1122 at Worms, Germany, forged a similar compromise between Henry V and Calixtus II. It marked the end of the first phase of conflict between Rome and what was becoming the Holy Roman Empire and made a clear distinction between the spiritual side of a prelate's office and his position as a landed magnate and vassal of the crown. Bishops and abbots were to be chosen by the clergy, but the emperor was to decide contested elections. Those selected were to be invested first with the powers and privileges of their office as vassal (granted by the emperor) and then with their ecclesiastical powers and lands (granted by church authority).

Bolesław then fled to Hungary, where he died. The cult of St. Stanislaus, who was canonized in 1253, became widespread in Poland and was invoked to defend the freedom of religion against the state and ethics against power.

Under Bolesław's brother and successor, Władysław I Herman, claims to the royal crown and a more ambitious foreign policy were abandoned. Efforts by the palatine, Sieciech, to maintain centralized power clashed with the ambitions of the rising magnate class. Following a period of internal conflict, Bolesław III (the Wry-Mouthed) emerged as the sole ruler (reigned 1102–38). Promoting Christianity, he expanded his influence over Western Pomerania, whose towns and harbours, such as Wolin, Kołobrzeg, and Szczecin, were already important centres of trade and crafts. Eastern, or Gdańsk, Pomerania came under direct Polish administration. After an invasion by Emperor Henry V was repelled, peace prevailed with the empire, and Bohemia renounced its claims to Silesia.

THE PERIOD OF DIVISIONS

The awareness of centrifugal trends and external dangers led Bolesław III to establish in his testament of 1138 a system meant to ensure greater stability. He divided the state among his sons; the oldest became the senior duke, whose domain included the capital in Kraków and who had general powers over military, foreign, and ecclesiastical matters.

COLLAPSE OF BOLESŁAW'S GOVERNING SYSTEM

By the early 13th century, however, the efforts of the grand duke to exert real controls had come to naught. The entire system was characterized by disputes, subdivisions, and fratricidal strife into which the neighbouring powers were frequently drawn.

During the period of divisions, lasting almost 200 years (until the rule of Casimir III), Poland underwent transformation in almost every sphere of life. The centrally controlled early Piast monarchy had been based on a system of fortified settlements from which an official called the castellan tended to the ruler's domain and acted as administrator, military commander, judge, and tax collector. Around some settlements there arose so-called service villages, in which artisans produced objects needed by the dukes and their retinues. The emerging social pyramid positioned the duke and his officials and leading warriors on top, with various categories of freemen, part-freemen, and slaves at the bottom. Between the 10th and the 12th century, this system slowly began to break down. Improved cultivation methods (notably the three-field system) enhanced the value of the land with which the ruler endowed the church and compensated his nobles, warriors, and officials. Estates cultivated by

a semiserf population grew significantly. The old *drużyna* changed into a smaller personal guard, the armed force being composed of nobles performing military service as landholders.

CULTURAL DEVELOPMENTS, 11TH–13TH CENTURY

The church was the principal proponent of learning and art. Romanesque and then Gothic architecture made their way into Poland. Religious orders such as the Benedictines arrived in the 11th century, the Cistercians in the 12th century, and the Dominicans and the first nuns in the 13th century. Cathedral and, later, parish schools appeared. During this time the earliest historical chronicles appeared. The first was compiled in the early 12th century by a Benedictine monk known as Gallus Anonymous. The second was completed by Wincenty Kadłubek at the beginning of the 13th century.

SOCIAL AND ECONOMIC DEVELOPMENTS

The 13th century marked a turning point in the history of medieval Poland. The agricultural boom was accompanied by the development of salt mining in Little Poland and of silver and gold mining in Silesia. The Polish lands were brought more fully into the European economy, participating in the west-east trade as well as in that of the Baltic region in the north and that along the Danube River in the south. The growth of large landed estates was partly the cause and partly the consequence of surplus production that could be sold on the market. It became profitable to have free tenant farmers, rather than serfs, cultivate the land, which attracted large groups of settlers from as far away as the Rhineland and the Low Countries. Demographic trends in western Europe facilitated this "colonization." The settlers—assured of personal freedom, fixed rents, and some measure of self-administration and operating under the so-called German Law—founded new villages and towns or reorganized old ones. Towns received formal charters (Wrocław in 1242, Poznań in 1253, Kraków in 1257) that provided for autonomy and self-government modeled on that of the German city of Magdeburg—hence the term Magdeburg Law.

Although the burgher population became largely German or German-speaking, the extent of settlement by Germans was restricted except in Silesia and Pomerania. Otherwise, most of the countryside remained Polish. Another alien group, however, began to play an important role in the country's economy—namely, the Jews escaping persecution in the west. Bolesław V (the Chaste) of Great Poland granted to the Jews the Kalisz Privilege (1264), which provided personal freedom, some legal autonomy, and safeguards against forcible baptism.

FEUDALISM

Economic and social transformation led to some forms of feudalism and organization of estates. A system in which the entire state structure was based on contractual personal arrangements between superiors and inferiors (lords and vassals)—with land (fiefs) being the traditional means of reward for services—did not really prevail in Poland. Nor did a typical feudal pyramid exist. Nevertheless, vassalage of sorts and customs of chivalry and knighthood developed. In view of the weakening of the rulers, the landowners, both ecclesiastical (the church in the 12th century) and lay (the nobility in the 13th century), succeeded in obtaining so-called immunities—i.e., exemptions for their estates from taxes, services, and the legal jurisdiction of the state.

During that period the church functioned as the only structure that transcended the divisions. Although the Silesian duchies gravitated toward Germany, the archbishopric of Gniezno continued to include the diocese of Wrocław. Several archbishops were active proponents of reunification of Poland, notably Jakób Świnka. The concepts of Corona Regni Poloniae, as divorced from the actual ruler, and of *gens polonica*—an early form of nationalism that identified the state with the Polish people and implied its indivisibility—began to make their appearance.

THE ARRIVAL OF THE TEUTONIC KNIGHTS

The chances of reunification were dim, as the various branches of the Piast dynasty pursued their vested interests and further subdivided their lands. Western Pomerania, with its native dynasty, and Eastern Pomerania were already largely severed from Poland and threatened by the aggressive and expansive margravate of Brandenburg. In the north the pagan Lithuanians, Prussians, and Jatvingians were harassing Mazovia. In 1226 Conrad of Mazovia called in the German crusading order, generally known as the Teutonic Order, provided them with a territorial base, and assumed that after a joint conquest of the Prussian lands (later known as East Prussia) they would become his vassals. The Teutonic Knights, however, tacitly secured imperial and papal recognition and forged Conrad's acquiescence to their independent status. After a series of ruthless campaigns, Prussia was conquered and resettled by Germans—the old Prussian population having been virtually wiped out. It became a powerful state of the Teutonic Knights. While German historians have traditionally stressed the civilizing and organizational achievements of the Knights, the Poles have emphasized their ruthlessness and aggressiveness. The arrival of the Teutonic Knights changed the balance of forces in that part of Europe and marked the beginning of the rise of Prussia as a great power.

In 1241 Little Poland and Silesia experienced a disastrous Mongol (Tatar) invasion. The duke of Silesia, Henry II (the Pious), who had been gathering forces to reunite Poland, perished in the Battle of Legnica (Liegnitz) in 1241, and the devastation wrought by the Mongols may have contributed to the above-mentioned colonization.

REVIVAL OF THE KINGDOM

The revival of the kingdom hinged upon the incorporation of a series of Polish principalities into a single kingdom. This would lay the foundation for a strong Polish nation.

THE CZECH DYNASTY

In the late 13th century, Bohemia emerged as the leading country in east-central Europe, and King Otakar II (Přemysl Otakar II) even tried to gain the imperial crown. His son Wenceslas II profited from the chaos prevailing in the Polish duchies—a bid for unification by Przemysł II of Great Poland (crowned king in 1295) was cut short by his assassination—to become king of Poland in 1300. Establishing an administration based on provincial royal officials (*starosta*)—a permanent feature of Polish administration in the centuries to come—he temporarily pacified the country. Wenceslas's grandiose plans to rule all of east-central Europe ended with his death in 1305, which was followed a year later by the assassination of his son Wenceslas III. This meant the end of the native Czech Přemyslid dynasty, and John of Luxembourg claimed the thrones of Bohemia and Poland. His pursuit of the latter was opposed by one of the minor dukes, Władysław the Short, who had earlier battled the two Wenceslases and their supporters. Allying himself with the new king of Hungary, Charles I, Władysław withstood the enmity of Bohemia, the Teutonic Knights, rival Polish dukes, and the mainly German patriciate of Kraków. At one point the struggle assumed the character of a Polish-German national conflict.

WŁADYSŁAW I

Władysław was crowned king of Poland in 1320, but he no longer controlled Silesia—whose dukes opted for John and which henceforth came under the Bohemian crown—and the Teutonic Knights seized Eastern Pomerania. The massacre the Knights perpetrated in Gdańsk in 1308 entered Polish folklore. Thus, the reunited Polish kingdom was deprived of two of its most developed provinces—Silesian Wrocław then had some 20,000 inhabitants—and was effectively cut off from the Baltic Sea. Cooperating closely with Hungary, Władysław sought unsuccessfully to regain Pomerania through lawsuits and papal arbitration, but the Knights ignored the verdicts. A major battle with the invading Knights fought at Płowce in 1331 was a Pyrrhic victory for Władysław.

CASIMIR THE GREAT

Under Władysław's son Casimir III (the Great), the only Polish ruler to bear this epithet, peace was made with John of Luxembourg, who gave up his claims to the Polish crown at the meeting of the kings of Poland, Hungary, and Bohemia at Visegrád, Hungary, in 1335. Casimir's simultaneous renunciation of Silesia was somewhat equivocal, and he sought later to regain the Silesian duchies by diplomacy and force. In 1343 Poland signed a peace treaty with the Teutonic Knights through which it recovered some land but retained only formal suzerainty over Pomerania. That policy of compromise was a tactical necessity on the part of a state still much weaker than the Teutonic Knights, Bohemia, or Hungary. Between 1340 and the 1360s, however, Poland expanded by roughly one-third, acquiring a larger part of Halicz, or Red, Ruthenia (the future eastern Galicia), which Hungary and Lithuania also coveted. That acquisition marked an expansion beyond ethnic Polish territory. Casimir's international prestige was evidenced by his acting as arbiter between the Luxembourgs, the Angevins, and the Habsburgs and subsequently hosting an international conference in Kraków in 1364 that dealt with general European issues. The sumptuous banquet given to the visiting rulers by the Kraków burgher Nicholas Wierzynek passed into popular lore.

The domestic achievements of Casimir may be subsumed under the slogan "One king, one law, one currency." His rule uncontested, Casimir presided over a process of unification and codification of laws in the mid-14th century for Great and Little Poland that is often called the Statute of Wiślica. In need of trained lawyers, he founded a university in Kraków (1364) modeled largely on that of Bologna.

It was the second university east of the Rhine River and north of the Alps.

The introduction of a new currency, the Kraków *grosz*, stimulated the economy and assisted the development of international trade. Many brick and stone structures arose in the country, as well as a large number of fortified castles. The population and its density increased. In view of a new wave of Jewish immigrants, the 1264 privilege was extended throughout the kingdom, and the town of Kazimierz, adjacent to Kraków, became a Jewish centre. The privileged condition of the Jews, although they were resented as competitors by the burghers (who staged anti-Jewish riots), eventually resulted in Poland's becoming the home of the largest Jewish population in Christendom.

LOUIS I

Casimir designated as his successor his nephew Louis I (the Great) of Hungary, who gained the support of influential nobles by granting them certain privileges in 1355. Louis's rule in Poland (1370–82), with his mother acting as regent, proved disappointing. Despite earlier promises, he definitely abandoned Silesia and Pomerania and sought to make Halicz Ruthenia directly dependent on Buda in Hungary. Eager to secure the succession to the Polish crown for one of his daughters, he granted privileges to the Polish nobility in the Pact of Koszyce (Hungarian: Kassa) in 1374. Among those privileges was the guarantee of

a minimum tax, which meant that any future increase would have to be negotiated with the nobles as an estate. Thus, the principle of representation was established, but it did not become operative for decades to come.

THE MARRIAGE OF JADWIGA

After Louis's death the lords of Little Poland selected his younger daughter, Jadwiga (Hungarian: Hedvig), over her sister Maria (the wife of King Sigismund of Hungary). Preventing Jadwiga's marriage to Wilhelm Habsburg, the lords chose for her husband Władysław II Jagiełło (Lithuanian: Jogaila), the grand duke of Lithuania. This momentous act opened a new chapter in Polish history by linking the relatively small kingdom with a huge and heterogeneous Lithuania, which then comprised most of Ukraine and Belarus. The threat posed by the Teutonic Knights to both Poland and Lithuania, and the aspiration of the Poles to achieve status as a great power, figured prominently in the calculations. The church and Jadwiga, who was later beatified, attached great importance to the extension of Christianity. The prospects of opening vast regions in the east for trade and settlement appealed to the lords and merchants of Kraków. In 1385 the negotiations were finalized through the Union of Krewo. Jagiełło accepted Roman Catholicism for himself and Lithuania proper—the other duchies were already Christian (Eastern Orthodox)— and promised to join (*applicare*) his

JADWIGA

The centuries-long union of Lithuania and Poland was created by the marriage of Jadwiga (born 1373/74—died July 17, 1399, Kraków, Poland). As the queen of Poland (1384–99), her marriage in 1386 to Jogaila, grand duke of Lithuania (Władysław II Jagiełło of Poland), cemented the bond between the two kingdoms.

Jadwiga (original Hungarian: Hedvig; German: Hedwig) was the daughter of Louis I, king of both Hungary and Poland, and Elizabeth of Poland. After Louis died on September 11, 1382, his elder daughter, Maria, was elected queen of Hungary, but the Poles opted to end the personal union between the two countries by choosing Jadwiga as their queen, though she was then but a child of nine years. On October 15, 1384, she was crowned *rex* ("king") of Poland. The Polish magnates further promoted her marriage to Jogaila in order to produce a union of territories larger than the former one with Hungary, and this new entity altered the balance of power in central Europe. The marriage also opened the way to the Christian conversion of the largely pagan Lithuanians. Jogaila was baptized in Kraków on February 15, 1386, married to Jadwiga on February 18, and crowned on March 4. While Jadwiga lived, however, she and her husband ruled jointly, with Jadwiga remaining the leading personality in the realm. She died in childbirth and without heir; her husband was then able to assert his authority in Poland.

A patron of religion and scholarship, Jadwiga sought to promote the religious development of the nations that she had united, founded a special college for Lithuanians in Prague, and financed the restoration of the university at Kraków, which was effected after her death and later named the Jagiellonian University. Chiefly Jadwiga's work, the university was modeled after the University of Paris and became the centre of Polish civilization and influence. Jadwiga was canonized by Pope John Paul II in Kraków on June 8, 1997. Her feast day is February 28.

Lithuanian and Ruthenian lands to the Polish crown. He became the king of Poland under the name of Władysław II Jagiełło upon marrying Jadwiga, with whom he at first ruled jointly.

THE STATES OF THE JAGIELLONIANS

The Polish clergy played a major role in the long process of Christianization—the bishopric of Wilno (Lithuanian: Vilnius) was set up in 1387—and Polish knights assisted Lithuania in its military campaigns; nevertheless, the Lithuanians were determined not to tolerate Polish interference, landowners, or troops. It was obvious that a simple incorporation of Lithuania into Poland was not possible.

THE RULE OF JAGIEŁŁO

Jagiełło's cousin Vytautas (Polish: Witold), who eventually controlled the various duchies that constituted the Lithuanian state before its union with

Poland, assumed the title of grand duke and made Lithuania a virtually independent state. He even aimed at a royal crown for himself. The defeat he suffered at the hands of the Tatars at Vorskla River in 1399, however, destroyed his plans. The union with Poland was renegotiated on the basis of partnership of two sovereign states under the reign of Władysław II, king and supreme duke.

The continuing struggles with the Teutonic Knights seeking to master eastern Lithuanian Samogitia (Polish: Żmudź)—on the pretext of Christianizing its inhabitants—led to the great war in which Poland and Lithuania joined forces. The result was a crushing defeat of the Knights at Tannenberg (Grunwald) in 1410. The victory had no immediate sequel, for the Knights ceded only Samogitia (temporarily), but it marked the beginning of their decline; the Prussian nobles and towns secretly opposed the ruthless rule of the Teutonic Order. Polish tolerance was manifest at the Council of Constance (1414–18), where the prominent theologian and rector of Kraków University Paweł Włodkowic (Paulus Vladimiri) denounced the Knights' policy of conversion by the sword and maintained that the pagans also had their rights. Similarly, the Poles were sympathetic to Jan Hus of Bohemia, who was condemned as a heretic by the council, and lent discreet support to his followers, the Hussites, in their struggles against the Holy Roman Empire and the papacy.

Because of his concerns over dynastic succession, Władysław II, who had no children with Jadwiga, granted new privileges to the *szlachta* (all those of noble rank). Called *neminem captivabimus* (comparable to habeas corpus), the measure guarded against arbitrary arrest or confiscation of property and distinguished between the executive and the judiciary. The Polish example also began to affect the internal evolution of magnate-dominated Lithuania. The lesser boyars, envious of the position of their Polish counterparts, favoured closer unity. At the Union of Horodło in 1413, Polish nobles offered their coats of arms to a number of Lithuanians as a gesture of solidarity.

Only Władysław's fourth wife, Sophia Holszańska, bore him male children. One of their sons, Władysław III Warneńczyk, ruled Poland (1434–44) under the regency of the powerful Zbigniew Cardinal Oleśnicki; the other son, Casimir, was the grand duke of Lithuania. Largely because of Oleśnicki, Władysław III was elected king of Hungary, became active in crusades against the Turks, and, after initial victories, died at the Battle of Varna in 1444. Casimir subsequently became the ruler of both Poland and Lithuania.

CASIMIR IV

The long and brilliant reign of Casimir IV Jagiellonian (1447–92) corresponded to the age of "new monarchies" in western Europe. By the 15th century Poland had narrowed the distance separating it from western Europe and become a significant factor in international relations. The demand for raw materials and semifinished goods stimulated trade (producing a positive balance) and contributed to the growth of crafts and mining. Townspeople in Poland proper constituted about 20 percent of the population—roughly the European average. Divisions between the nobles, the burghers, and the peasants were still somewhat fluid. Coexistence of the ruler and the estates was relatively smooth and stable.

Cultural progress was striking, with the reconstituted and enlarged University of Kraków playing a major role. Humanist trends found a promoter at Kraków in the Italian scholar Filippo de Buonacorsi, known as Callimachus. From the pen of Jan Długosz came the first major history of Poland.

Casimir's foreign policy centred on the conflict with the Teutonic Knights and succession in Hungary and Bohemia. When the rebellious Prussian towns and nobility turned to Casimir, he decreed an incorporation of the Knights' state into Poland (1454). Unable to decisively defeat the Teutonic Order during the Thirteen Years' War (1454–66), he had to sign the compromise Treaty of Toruń in 1466. Gdańsk Pomerania, renamed Royal Prussia and endowed with far-reaching autonomy, became Polish once again. This opened

JAN DŁUGOSZ

The Polish diplomat and historian Jan Długosz (born 1415, Brzeźnica, Poland—died May 19, 1480, Kraków) wrote a monumental history of Poland. The first of its kind, the history inspired Poles with pride in their past and helped to favourably change the attitude of educated Europeans toward Poland.

Długosz entered the service of Zbigniew Oleśnicki, bishop of Kraków, and eventually became the head of his chancery. Appointed canon of Kraków (1436), Długosz in 1449 brought back from Rome a cardinal's hat for Oleśnicki and was thereafter entrusted with a succession of missions on behalf of church and state. After Oleśnicki's death, Długosz upheld his patron's theocratic views and suffered a period of disgrace (1461–63). Unlike Oleśnicki, however, Długosz had from the start supported King Casimir IV in his Prussian policy, assisting him in the negotiations with the Teutonic Order before and during the Thirteen Years' War (1454–66) and at the peace negotiations. His relations with the king having gradually improved, Długosz was charged with the education of the royal princes in 1467.

Długosz wrote *Liber beneficiorum ecclesiae Craceviensis* ("Book of the Benefices of the Bishopric of Kraków"), which is now a primary source for economic history. His *Historiae Polonicae* originally appeared in 12 books between 1455 and 1480 but was not published in full until 1711–12 (2 vol.). Although the work is deeply patriotic and often tendentious, it is valued as evidence of many documents no longer extant in the original.

the route to the Baltic. The other territories (most of the future East Prussia), with the capital at Königsberg (now Kaliningrad, Russia), remained with the Knights, albeit as a Polish fief.

Casimir's dependence on the noble levies in wartime enabled the *szlachta* to extract new concessions. They culminated in the Privilege of Nieszawa (1454), which gave the provincial diets (*sejmiki*) the right to declare the levies and raise new taxes. In 1493–96 a bicameral general diet (Sejm) marked the beginning of Polish parliamentarism. The representatives of the *sejmiki* formed the lower house, while the king's appointees constituted the senate.

The question of succession in Bohemia and Hungary was resolved toward the end of the 15th century when one of Casimir's sons, Vladislas II, was elected to the throne of Bohemia in 1471 and Hungary in 1490. His other sons John I Albert and Alexander succeeded each other in Poland and Lithuania from 1492 to 1506. A Jagiellonian bloc had come into existence, but its effectiveness was marred by the fact that the four countries were guided by divergent interests and faced different problems

THE GOLDEN AGE OF THE SIGISMUNDS

The last two Jagiellonian kings were Sigismund the Old and Sigismund II Augustus. It was under the reign of these kings that Poland reached its apogee.

POLITICAL DEVELOPMENTS

The king was the source of law (usually in tandem with the Sejm, though some decrees did not require the Sejm's assent), supreme judge, chief executive, and supreme commander, free to declare war and peace. He ruled Lithuania as a hereditary domain. Royal administration was quite effective, and Casimir's youngest son, Sigismund the Old (reigned 1506–48), tried to improve the nation's finances and taxation. An inadequate financial base and an undersized standing army limited the actual power of the king.

Domestic politics under Sigismund— and even more so under his son and successor, Sigismund II Augustus (reigned 1548–72)—centred on a contest between the fast-growing magnate oligarchy and the dynamic gentry, with the rulers generally favouring the former. The option of relying on the burghers, as was done by western European rulers, was not available because the towns (Gdańsk and some Royal Prussian towns excepted) allowed themselves to be eliminated from political struggles. The reformers among the lesser nobles focused on the program of the "execution" (enforcement) of laws that prohibited the transfer of crown lands and the accumulation of offices that profited the oligarchy. Wishing to emancipate itself from the magnates' political tutelage, the gentry strove for real partnership in government.

The Nihil Novi constitution (1505) achieved some of these aims, but it also stipulated that no new laws could be passed without the consent of the Sejm. The way was opened for parliamentary dominance that would eventually undermine the existing system of checks and balances. The growing political and economic power of the landowners had pernicious effects on the lot of the peasantry. Beginning with edicts issued in 1496 and repeatedly throughout the 16th century, the peasants' mobility was curtailed, labour obligations (corvée) were increased, and subjection to the lord's jurisdiction was affirmed. The degree of evasion of these burdens, however, was probably high. The impoverishment of the peasantry from the late 16th century became pronounced, while the barriers between the burghers and the *szlachta* became more rigid.

FOREIGN AFFAIRS

Sixteenth-century foreign policies had to take into consideration an alliance between the Habsburgs, Moscow, and the Teutonic Order that was directed against Poland. Muscovite expansion threatened Lithuania, and only a major victory at Orsza in 1514 averted a catastrophe. The victory allowed Sigismund I to detach the Habsburgs from Moscow through the Vienna accords of 1515. Providing for dynastic marriages, the accords opened the way for Habsburg succession in Bohemia and Hungary should the Jagiellonians die out. Eleven years later Louis II, the Jagiellonian king

of Hungary and Bohemia, perished at Mohács fighting the Turks. Thus ended the Jagiellonian bloc.

One year before Mohács, however, the matter of the Teutonic Knights had found a controversial resolution. The grand master of the order, Albert Hohenzollern, became a Lutheran and, isolated from the empire and papacy, offered to secularize his state as a vassal of the king of Poland. His act of homage in 1525 seemed a realistic arrangement that left the way open for the eventual absorption of Ducal Prussia (as East Prussia was thereafter called) into Poland. However, subsequent concessions to the Hohenzollerns allowed them to rule both Prussia and Brandenburg, on the flanks of the "corridor" that provided Polish access to the Baltic.

Polish concern with Baltic issues led to the creation of a small navy and to wars with Muscovy over Livonia (present-day Latvia and Estonia), which was controlled by the Knights of the Sword and coveted by the Muscovite tsar Ivan the Terrible. Eventually the region was partitioned. The union of 1561 brought the southern part to Poland and Lithuania and established a duchy of Courland, ruled as a Polish fief by the former grand master of the secularized Knights of the Sword. Meanwhile, Sweden expanded in the north.

Since Sigismund Augustus was childless, the future of the Polish-Lithuanian union became a paramount issue. Lithuanian socioeconomic, legal, and administrative structures came to resemble those of Poland, but the Lithuanians still opposed a simple incorporation. Their gentry, wishing to share in the privileges of the Polish *szlachta*, wanted a real union, but the powerful magnates opposed it. Fear of discrimination on religious grounds on the part of the Orthodox gentry (in Ukraine and the region that would become modern-day Belarus) was dispelled by granting them equality. The opposition of the magnates was finally broken by the king, who detached Podlasie, Volhynia, and the Kiev and Bracław regions from Lithuania and incorporated them into Poland. Facing the threat of complete annexation, the Lithuanian opposition gave in. The Union of Lublin (1569) established a federative state of two nations with a jointly elected mutual king–grand duke and legislature (a unique feature in Europe) and a customs union but with separate territories, laws, administrations, treasuries, and armies.

SOCIAL AND CULTURAL DEVELOPMENTS

Polish culture, highly praised by Desiderius Erasmus of Rotterdam, continued to flourish. Renaissance art and architecture, promoted by Sigismund I's wife Bona Sforza, became the style for numerous churches and castles. From Kraków University came Nicolaus Copernicus, who revolutionized astronomical concepts. After 1513 a large number of books were printed in Polish, including translations of the Bible. During the 16th century the writings of

NICOLAUS COPERNICUS

The Polish astronomer Nicolaus Copernicus (born February 19, 1473, Torun, Poland—died May 24, 1543, Frauenburg, East Prussia [now Frombork, Poland]) is often considered the founder of modern astronomy. His study led to his theory that Earth and the other planets revolve around the Sun.

Copernicus' father was a well-to-do merchant, and his mother also came from a leading merchant family. After his father's death, the boy was reared by his uncle, a wealthy Catholic bishop, who sent him to the University of Kraków. There he studied liberal arts, including astronomy and astrology. Copernicus also studied law at Bologna and medicine at Padua in Italy. Following his studies, he became an officer in the Roman Catholic Church. In 1500 he lectured on mathematical subjects in Rome. He returned to his uncle's castle near Frauenburg in 1507 as attending physician to the elderly man. Copernicus spent his spare time studying the heavens.

For centuries before Copernicus' time, astronomy had been based on Ptolemy's theory that Earth was the center of the universe and motionless. The problem was to explain how the other planets and heavenly bodies moved. At first it was thought that they simply moved in circular orbits around Earth. Calculations based on this view, however, did not agree with actual observations. Then it was thought that the other planets traveled in small circular orbits. These in turn were believed to move along larger orbits around Earth. With this theory, however, it could not be proved that Earth was the center of the universe.

Copernicus' revolutionary idea was that Earth should be regarded as one of the planets that revolved around the Sun. He also stated that Earth rotated on an axis. Copernicus, however, still clung to the ideas of planets traveling in small circular orbits that moved along larger orbits.

Copernicus probably hit upon his main idea sometime between 1508 and 1514. For years, however, he delayed publication of his controversial work, which contradicted all the authorities of the time. The historic book that contains the final version of his theory, *De revolutionibus orbium coelestium libri vi* ("Six Books Concerning the Revolutions of the Heavenly Orbs"), did not appear in print until 1543, the year of his death. According to legend, Copernicus received a copy as he was dying, on May 24, 1543. The book opened the way to a truly scientific approach to astronomy. It had a profound influence on later thinkers of the scientific revolution, including such major figures as Galileo, Johannes Kepler, and Isaac Newton.

Mikołaj Rej, the father of Polish literature, and of the great poet Jan Kochanowski helped establish the period as the golden age of Polish literature. The Renaissance and the Reformation had a major impact on Lithuania, marking its absorption into western European culture.

Under the tolerant policies of Sigismund II, to whom John Calvin dedicated one of his works, Lutheranism spread mainly in the cities and Calvinism among the nobles of Lithuania and Little Poland. The Sandomierz Agreement of 1570, which defended religious freedom, marked the cooperation of Polish Lutherans and Calvinists. The Polish Brethren (known also as Arians and Anti-Trinitarians) made a major contribution by preaching social egalitarianism and pacifism. In 1573 the *szlachta* concluded the Compact of Warsaw, which provided for the maintenance of religious toleration. These victories for the Reformation, however, were gradually canceled by the Catholic Counter-Reformation under the leadership of Stanisław Cardinal Hozjusz (Stanislaus Hosius). In the 1560s the Jesuits arrived in Poland (their greatest preacher was Piotr Skarga), and their network of schools and colleges included the future University of Wilno (now Vilnius, Lithuania), founded in 1579.

CHAPTER 21

THE POLISH-LITHUANIAN STATE OF THE COMMONWEALTH

The dual Polish-Lithuanian state, Respublica, or "Commonwealth" (Polish: Rzeczpospolita), was one of the largest states in Europe. While Poland in the mid-16th century occupied an area of about 100,000 square miles (260,000 sq km), with some 3.5 million inhabitants, the Commonwealth at its largest point in the early 17th century comprised nearly 400,000 square miles (1,040,000 sq km) and some 11 million inhabitants.

BÁTHORY AND THE VASAS

For some time, the Commonwealth was under the rule of Stephen Báthory, a soldier and the prince of Transylvania, and members of the Swedish and Polish dynasty. The latter were known as members of the House of Vasa.

SOCIAL AND POLITICAL STRUCTURE

Given the great expanse of the Commonwealth, it was a multiethnic country inhabited by Poles, Lithuanians, Ruthenians, Germans, Jews, and small numbers of Tatars, Armenians, and Scots. It was also a multifaith country, with Roman Catholics, Protestants, Eastern Orthodox, Jews, and Muslims living within its boundaries. Certain communities lived under their own laws; the Jews, for example, enjoyed self-administration through the Council of the Four Lands.

The term "Poland" was used for both the entire state and the strictly Polish part of it (though the latter was officially

Poland's territory in 1634, during the reign of Władysław IV Vasa. Encyclopædia Britannica, Inc.

called the Crown). This could be confusing. A supranational term like "British" was missing. The Commonwealth gradually came to be dominated by the *szlachta*, which regarded the state as an embodiment of its rights and privileges. Ranging from the poorest landless yeomen to the great magnates, the *szlachta* insisted on the equality of all its members. As a political nation it was more numerous (8–10 percent) than the electorate of most European states even in the early 19th century.

Throughout most of Europe the medieval system of estates evolved into absolutism, but in the Commonwealth it led to a *szlachta* democracy inspired by the ideals of ancient Rome, to which parallels were constantly drawn. The *szlachta* came to see in its state a perfect constitutional model, a granary for Europe, and a bulwark against eastern barbarism. Its inherent weaknesses in finance, administration, and the military were ignored.

The end of the Jagiellonian dynasty meant the beginning of unrestricted election to the throne. The first king elected *viritim* (i.e., by direct vote of the *szlachta*) was Henry of Valois, the brother of the king of France. On his accession to the throne (reigned 1573–74), which he quickly abandoned to become Henry III of France, he accepted the so-called Henrician Articles and Pacta Conventa. Presented henceforth to every new king as a contract with the noble nation, the former document provided for free election (but not during the reigning monarch's lifetime), religious peace, biennial meetings of the Sejm (with a standing body of senators active in the interval), and the right to renounce the allegiance to the king should he break the contract.

STEPHEN BÁTHORY

In 1576 the prince of Transylvania, Stephen Báthory (Stefan Batory), became king. A brilliant soldier, he closely cooperated with Jan Zamoyski, chancellor of the Crown and grand hetman (commander in chief). The most spectacular achievement of Báthory's reign was a series of military victories (1579–81) over Ivan the Terrible of Russia. Yet it is likely that the king's eastern policies were inspired by the ultimate goal of liberation of Hungary, which was not necessarily a Polish concern.

SIGISMUND III VASA

The long reign of his successor, Sigismund III Vasa (1587–1632), raised hopes of a union with Sweden that would strengthen Poland's standing in the north. Sigismund was the grandson of the legendary Swedish ruler Gustav I Vasa, but, as an ardent Roman Catholic and champion of the Counter-Reformation, he was unable to hold on to the crown of Lutheran Sweden, and a 10-year succession struggle ensued. His attempts to secure the throne involved Poland in a series of wars with Sweden. Although one of Lithuania's great military commanders, Jan Karol Chodkiewicz, triumphed at Kirchholm (1605), and the Gdańsk-based navy defeated the Swedish fleet near Oliwa (1627), the truce that followed was inconclusive. The same was true for most settlements in foreign and domestic affairs.

Although Poland remained neutral in the Thirty Years' War (1618–48), Sigismund stealthily supported the Habsburgs, a policy that contributed to a war with Turkey. Poland suffered a major defeat at Cecora in 1620 but was victorious at Chocim (now in Khotyn, Ukraine) and negotiated peace a year later. The victory at Chocim was memorialized by poet Wacław Potocki a half century later.

There was, however, no real peace with Muscovy, then going through its

The Thirty Years' War. Encyclopædia Britannica, Inc.

Time of Troubles. The support extended by some Polish magnates to the False Dmitry (who claimed to be the son of Ivan the Terrible) eventually embroiled Poland in hostilities. The victory at Klushino in 1610 by Hetman Stanisław Żółkiewski resulted in a Polish occupation of Moscow and the election by Moscow's boyars of Sigismund's son Władysław as tsar. Sigismund's veto wasted this opportunity and instead left a residue of Russian hatred of Poland.

Suspicions that Sigismund's policies were guided by his dynastic interests contributed to a domestic confrontation: the 1606–08 *rokosz* ("rebellion"). Accusing the king of absolutist designs, the *rokosz* brought together sincere reformers (who demanded the "execution" of the laws), Roman Catholics, and Protestants, as well as magnates pursuing their own ends. Although the royal forces triumphed in battle, both the king and the reformers were losers in the political realm to the magnates posing as defenders of freedom.

WŁADYSŁAW IV

Władysław IV Vasa (reigned 1632–48) continued his father's policy of strengthening the monarchy and of insisting on the rights to the Swedish throne. Some of the bellicose plans he formulated to increase his power were thwarted by the Sejm and by international circumstances. The anti-Turkish crusade he planned, however, in which Cossacks were to play a major role, contributed to the upheaval that shook the Commonwealth between 1648 and 1660—the uprising in Ukraine and war in the northeast.

Transferred as a result of the Union of Lublin from the grand duchy of Lithuania to the more ethnically homogeneous Crown, Ukraine was "colonized" by both Polish and Ukrainian great nobles. Most of the latter gradually abandoned Orthodoxy to become Roman Catholic and Polish. These "little kings" of Ukraine controlled hundreds of thousands of "subjects" and commanded armies larger than those of the regular Crown troops. In 1596 the Union of Brest-Litovsk subordinated the Eastern Orthodox church of the Commonwealth to the papacy by creating the Eastern rite (Uniate) church.

Politically, this was intended to cement the cohesion of the state vis-à-vis Moscow; instead it led to internal divisions among the Orthodox. The new Eastern rite church became a hierarchy without followers, while the forbidden Eastern Orthodox church was driven underground. Władysław's recognition of the latter's existence in 1632 may have come too late. The Orthodox masses—deprived of their native protectors, who had become Polonized and Catholic—turned to the Cossacks.

THE COSSACKS

The Zaporozhian Cossacks were frontiersmen who organized themselves in a self-governing centre at modern Zaporizhzhya, Ukraine, first to resist Tatar raids and then to plunder as far away as Constantinople (modern Istanbul). Their prowess was recognized by Sigismund Augustus and Báthory, who "registered" a number of Cossacks for military duty. Other Cossacks and all those diverse groups of settlers or tenants whom the lords tried to turn into serfs coveted this privileged status. Even small nobles and burghers resented the heavy-handed behaviour of the "little kings," who were bent on realizing maximum profits and employing Jews as middlemen and overseers. Growing socioeconomic antagonisms combined with religious tensions.

In the Polish-Turkish war of 1620–21, the victory in the Battle of Chocim had been largely due to the participation of some 40,000 Zaporozhian Cossacks, whom Petro Konashevych-Sahaydachny had brought to aid the Poles. Nonetheless, some 12 years later Cossack demands to be placed on an equal footing with the *szlachta* were contemptuously rejected by the Sejm. The king and the magnates needed the Cossacks in wartime but feared them as an unruly and seditious group that was embroiling the Commonwealth in hostilities with Turkey and the Tatars. Complaints about the enlargement of the military register and about mistreatment led to several Cossack uprisings. After the rebellion of 1638 was put down by Polish troops, Cossack privileges were greatly curtailed.

The undertaking of an anti-Turkish crusade opened new vistas. There was talk of massive Cossack participation, provided that some 20,000 men be "registered," social grievances redressed, and a military border free of Polish troops established. Whatever the exact encouragements proffered by Władysław IV, the Sejm and the *szlachta* were adamantly opposed and frightened lest the king use the Cossacks for his own ends.

BOHDAN KHMELNYTSKY

In 1648 Bohdan Khmelnytsky, whom contemporaries likened to Oliver Cromwell, assumed the leadership of the Zaporozhian Cossacks and, allied with the Tatars, defeated the troops of the Commonwealth and some magnate contingents. Khmelnytsky became the master of Ukraine, and its peasant masses, many of its townsmen, and even lesser noblemen were among his followers. The city of Kiev hailed him as a prince and the defender of the Orthodox faith. His objective became the creation of a separate Ukraine under the direct rule of a king.

In Poland, where the sudden death of Władysław IV left the country leaderless, a policy of compromise represented by the chancellor, Jerzy Ossoliński, and the last Orthodox senator, Adam Kisiel (Kysil), clashed with warlike operations of the leading "little king," Prince Jeremi Wiśniowiecki. The nature of temporary agreements, which intervened between the Commonwealth and the Cossacks, varied depending on the changing fortunes of war. The Polish victory at the Battle of Beresteczko in 1651 was followed by the pact of Biała Cerkiew, which the Cossacks found hard to accept.

In 1654 Khmelnytsky submitted to Tsar Alexis in the Pereyaslav Agreement. Russian historiography characterizes that agreement as the reunification of Ukraine with Russia; the Ukrainians interpret it as an alliance based on expediency. At any rate, war began between Muscovy and the Commonwealth, and Alexis's armies drove deep into Lithuania. In 1655 they occupied its capital, Wilno. For the first time in nearly two centuries, an enemy invasion had taken place,

BATTLE OF BERESTECZKO

The Polish king John Casimir (reigned 1648–68) inflicted a severe defeat upon the rebel Cossack leader Bohdan Khmelnytsky at the Battle of Beresteczko. The military engagement took place on June 28–30, 1651.

In 1648 Khmelnytsky organized an insurrection among the Zaporozhian Cossacks, who lived along the Dnieper River, against their Polish rulers, who had been trying to limit the Cossacks' autonomy by reducing their numbers, restraining them from conducting lucrative raids upon their Turkish and Crimean Tatar neighbours, and forcing them into a condition of serfdom. After a series of military victories, the Cossacks exacted the Compact of Zborów (1649) from the Polish king.

Although that settlement granted a large degree of autonomy to the "registered" Cossacks (i.e., those forming a privileged class), it failed to satisfy either the Poles or the "unregistered" Cossacks. Within 18 months, hostilities were resumed. The Cossacks were formally taken under the protection of the Turkish sultan (April 1651) and were reinforced by the sultan's vassal, the khan of the Crimean Tatars. In June the Cossack-Tatar force advanced against the Poles and engaged them in battle at Beresteczko, on the Styr River in Volhynia south of Lutsk. The Cossacks' army was approximately three times larger than the Poles'. But in the midst of the fighting the Tatar khan and his force left the field of battle. This action, which has been described by some historians as treasonous desertion and by others as a maneuver to establish another line of defense closer to the Dnieper to protect Kiev from an advancing Lithuanian army, enabled the numerically inferior Polish army to gain a victory over the Cossacks.

Subsequently, the defeated rebels accepted a new peace settlement, concluded at Biała Cerkiew (September 28, 1651), which reduced the number of "registered" Cossacks from 40,000 to 20,000 and deprived them of the right to settle in and control various provinces that had been designated in the Compact of Zborów. Neither the Cossacks nor the Polish Sejm (parliament) accepted the new treaty, and in January 1654 the Cossacks chose to recognize the suzerainty of the Russian tsar and to incorporate their community into the Muscovite state (Union of Pereyaslav).

and, when it was followed by a Swedish aggression, a veritable "deluge" overtook the Commonwealth.

JOHN II CASIMIR VASA

The belligerent and ambitious Charles X Gustav of Sweden worried lest the extension of Muscovy upset the balance of power in the Baltic, which he aimed to turn into a Swedish lake. The refusal of King John II Casimir Vasa, the successor and brother of Władysław IV, to give up his claims to the Swedish crown offered a good pretext for resuming hostilities with the Commonwealth. Aiming originally to seize Polish and Prussian harbours, Charles Gustav saw, after the first successes, the possibility of gaining the Polish crown and the mastery of the Commonwealth.

The magnates and gentry of Great Poland capitulated to the Swedes in July 1655. Prince Janusz Radziwiłł, a leading Calvinist and the greatest magnate of Lithuania, hard-pressed by the Russians, broke off the union with Poland and signed one with Sweden. His motives were a combination of Lithuanian and Protestant interests coloured by his own ambition to rule the grand duchy.

The nearly bloodless conquest of the huge Commonwealth came as a shock to many Poles and foreigners. Yet Polish resistance to what turned out to be a regime of brutal occupation developed very quickly. The successful defense of the fortified monastery of Jasna Góra (now in Częstochowa) became a rallying point and provided a symbolic religious-ideological banner. Although the Poles were seldom a match for the Swedish professional troops, they excelled at partisan warfare and at winning minor battles. Not only the *szlachta* but also the peasants fought the foreigner and enemy of Roman Catholicism. Stefan Czarniecki became the hero of the war.

Returning from exile in Silesia, John Casimir built an international coalition against the Swedes, whose successes were upsetting the balance of power. A cease-fire intervened on the Russian front, and the Cossacks were neutralized by the Tatars, while the Habsburgs, Denmark, and Brandenburg-Prussia went to Poland's aid. The Swedes were gradually driven out of the Commonwealth, despite an armed intervention on their side by Transylvania's Prince György II Rákóczi, who aspired to the Polish crown. The war ended with the Treaty of Oliwa (1660), which restored the territorial status quo before the Swedish invasion and brought the final renunciation of John Casimir's claim to the crown of Sweden.

The real winner in the conflict proved to be Frederick William, the elector of Brandenburg and duke of Prussia. Adroitly maneuvering between Sweden and Poland and extracting a price for his collaboration from both sides, the "Great Elector" finally switched his support to John Casimir and thereby received the recognition of full sovereignty over Prussia for himself and his male descendants through the treaties of Wehlau (Welawa) and Bromberg (Bydgoszcz) in 1657.

Eastern wars still continued for Poland for several years. In Ukraine the Hadziacz agreement of 1658 with Khmelnytsky's successor provided for the creation of a Ukrainian state as a third member of the Commonwealth with its own offices and army, as well as mass ennoblements of Cossacks and the suspension of the Union of Brest-Litovsk. The accord was short-lived. A pro-Russian faction in Ukraine denounced and nullified the pact, which led to a renewal of hostilities with Muscovy that ended in 1667 with the Truce of Andrusovo and was confirmed by a treaty in 1686. Restoring the occupied parts of Lithuania to the Commonwealth, the truce divided Ukraine along the Dnieper River. Together with the Treaty of Oliwa, that agreement marked the beginning of the decline of the Commonwealth's international standing.

THE 17TH-CENTURY CRISIS

The two decades of war and occupation in the mid-17th century ruined and exhausted the Commonwealth. In the case of Lithuania, they also provided a foretaste of the 18th-century partitions.

SOCIAL AND ECONOMIC CHANGES

Famines and epidemics followed hostilities, and the population dropped from roughly 11 to 7 million. The number of inhabitants of Kraków and Warsaw fell by two-thirds and one-half, respectively. Wilno was burned down. The Khmelnytsky uprising decimated the Jews in Ukraine, even if they recovered fairly rapidly demographically. The productivity of agriculture diminished dramatically owing to labour shortages, the destruction of many farm buildings and farming implements, and the loss of numerous cattle. The dynamic network of international trade fairs also collapsed. Grain exports, which had reached their peak in the early 17th century, could not redress the unfavourable balance of trade with western Europe. Losses of art treasures—the Swedes engaged in systematic looting—were irreplaceable.

The Commonwealth never fully recovered, unlike Muscovy, which had suffered almost as much during the Time of Troubles. Twentieth-century Marxist historians blamed the manorial economy based on serf labour for pauperizing the masses and undermining the towns, yet the Polish economy was not unique in that respect. Moreover, some attempts to replace serfs with rent-paying tenants did not prove to be a panacea. The economic factor must therefore be treated jointly with other structural weaknesses of the Commonwealth that militated against recovery.

The 17th-century crisis—a European phenomenon—was basically a crisis of political authority. In the Commonwealth the perennial financial weakness was the central issue. The state budget in the second half of the century amounted to 10–11 million złotys, as compared with the equivalent of about 360 million in France or 240 million in England. About nine-tenths of it went for military purposes, compared with half in Brandenburg and more than three-fifths in France and Russia. Equating a large army with royal absolutism and extolling the virtue of noble levies, the *szlachta* was unwilling to devise defensive mechanisms. This was true even after the chastising experience of the Swedish "deluge." Most nobles contented themselves with invoking the special protection of St. Mary, symbolically crowned queen of Poland, as a sufficient safeguard.

POLITICAL STAGNATION

Those wishing to reform the state without strengthening the monarchy wanted to make the Sejm an effective centre of power. The *szlachta*, however, refused to accept the notion that liberty could be better preserved in a stronger state. In 1652 the notorious and often misunderstood practice of liberum veto (free veto) appeared: a single negative vote by a member of the Sejm was considered sufficient to block the proceedings. It was argued that unanimity was essential for passing laws, for deputies, as representatives of the local *sejmiki*, were bound by instructions. Moreover, a majority could disregard local interests and be corrupted by the administration. Hence, liberum veto came to be regarded as the kernel of liberty and a safeguard against tyranny. In reality, the dissenting deputy was usually an instrument of a magnate or even of the king.

The liberum veto could paralyze the functioning of the state, and in the 17th century it was used sparingly. The weakening of the Sejm meant that some of its functions, notably in matters of taxation, had to pass to local *sejmiki*. Without a central bureaucracy and with a dual structure of offices in the Crown and Lithuania, the fragmentation of sovereignty became increasingly ominous. The attempts at reform by John Casimir and his energetic wife, Marie Louise, may have been ill-conceived, but, given the factional strife within the oligarchy, it was difficult for the monarch to find a stable base of support. The *szlachta*, ever suspicious of anything that could smack of absolutism, was naturally opposed. The royal plans were defeated by a *rokosz* in 1665–66 led by Marshal Jerzy Lubomirski. Two years later the frustrated John Casimir abdicated and settled in France, having prophetically warned the Sejm that Poland would fall victim to its rapacious neighbours unless it reformed its ways.

CULTURAL CHANGES

The prevalent mentality in the Commonwealth in the 17th century manifested itself in Sarmatism. The name came from alleged ancestors of the *szlachta* (Sarmatians), and the concept served to integrate the multiethnic nobility. Representing a symbiosis of a political ideology and a lifestyle typical of a landowning, rather provincial, tightly knit, and increasingly xenophobic culture, Sarmatism extolled the virtues of the *szlachta* and contrasted them with Western values. An Orientalization of Polish-Lithuanian culture (including modes and manners) was occurring. Roman Catholicism was Sarmatized in its turn, assuming a more intolerant posture toward other denominations. The struggles against Lutheran Swedes and Prussians, Orthodox Russians, and

Muslim Turks and Tatars strength-ened the belief in Poland's mission as a Catholic bastion. The expulsion in 1658 of Polish Brethren—accused of col-laboration with the Swedes—when taken together with the virtual elimination of non-Catholics from public offices, was the first harbinger of the Pole-Catholic syndrome (the notion that a true Pole must be a Catholic).

DECLINE AND ATTEMPTS AT REFORM

The Lubomirski *rokosz* was barely over and the truce with Muscovy newly signed when the Cossacks in the Polish part of divided Ukraine submitted to Turkey and called for Tatar aid against Poland. Victories won by Hetman Jan (John III) Sobieski only temporarily forestalled the threat, and in 1672 the Commonwealth faced a major invasion by Turkey. The fall of the key border fortress Kamieniec Podolski was followed by the humiliating Peace of Buczacz. The Commonwealth lost the provinces of Podolia and Bratslav and part of Kiev, which remained under Turkish rule for more than 20 years, and it had to pay a tribute to the Sublime Porte. Sobieski's victory over the Turks at Chocim in 1673 was not exploited, because of the lack of financial means, but it paved the way for Sobieski's elec-tion to the Polish throne. His predecessor, Michael Korybut Wiśniowiecki—who had followed John Casimir—reigned for only four years (1669–73) and proved utterly incapable.

Sobieski, ruling as John III (1674–96), sought to improve Poland's position and at first considered conquering Prussia in alliance with France. But that plan did not succeed. With the papacy and the Habsburgs preparing for all-out war against Turkey, John reverted to an anti-Turkish policy and concluded an alliance with Austria. In 1683 he led a relief army to a Vienna besieged by the Turks and, as supreme commander of the allied forces, won a resounding victory that marked the beginning of Turkish withdrawal from Europe. The Commonwealth, however, did not share in the subsequent victorious Austrian campaigns. Poland became a secondary partner, and, when the final peace with Turkey was concluded with the Treaty of Carlowitz in 1699, the Poles recov-ered only the lost Ukrainian lands. By that time John was no longer alive, and Augustus II, the elector of Saxony, had succeeded him on the throne (reigned 1697–1733).

THE SAXONS

The "Saxon Era" lasted for more than 60 years and marked the lowest point in Polish history. Research since the 1980s has somewhat corrected the largely nega-tive picture of Augustus II and Augustus III by stressing that they were operat-ing in a context of political anarchy, dominated by factions of struggling oli-garchs and subject to the meddling of neighbouring powers. The neighbour-ing states signed agreements among themselves to promote weakness within the Commonwealth, as for instance the Austro-Russian accord of 1675 and the Swedish-Brandenburg pacts of 1686 and 1696, which were followed by others in the 1720s.

Foreign interlopers corrupted politicians and fomented disorder. During the reign of Augustus II, 10 out of 18 Sejms were paralyzed by liberum veto. In 1724 a Protestant-Catholic riot in Toruń resulted in Protestant officials' being sentenced to death. Prussian and Russian propagandists spoke of a "bloodbath" and used the situation as an opportunity to denounce Polish intolerance. Posing as a protector of non-Catholics, St. Petersburg was in fact using them as a political instrument. Polish politics, ways, and manners, as well as declining education and rampant religious bigotry, were increasingly pictured as exotically anachronistic. The Polish nobles became the laughingstock of Europe. Because the promises John Casimir made during the darkest days of Swedish invasion to improve the lot of the peasantry had remained empty, the oppressed peasants were largely alienated from the nation.

AUGUSTUS II

A personal union with Saxony, where Augustus II was a strong ruler, seemed at first to offer some advantages to Poland. A king with a power base of his own might reform the Commonwealth, which was still a huge state and potentially a great power. But such hopes proved vain. Pursuing schemes of dynastic greatness, Augustus II involved unwilling Poland in a coalition war against Charles XII of Sweden that proved disastrous. In 1702 Charles invaded the country, forced Augustus out, and staged an election of the youthful Stanisław I Leszczyński as king.

The country, split between two rival monarchs, plunged into chaos. The slowly proceeding demographic and economic recovery was reversed as the looting armies and an outbreak of bubonic plague decimated the people. A crushing defeat of Sweden by Peter I (the Great) of Russia at the Battle of Poltava (Ukraine, Russian Empire) in 1709 eventually restored Augustus to the throne but made him dependent on the tsar. Having failed to strengthen his position through war and territorial acquisitions, Augustus contemplated domestic reforms while his entourage played with the idea of a coup backed by Saxon troops. Peter intervened as an arbiter between the king and his noble opponents. A settlement at the "silent Sejm" surrounded by Russian troops removed Saxon contingents from Poland, but it brought about certain reforms. Subsequent attempts by Augustus to mount a coalition against the rising might of Russia foundered on the distrust of the king's motives. He was even suspected of plotting partitions of the Commonwealth. During the remaining years of his reign, Augustus' main preoccupation was to ensure the succession of his son.

AUGUSTUS III

Upon Augustus' death in 1733, Stanisław I, seen this time as a symbol of Poland's independence and supported by France (his daughter, Marie Leszczyńska, married Louis XV), was elected once again. The counterelection of Augustus III followed, and Russian troops drove Stanisław out of the country. He abdicated, receiving as compensation (after the so-called War of the Polish Succession) the duchy of Lorraine.

The reign of Augustus III (1733–63)—during which 5 out of 15 Sejms were dissolved while the remainder took no decisions—witnessed the nadir of Polish statehood. The Commonwealth no longer could be counted as an independent participant in international relations; the king's diplomacy was conducted from Dresden in Saxony. Poland passively watched the once-Polish territory of Silesia pass from the Habsburgs to Prussia as a result of the War of the Austrian Succession. Prussia, under Frederick II (the Great), whose grandfather had already been recognized in 1701 as "king in Prussia" by Augustus II, was becoming a great power. During the Seven Years' War (1756–63), Austrian and Russian troops marched through Poland, and Frederick flooded the country with counterfeit money. The Commonwealth was being treated as a wayside inn.

And yet there were also the first signs of economic recovery and population growth, the beginnings of a transition from Sarmatism to Enlightenment, and the appearance of a reformist political

FAMILIA

Familia (English: Family) was the name by which the Czartoryski family was popularly known. The Familia, the leading noble family of Poland in the 18th century, eclipsed the rival Potocki family in both power and prestige.

Although the members of the Czartoryski family trace their lineage back to the 14th-century noble Gedymin (Gediminas) of Lithuania, they first achieved widespread power through the efforts of Michał Fryderyk Czartoryski and his brother August Aleksander during the reigns of Kings Augustus II and Stanisław I in the early 18th century. The family, which sought the enactment of such constitutional reforms as the abolition of the liberum veto, attained the height of its influence in the mid-18th century in the court of Augustus III. The Czartoryski brothers possessed a very powerful ally in their brother-in-law, Stanisław Poniatowski, whose son became the last king of independent Poland, as Stanisław II, at the end of the century.

Although the Czartoryski family estate at Puławy was confiscated in 1794, during the Third Partition of Poland, the family continued to wield significant cultural power, notably through the princes Adam Kazimierz Czartoryski and Adam Jerzy Czartoryski.

literature. In 1740 Stanisław Konarski, a member of the Roman Catholic Piarist teaching order, founded the Collegium Nobilium, which was to train the future elite. A network of Piarist schools followed, while the ideas of the Enlightenment were being spread, often through Freemasonry. Konarski's writings, as well as those coming from the circle of Stanisław I in Lorraine, attacked the liberum veto and advocated an improvement of the lot of towns and peasantry. After the 1740s, from the medley of factions, coteries, and partisan groups, two major camps were emerging: the so-called Familia, led by the Czartoryskis, and the Republicans, with the Potockis and Radziwiłłs at their head.

REFORMS, AGONY, AND PARTITIONS

The election of Stanisław II August Poniatowski as the last king of Poland (reigned 1764–95) was the work of the powerful Familia. Rising from the middle nobility (though his mother was a Czartoryska), the candidate was handpicked by Catherine II (the Great) of Russia not only because he had been her lover but because she felt that he would be completely dependent on her. The Czartoryskis in turn saw him as their puppet. Thus, from the beginning Stanisław II—a highly intelligent man, a patron of the arts, and a reformer in the spirit of the Enlightenment—had to operate under most-difficult conditions. The magnates resented him as an upstart;

the conservative *szlachta* viewed him as Catherine's tool and as a threat to their liberties. The king's adroitness and personal charm allowed him in time to win over some of his adversaries, but he lacked a strong will and showed none of the military inclination so cherished by the Poles.

REFORM UNDER STANISŁAW II

The reforms that accompanied the election were limited. Stanisław sought to reform the state by strengthening the monarchy; the Czartoryskis wished to reform it by strengthening the Sejm. The king embarked on a vast program of modernization, encouraging initiatives in the economic, financial, and military spheres. But above all he waged a nationwide campaign, using the press, literature, and the new National Theatre to change the conservative mentality of the *szlachta*. In 1765 Stanisław established the Knights' School—the first truly secular college, which promoted civil virtues and religious toleration—and criticized the treatment of towns and peasantry.

The king's policies, however, were constantly undermined by neighbouring powers. Frederick II's view that Poland ought to be kept in lethargy was shared by St. Petersburg, which sought to isolate Stanisław by encouraging both religious dissenters (i.e., non-Catholics) and the conservative circles to form confederations. The presence of Russian troops terrorized the Sejm, and Russia formally guaranteed as immutable such principles of Polish politics as liberum veto, elective monarchy, and dominance of the *szlachta*.

THE FIRST PARTITION

In 1768 the Confederation of Bar was formed. Its antiroyalist and anti-Russian program mingled patriotic and conservative overtones with religious objectives (namely, the defense of the privileged status of Roman Catholicism vis-à-vis the religious and political equality for non-Catholics advocated by Russia). Civil war erupted and lasted until 1772. Royal

The Partitions of Poland, 1772–95. Encyclopædia Britannica, Inc.

troops assisted the Russians—at one point the king was kidnapped by the confederates—and France and Turkey helped the confederates. The movement strengthened Polish national consciousness and produced the first martyrs sent to Siberia, but, at the same time, it created such chaotic conditions that St. Petersburg began to listen when Frederick repeatedly proposed partitioning Poland. With Russia and Austria on the brink of war over Turkish matters, Berlin suggested a resolution of the eastern crisis through mutually agreeable compensations at Poland's expense. Austria, which had opposed the scheme (Maria Theresa had found it immoral), unwittingly created a precedent by annexing some Polish border areas.

As a result of the First Partition (1772), Poland lost almost one-third of its territory and more than one-third of its population. Russia received the largest but least-important area economically, in the northeast. Austria gained the densely populated Little Poland (renamed Galicia). Prussia's share was the smallest, but the annexation of Eastern Pomerania (although without Gdańsk) cut off Poland from the sea and allowed Frederick to put a veritable stranglehold on the Polish economy. Except for individual protests the helpless Sejm, fearing additional territorial losses, ratified the partition. Despite some British concern about Gdańsk and the Baltic trade, the European powers reacted to the partition with utmost indifference. The British political philosopher Edmund Burke was alone in criticizing the immorality of the act and in recognizing in it the beginning of a revolutionary change in the European balance of power.

SOCIAL AND ECONOMIC CHANGES

During the two decades that separated the First and Second Partitions, the country experienced a remarkable revival. The dissolution of the Jesuit order in 1773 allowed a complete reorganization of the Polish educational system under the Commission of National Education, one of the first ministries of education in Europe. Cut off from the Baltic, Poland reoriented its trade toward the Black Sea. Producing for the national market, early manufacturing concerns grew on both royal and magnate land. Many estates began to operate with tenant farmers rather than serfs. Banks and joint stock companies appeared, canals were built, and roads improved. The position of the towns began to change, and Warsaw with its 100,000 inhabitants became a centre radiating into the country.

Under the king's patronage, arts and literature flourished. Learning made important strides. The satiric poet Bishop Ignacy Krasicki headed a long list of important authors. Political literature reached its summit with the writings of Stanisław Staszic (a burgher) and Hugo Kołłątaj. There was discussion of a reform of towns (including a Jewish reform) and changes in the status of the peasantry by extending to them rights and representation as well as state protection.

The newly created Permanent Council, a collegial body composed of five ministries, was the first executive organ for both the Crown and Lithuania. The council achieved progress in financial, police, and administrative fields, although it was seen as a channel for Russian influence and was attacked by the oligarchic opposition, who believed it strengthened the position of the king. However, because Stanisław II was convinced that only close collaboration with St. Petersburg constituted a guarantee against further partitions, reforms had to meet with Russian approval. The failure of a projected new code of laws reforming the social system and state-church relations showed the limits of tolerated reform. St. Petersburg seemed to regard its tutelage as firm enough to withdraw its troops from the country in 1780.

THE CONSTITUTION OF 1791

A Russo-Turkish war that began in 1787 created a situation that both the king and the magnate opposition tried to exploit. With Prussia proposing an alliance with the Poles (signed in 1790) and Austria becoming preoccupied with the French Revolution, the so-called Great Sejm, which met in 1788, embarked on sweeping reforms. The king aspired to constitutional monarchy, and the "patriots" preferred a republic presided over by a monarch, while the die-hard conservatives ("false patriots") opposed all modernization and change. It took the Sejm four years of heated debates, in the course of which the example of the American Revolution was frequently invoked, to demolish the old system and enact a new one. The king, although fearful that the Sejm would go too far and antagonize Russia, eventually joined with the patriots in approving, on May 3, 1791, the first modern written constitution in Europe.

The new constitution was a revolutionary document that created a constitutional parliamentary monarchy and gave a new meaning to the term *political nation*. It combined Polish traditions with the ideas of the Enlightenment. Dynasties, not individuals, would henceforth be elected, beginning with the house of Wettin. The king's decrees had to be countersigned by ministers responsible to the Sejm, which was partly elected on the basis of property qualifications. Since burghers gained some political rights and the poorest gentry—clients of the magnates—lost some of theirs, birth alone would no longer be a determinant of citizenship. The liberum veto was abolished, as was discrimination on religious grounds. An army 100,000 strong was to be raised. Royal towns recovered their autonomy, but the peasantry was only taken under the protection of the law. Additional laws applying to social and economic problems were to follow.

Although the constitution was passed through a quasi-coup (1791–92), Stanisław gained for it the approval of most of the *sejmiki*. It was, however, unacceptable to Russia and Prussia, both of which were fearful lest a revived, strong Poland reclaim its lost lands. Driven by pride and doctrine, a number of die-hard conservatives—among them high dignitaries such as Stanisław Szczęsny Potocki, Seweryn Rzewuski, and Ksawery Branicki—formed the Confederation of Targowica (in St. Petersburg) to overthrow the May constitution. Acting as guarantor of the old Polish regime, Catherine ordered her armies to invade Poland in 1792. There they fought the outnumbered Polish troops under Prince Józef Poniatowski and Gen. Tadeusz Kościuszko, a hero of the American Revolution.

THE SECOND AND THIRD PARTITIONS

Intimidated, the king and the government capitulated; the May constitution was abolished; and leading patriots emigrated. All this did not prevent Russia and Prussia from further diminishing Poland's territory with the Second Partition in 1793. In 1794 Kościuszko, returning from abroad, raised the banner of insurrection in the rump Commonwealth. It may have been a hopeless undertaking, but the Poles could not see their state destroyed without making a last stand. Kościuszko, assuming the title of chief (*naczelnik*),

ignored the king, but crowds in Warsaw, inspired by the example of revolutionary France, summarily executed a number of Targowica leaders. Offering emancipation measures to the peasants, Kościuszko brought a large number of them under his banner. After winning the battle of Racławice and capturing Warsaw and Wilno, the insurrectionists were defeated by Russian and Prussian forces. The wounded Kościuszko was taken prisoner, and Aleksandr Suvorov's Russian army carried out a wholesale massacre of the population in the Warsaw suburb of Praga.

The Third Partition followed in 1795, and, as in the preceding cases, the Polish Sejm was obliged to give its consent. Stanisław abdicated and left for St. Petersburg, where he died. In the final count Russia annexed 62 percent of Poland's area and 45 percent of the population, Prussia 20 percent of the area and 23 percent of the population, and Austria 18 and 32 percent, respectively. The three monarchs engaged themselves not to include Poland in their respective titles and thus obliterated its very name. But, while Poland disappeared, the "Polish question," as the controversy over Poland's status was called, was born, affecting both European diplomacy and the growth of Polish nationalism.

CHAPTER 22

PARTIONED POLAND

The 123 years during which Poland existed only as a partitioned land had a profound impact on the Polish psyche. Moreover, major 19th-century developments such as industrialization and modernization were uneven in Poland and proved to be a mixed blessing. Growing Polish nationalism was by necessity that of an oppressed nation and displayed the tendency of "all or nothing." Compromise became a dirty word, for it implied collaboration with the partitioners; a distrust of authority grew. The tradition of the Polish nobles' republic militated against submission and engendered an attitude of revolutionary defiance.

Beginning with the Kościuszko Insurrection, the Poles staged uprisings in 1806, 1830, 1846, 1848, and 1863 and a revolution in 1905. Defeats were followed by "organic work" that aimed at strengthening the society and its economy by peaceful means. This other major trend of nationalist aspiration was linked with Positivism, while the insurrectionary tradition became closely connected with Romanticism, but it is an oversimplification to identify the former with realism and the latter with idealism.

The survival of the Polish nation, which during the 19th century absorbed the peasant masses, was due in no small degree to a culture that continued to be all-Polish and dedicated to the Roman Catholic Church, whose role in maintaining "Polishness" was very important. Numerous writers, from the Romantic poets to Henryk Sienkiewicz, winner of the 1905 Nobel Prize for Literature, shaped the Polish mentality. For a stateless nation, ideas and imponderables acquired special importance. A rebirth of statehood, however, could be achieved only under the conditions of a major European upheaval, which would mean a collapse of the partitioning powers; this did not happen until 1918.

THE LEGIONS AND THE DUCHY OF WARSAW

Proud and politically conscious Poles never reconciled themselves to the loss of independence. Conspiracies and attempts to exploit the differences between the partitioning powers arose. Émigrés looked to revolutionary France for assistance, and Gen. Jan Henryk Dąbrowski succeeded in 1797 in persuading Napoleon Bonaparte, then waging his Italian campaign, to create auxiliary Polish legions. In their headquarters the future Polish national anthem—"Jeszcze Polska nie zginęła" ("Poland Has Not Yet Perished")—was sung for the first time.

Territory of the Polish state known as the Duchy of Warsaw, 1812. Encyclopædia Britannica, Inc.

Hopes placed on a French victory over Austria that would open the Polish question were, however, quashed by the Treaty of Campo Formio. In subsequent struggles Polish legionnaires were employed to fight French battles in Germany and in Santo Domingo, but Poland gained no political commitments. Yet the Poles' struggles did have a meaning in the long run, keeping a democratic Polish spirit alive and furnishing cadres to a future Polish army under Napoleon.

The pro-French military option had a counterpart in the ideas and policies of Prince Adam Jerzy Czartoryski. Appointed Russian foreign minister by Tsar Alexander I, the prince advocated redrawing the map of Europe to take into account national feelings and reconstitute Poland in union with Russia. This approach failed when Alexander committed himself to a struggle against France on the side of Prussia.

After Napoleon's victories over Prussia in 1806, French troops entered the Prussian part of Poland. Responding to somewhat vague promises by Napoleon, Dąbrowski called on the Poles to rise and organize armed units. In the campaigns that followed, Polish troops played a significant role, and Napoleon could not avoid making some gesture toward the Poles. In 1807, as a result of the compromise peace with Alexander at Tilsit, Prussia (now Sovetsk, Russia), a small state was created out of the Prussian shares in the First and Second Partitions and called the Duchy of Warsaw. Its ruler was the king of Saxony, Frederick Augustus I. Gdańsk was made a free city.

The Duchy of Warsaw, so named in order not to offend the partitioners, appeared to the Poles as a nucleus of a revived Poland. Doubled in size after a victorious war against Austria in 1809, it numbered more than four million people and had within its borders Warsaw, Kraków, and Poznań. The constitution imposed by Napoleon was comparable to his other authoritarian constitutions but took into account Polish traditions and customs. The ruler was absolute but used his powers with discretion and later delegated them to his ministers. The Napoleonic Code was introduced, and the constitution abolished "slavery." But this was interpreted to imply only the personal emancipation of the peasants without transferring to them the land they cultivated. Hence, servile obligations for those who stayed on the land continued in practice.

Napoleon regarded the duchy as a French outpost in the east, which required the maintenance of a disproportionately large army. The costs of maintaining it, together with the adverse effects of the Continental System, brought the duchy's economy to the brink of ruin. The emperor then took some Polish troops on his payroll, and they fought in Spain, where the charge of the light horse guards at Somosierra in 1808 passed into national legend.

Napoleon's invasion of Russia in 1812, in which nearly 100,000 Polish soldiers participated, seemed to promise the re-creation of Poland. Napoleon encouraged the Poles to proclaim the restoration of their country but did not commit himself to that goal. In reality, the emperor waged war not to destroy Russia but to force the tsar back into a policy of collaboration with France. Only in his exile at St. Helena did Napoleon speak of the key importance of Poland. His defeat in Russia brought the victorious Russian troops into the Duchy of Warsaw. While other allies of Napoleon were abandoning the sinking ship, Prince

Józef Poniatowski, who commanded the Polish army, remained loyal and died fighting at the Battle of Leipzig (1813) as a marshal of France.

FROM THE CONGRESS OF VIENNA TO 1848

The victory of the anti-Napoleonic coalition led to a redrafting of the map of Europe at the Congress of Vienna (1814–15). The Congress paid lip service

Territory of the Russian-ruled Polish state known as the Congress Kingdom of Poland, 1815–74. Encyclopædia Britannica, Inc.

to Poland by enjoining the partitioning powers to respect the national rights of their Polish subjects (insofar as was compatible with the partitioners' state interests) and by providing for free trade and communications within the borders of the old Commonwealth. The latter turned out to be a dead letter. The territorial issue caused dissent among the powers, but eventually a compromise arrangement left the former Duchy of Warsaw, minus Poznania (which went to Prussia) and Kraków (made a free city), to Tsar Alexander under the name of the Kingdom of Poland. The tsar now controlled about two-thirds of the old Commonwealth—both the area commonly called Congress Kingdom, or Congress Poland, and the former Commonwealth (Lithuanian, Ukrainian, and Belarusian) provinces that had been annexed during the partitions.

EARLY RUSSIAN RULE

Endowed with a liberal constitution, which was increasingly violated in practice, the settlement satisfied neither the Poles nor the Russians. The former hoped for the kingdom to be united with the eastern "lost lands" and to become a junior partner of the empire. Alexander, who played with the idea, abandoned it under the pressure of Russian circles that were unwilling to give up any of the annexed provinces. The Wilno educational district, which comprised most of them, originally had been chaired by Czartoryski and had been seen as a

model for educational reform in Russia. The university in Wilno was the largest in the empire. In 1823 it came under attack; students accused of sedition were jailed or exiled. One of the victims was the great Polish poet Adam Mickiewicz. Thus, basic disagreement about the territorial question was augmented by the anomalous union of an autocratic empire with a liberal kingdom. In the long run a confrontation may have been inevitable, but it was hastened by a gradual deterioration of the position of the Poles.

The post of viceroy did not go to Prince Czartoryski, by then estranged from Alexander, but went to a servile political nonentity, Gen. Józef Zajączek. The tsar's brother Constantine, the brutal and neurotic grand duke, was made commander in chief. Together with a special representative of the tsar, the intriguing and unscrupulous Nikolay Novosiltsev, they dominated the kingdom while usually at odds with one another. Alexander, autocratic by temperament, was revolted by the phenomenon of a liberal opposition in the Sejm, which he regarded as ingratitude.

Out of Freemasonry, which the tsar at first patronized, there grew a secret Polish Patriotic Society whose aims could hardly be qualified as treason. Nevertheless, its leader, Major Walerian Łukasiński, became a national martyr when he was thrown into prison, where he languished half-forgotten for more than 40 years until his death. Other conspiracies of more radical character began to spread.

NOVEMBER INSURRECTION

The Polish rebellion known as the November Insurrection occurred in 1830–31. The revolt was unsuccessful in its attempt to overthrow Russian rule in the Congress Kingdom of Poland as well as in the Polish provinces of western Russia and parts of Lithuania, Belorussia (now Belarus), and Ukraine.

When a revolution broke out in Paris (July 1830) and the Russian emperor Nicholas I indicated his intention of using the Polish army to suppress it, a Polish secret society of infantry cadets staged an uprising in Warsaw on November 29, 1830. Although the cadets and their civilian supporters failed to assassinate the emperor's brother Grand Duke Constantine (who was commander in chief of the armed forces in Poland) or to capture the barracks of the Russian cavalry, they did manage to seize weapons from the arsenal, arm the city's civilian population, and gain control of the northern section of Warsaw.

The insurgents' partial success was aided by the grand duke's reluctance to take action against them and his eagerness to retreat to safety. But lacking definite plans, unity of purpose, and decisive leadership, the rebels lost control of the situation to moderate political figures, who restored order in the city and futilely hoped to negotiate with Nicholas for political concessions. Although the rebellion gained widespread support and its new leaders formally deposed Nicholas as king of Poland on January 25, 1831, the conservative military commanders were unprepared when Nicholas's army of 115,000 troops moved in on February 5–6, 1831. The Polish army of 40,000 offered strong resistance at several battles, but it was unable to stop the Russian advance toward Warsaw until February 25, when it fought a major but indecisive battle at Grochów.

The Russians then settled into winter camps, and uprisings sympathetic to the Poles broke out in Russian-controlled Lithuania, Belorussia, and Ukraine (spring 1831). Nevertheless, the Polish commanders hesitated to strike and then quickly retreated. Furthermore, the divided political leaders not only refused to pass reforms to win the support of the peasantry but also failed to gain the foreign aid that the generals were depending on.

As a consequence, the rebellion lost its impetus, particularly after a major Russian victory at Ostrołęka on May 26, 1831. The uprisings in the western Russian provinces were crushed, and people in the cities began losing confidence in the revolution's leaders. When the Russians finally attacked Warsaw on September 6, the Polish army withdrew to the north two days later. Leaving the territory of Congress Poland, which subsequently fell under stricter and more repressive Russian control, the Poles crossed the border into Prussia on October 5 and surrendered, thus ending the November Insurrection.

The economy of the kingdom, however, developed, and its finances were put in order by the able though heavy-handed Prince Ksawery Drucki-Lubecki. He showed that Congress Poland was not a burden on the empire.

The Decembrist uprising in Russia in 1825, which accompanied the succession to the throne of Nicholas I, had repercussions in Congress Poland. A public trial exonerated the Polish leaders of complicity but made Russo-Polish relations tense. The outbreak of revolutions in Belgium and France in 1830 hastened the arrival of the November Insurrection. After its inception as a conspiratorial act at the cadet school in Warsaw (November 29, 1830), this uprising developed into a national revolt, marked by the dethronement of the Romanovs in Poland and the onset of a full-fledged Russo-Polish war. Hostilities spread into Lithuania and lasted until September 1831.

Russian victory was followed by severe reprisals, confiscations, arrests, and deportations. The kingdom's constitution was suspended, which meant the end of a separate Polish Sejm, government, and army. The University of Warsaw (founded 1817) was closed, as was the University of Wilno. Cultural Russification in the empire's former Polish provinces involved the liquidation of the Uniate church in 1839 and the abolition of the statute that had preserved the Lithuanian code of law. The Uniate church continued to exist only within the Congress Kingdom (until 1875) and in Galicia (until 1945).

EMIGRATION AND REVOLT

Several thousand Poles, including the political and intellectual elite, emigrated. When they passed through Germany, these émigrés were hailed as champions of freedom, and many of them came to believe in the idea of the solidarity of nations. The émigrés, settling mainly in France, splintered into many factions but grouped mainly around two figures: the moderate conservatives followed Prince Czartoryski, and the leftists were led at first by the great historian Joachim Lelewel. Later these leftists took a more radical stance as the Polish Democratic Society. Czartoryski concentrated on seeking the support of Britain and France for the Polish cause against Russia. The democrats, distrusting governments and blaming the conservatives for the defeat of the November Insurrection, preached a national and social revolution in cooperation with other peoples that would emancipate the peasantry. The Polish Democratic Society, whose program was embodied in the Poitiers Manifesto of 1836, became the first democratically run, centralized, and disciplined political party of east-central Europe. Karl Marx regarded its concept of agrarian revolution as a major Polish contribution to European revolutionary thought.

Political and philosophical writings and belles lettres of the émigrés were imbued with an intense patriotic message. The three greatest Polish Romantic poets—Mickiewicz, Juliusz Słowacki, and Zygmunt Krasiński—were the national "bards" (wieszcz) who influenced entire generations of Poles. They were followed by the much-later-discovered poet Cyprian Norwid. In music the emigration was epitomized by the compositions of

PRINCE ADAM JERZY CZARTORYSKI

Polish Prince Adam Jerzy Czartoryski (born January 14, 1770, Warsaw, Poland—died July 15, 1861, Montfermeil, France) worked unceasingly for the restoration of Poland when Russia, Prussia, and Austria had partitioned his country's former lands among themselves. Czartoryski was the most renowned member of a princely family, descended from the Lithuanian royal house, which wielded great power in Poland in the 18th century. He received a thorough education in his native country and traveled widely in western Europe. On returning to Poland in 1791, he played a distinguished part in the anti-Russian 1792 campaign that precipitated the second partition of Poland (1793). Although neither he nor his father took an active part in the 1794 insurrection that resulted in the third partition of Poland (1795), their palace at Puławy was destroyed and the family estates confiscated.

Seeking the recovery of his property, Czartoryski went in 1795 to St. Petersburg, where he joined the Russian government service and became friendly with the grand duke Alexander. When Alexander became tsar, he called upon Czartoryski, who had become one of his close advisers, to work on plans for the reform of the government, naming him deputy minister of foreign affairs in 1802 and minister in 1804. Czartoryski's hostility to Russia's alliance with Prussia and the Russian military defeat in the 1805 campaign against Napoleon (undertaken against his advice), caused his dismissal in 1806; but he remained in Russian service as curator (from 1803) of the educational region of Wilno (Vilnius), which embraced the eastern provinces of the former Polish state.

After Napoleon's downfall, Czartoryski resumed his efforts to restore Poland. With Alexander's consent, he was Poland's spokesman at the Congress of Vienna in 1815, obtaining as much as was possible—the creation of a new Kingdom of Poland with Alexander as king. He helped to prepare a liberal constitution for the kingdom and became a senator and member of the executive council, but in 1816, disillusioned with Alexander, he largely withdrew from public life.

Czartoryski did not want a Polish rebellion against Russia and knew success would depend more on Western diplomatic intervention than on fighting by the Poles, but he found himself at the head of the Poles' November Insurrection that broke out on November 29, 1830. On the collapse of the rebellion, sentenced to death by the Russians and deprived of his estates, he went into exile on August 15, 1831. His Paris residence, the Hôtel Lambert, became the centre of the political activity of the Polish exiles. He was unofficially acknowledged as "Polish king in exile" and maintained unofficial representatives in Constantinople, Rome, and other European capitals. Czartoryski wrote his memoirs, in addition to other literary and historical books and essays.

Frédéric Chopin. A messianic conception of the Polish nation arose, which in its most extreme and mystical form characterized Poland as the Christ of nations, redeeming all oppressed peoples through its suffering and transcendence.

In partitioned Poland émigré emissaries inspired conspiratorial activities. After the failure of several other attempts, an uprising was planned for 1846. Stanched by arrests in Poznań, it got off the ground only in Kraków (where a national government was proclaimed) and in the neighbouring districts of western Galicia. The Kraków rising was put down by Austrian troops, and the city was annexed; elsewhere peasant antagonism toward the landowners was channeled by Austrian officials against the mostly noble rebels. A jacquerie (peasant revolt) developed, in the course of which many manors were burned down and landowners killed. This came as a shock to Polish democrats, who had extolled the people (*lud*) as the backbone and the hope of the nation, and to conservatives, who had warned against a social upheaval.

The liberal and democratic Revolutions of 1848, which spread over most of Europe, raised hopes for the revival of the Polish cause. Poles were in the forefront of numerous struggles, and Gen. Józef Bem became a hero of the Hungarian Revolution. While the tsar threatened to punish the revolutionaries in Germany and in the Habsburg monarchy, liberals in Berlin and Vienna saw the advantage of a Polish buffer state against Russia. In Prussian Poland the authorities tolerated the emergence of a virtual Polish takeover of Poznania, including the formation of an armed militia. However, when the Russian danger receded, Polish nationalism appeared as the main threat, and Prussian troops crushed the militia. The Germans had opted for "healthy national egoism," which meant that henceforth the Polish strife with the Prussian officialdom would become a nationalist German-Polish struggle.

Some circles in revolutionary Vienna seemed to consider the possibility of giving up Galicia to a revived Poland. The governor of Galicia was interested mainly in ensuring control over the province. Forestalling Polish plans, he abolished serfdom and used the nascent Ruthenian-Ukrainian movement in eastern Galicia to oppose national aspirations. A limited Polish resistance was broken by bombardments of Kraków and Lemberg (now Lviv, Ukraine).

After the Revolutions of 1848, which revealed the sharpness of national conflicts, the Poles began to realize that a Poland within the prepartitions borders—a smaller Polish state was out of the question not only for Poles but also for Marx and Friedrich Engels—might have to be a federation of distinct nationalities and no longer a unitary country. The emancipation of the peasantry in Galicia (already emancipated under Prussia some two decades earlier) made the peasant question a central issue—namely, whether the peasants could be absorbed into the Polish national fabric or whether their first loyalty would be to the partitioning monarchs. The issue became acute in the Russian partition, which had remained passive in 1848.

THE JANUARY 1863 UPRISING AND ITS AFTERMATH

After humiliating defeats in the Crimean War, the Russian Empire under Tsar Alexander II embarked on major liberal reforms. For Congress Poland this meant political amnesty, conciliatory measures in cultural and religious matters, and the creation of the Agricultural Society to tackle the peasant question. Simultaneously, Alexander II warned the Poles against political "daydreaming." The Agricultural Society, a union of reformist landowners headed by the popular Hrabia (count) Andrzej Zamoyski, debated changes in the agrarian sector but found it hard to avoid politics. A patriotic movement later known as the Whites grew around and partly out of the society. It included landowners and members of the bourgeoisie (often of German or Jewish origin), such as the banker Leopold Kronenberg. At this time a Polish-Jewish dialogue promoted close cooperation.

On the other side of the political spectrum, there developed a number of conspiratorial groups composed of students, younger army officers, artisans, and members of the lesser gentry. Subsequently called the Reds, these radicals acted as a pressure group on the Agricultural Society and staged demonstrations commemorating Polish patriots or historic events. In 1861, the year of the peasant emancipation decree in the Russian Empire, demonstrators in Warsaw clashed with Russian troops, and several were killed or wounded.

The Russians, determined to be firm with the radicals, sought a dialogue with the upper classes. But Zamoyski, worried lest he appear subservient to the Russians, demanded a return to the guarantees of the 1815 constitution. Such demands were rejected, and Zamoyski was eventually ordered to leave the country. The Russian viceroy turned to Zamoyski's rival, Margrabia (margrave) Aleksander Wielopolski, whose program of limited concessions (Polonization of education, restoration of local self-government, transformation of the peasants into tenants, and emancipation of the Jews) was acceptable to St. Petersburg. Wielopolski's contempt for public opinion and high-handed methods—especially the disbanding of the Agricultural Society and a showdown with the Roman Catholic Church—estranged him from the Poles. Tension grew after a massacre of demonstrators near the castle square.

Wielopolski, appointed the head of government in 1862, introduced reforms that were not insignificant but did not include peasant emancipation. He was viewed as an enemy by both the Reds, who created an underground National Committee, and the Whites, who also set up a clandestine organization. Wielopolski decided to break the Reds by drafting large numbers of them into the Russian army. In January 1863 the National Committee, left with no choice but to take up the challenge, called on the peoples of Poland, Lithuania, and Rus (Ukraine) to rise, decreed peasant emancipation, and appealed for support from the Jews ("Poles of Mosaic faith").

Thousands responded to the call; however, because the insurgents had failed to capture any town or compact territory, the National Committee, transformed into the National Government, had to operate anonymously underground. In the spring the Whites joined the uprising, contributing finances and international contacts but also seeking to control the movement. Fighting extended into Lithuanian and Belarusian lands but not into Ukraine. In some instances the peasantry participated in the struggle, and in others they cooperated with the Russians. France proffered encouragement and hinted that the blood of the insurgents would mark the boundaries of an independent Poland. But in practice France, Britain, and Austria did not go beyond joint diplomatic démarches in St. Petersburg. Prussia sided with Russia. The insurgents, equipped with primitive weapons, fought doggedly as partisans in small detachments and succeeded in keeping the rising going until the autumn of 1864, when its last and most prominent leader, Romuald Traugutt, was captured and executed.

The decades that followed the January Insurrection opened a new phase in the history of partitioned Poland. Harsh reprisals in the kingdom—now called the Vistula Land—were designed to reduce it to a mere province of Russia, denied even the benefits of subsequent reforms in Russia proper. Large garrisons and emergency legislation kept the Poles down. Many individuals involved in the rising were executed or deported to Siberia; thousands of landed estates were confiscated. The Uniate church was abolished, and the Roman Catholic hierarchy was harassed. A huge Orthodox church emerged in the centre of Warsaw.

The government believed that it could resolve the Polish question by winning over the peasantry (emancipated in 1864) and pitting them against the *szlachta* and the Catholic Church, as well as by eradicating the historical ties between the "western provinces" and Poland. Catholics could no longer buy land there. In Lithuania the brutal governor Mikhail Muravyov was nicknamed "the hangman." The post-1863 period marked the beginning of a final parting of the ways between the Poles and the Lithuanians and Ukrainians (the latter also were undergoing a national revival), but in the long run Russian policies did not accomplish their aims.

The emancipated peasantry, coming into direct contact with the Russian officialdom and antagonized by anti-Catholic and Russification policies, became more self-consciously Polish. The dispossessed gentry moved to towns, transmitting their values to a growing intelligentsia, which assumed national leadership. As the Industrial Revolution penetrated Congress Poland, the growth of a bourgeoisie and of an industrial proletariat was accelerated.

The fastest and greatest development was in textiles and was centred on Łódź—the Polish Manchester—the population of which increased 10-fold between 1865 and 1897. Mining, metallurgy, and food-processing industries followed suit. Vistula Land became the most developed part of the Russian Empire, but its development was uneven and its modernization partial. Moreover, its reliance on the eastern markets made the country dependent on Russia.

Socioeconomic progress contrasted with political stagnation. The Polish question largely disappeared from the European agenda after 1870. Blaming romantic idealism for the catastrophic uprising, people rejected political activities and extolled the value of "organic work," progress, and modernization. Warsaw Positivism, deriving its name and inspiration from the thought of Auguste Comte, provided the rationale for these views.

ACCOMMODATION WITH THE RULING GOVERNMENTS

Uprisings also were condemned as folly by conservatives in Galicia, where the Kraków historical school critically reinterpreted Poland's history. The conservatives were willing to cooperate with Vienna in exchange for concessions, and, as the Habsburg monarchy transformed itself into a dual Austro-Hungarian Empire in 1867, Galicia obtained local autonomy. From the 1860s the province was largely Polonized. Persecuted

elsewhere, Polish culture could flourish there; the Universities of Kraków and Lwów (Lemberg) and the Academy of Arts and Sciences became cultural beacons radiating across the partition borders. There was less progress in the socioeconomic field. Ruled by conservative landowners, Galicia remained a poor and backward province. In its eastern part nascent Ukrainian nationalism clashed with that of the Poles.

The situation for Poles in Prussia at times appeared critical. German Chancellor Otto von Bismarck's anti-Polish policies culminated in the Kulturkampf, designed to strengthen the cohesion of the newly created German Empire. In addition, policies of cultural and linguistic Germanization and German settlement in the provinces continuously threatened the Polish and Roman Catholic character of Poznania and West Prussia. A colonization commission was set up in 1886. Eight years later a society for the promotion of German interests in the east came into being. The Poles called it Hakata, after the initials of its founders. The Polish response took the form of credit unions, cooperative associations, and self-help institutions. Showing great solidarity and organizational talents, working hard, and raising socioeconomic standards, Prussian Poles developed characteristics that distinguished them from their countrymen under Russian or Austrian rule.

In the post-1863 decades, prevailing political attitudes took the form of Triple Loyalism, the belief that material and cultural progress in each part of divided Poland was predicated on loyalty to the ruling governments. This policy seemed to produce beneficial results only under Austria. The pursuit of riches was being represented as essentially patriotic even if realized under the harsh conditions of early capitalism. For the masses, with their rapid population growth, living conditions were deplorable. This led to their radicalization on the one hand and to a sizable emigration on the other. In the period 1870–1914, about 3.6 million people, mostly peasants, emigrated from Polish lands to the United States.

A reaction to that situation developed in the 1890s that had both a nationalist and a socialist character. The National Democratic movement originated with a Polish League organized in Switzerland; by 1893 the organization had transformed into the clandestine National League, based in Warsaw. It stressed its all-Polish character, rejected loyalism, and promoted national resistance, even uprisings, when opportune. Its nationalist ideology tinged with populism gradually evolved into "integral" nationalism, which placed national interest and national egoism above everything else. Affected by social Darwinist theories of survival of the fittest and natural selection, Polish nationalism advocated a struggle not only against the partitioning powers but also against the Ukrainians and the Jews, whose interests were seen as opposed to those of the Poles. The father of this integral nationalism was Roman Dmowski, whose writings stressed the need to create a modern Polish nation deriving its strength from the ethnically Polish masses.

Polish socialism, which in its early manifestations was purely a class movement with an emphasis on internationalism, began by the 1890s to stress an indissoluble connection between social revolution and Poland's independence. At a conference held in Paris in 1892, the Polish Socialist Party (PPS) came into existence. Illegal under Russian rule, it had a counterpart in Galicia in the Polish Social Democratic Party led by Ignacy Daszyński. The dominant figure in the PPS was Józef Piłsudski, who saw the historic role of socialism in Poland as that of a destroyer of reactionary tsardom.

Doubly oppressed (nationally and socially), the Polish proletariat was to be the force to carry the struggle for social justice and national liberation. Opposing such views was the Social Democracy of the Kingdom of Poland and Lithuania, the forerunner of Polish communism. Its leading theorist, Rosa Luxemburg, argued that national independence would not promote the interests of the proletariat, who were integrated economically into the three partitioning states.

CHAPTER 23

POLAND IN THE 20TH CENTURY AND BEYOND

The outbreak of the Russo-Japanese War in 1904 created a tense atmosphere and sharpened the basic differences between the major political trends. While Dmowski and his supporters sought to extract concessions from the tsarist regime, Piłsudski promoted revolutionary nationalistic tactics. Both politicians went to Tokyo, where they presented their opposite programs to the Japanese. At the beginning of 1905, just as the revolution began to sweep Russia, Congress Poland responded to events with a school strike and a general workers' strike, while Piłsudski's PPS squads battled with Russian troops and police. The government offered limited concessions to the Poles in Congress Poland and the western provinces. Dmowski's larger hopes, bound with the creation of the Russian Duma—in which the Poles were mainly represented by National Democrats—proved unfounded. The PPS, in turn, suffered internal splits, Piłsudski moving increasingly in an insurrectionary (national), as opposed to a revolutionary (social), direction.

During the first decade of the 20th century, a mass political culture developed in Polish lands. The Russian Revolution of 1905 contributed to the growth of a civil society in Congress Poland (with legal political parties and trade unions), though it was constantly undermined by Russian rule. In Austria the introduction of universal manhood suffrage in 1907 widened the political involvement of the masses. The Polish peasant movement that had risen in Galicia in the 1890s was beset by schisms. In 1913 there emerged from it the Polish Peasant Party led by Wincenty

Witos. In the German partition a Polish national revival in Upper Silesia led by Wojciech Korfanty and one on a lesser scale in East Prussia affected for the first time regions that had not been part of the prepartition Commonwealth.

THE REBIRTH OF POLAND

With the outbreak of World War I, two major political trends emerged among the Poles. Józef Piłsudski, distancing himself from socialist politics, became a military leader and commander of a brigade that fought on the Austrian side. His cooperation with the Central Powers was tactical, part of his pursuit of the goal of complete independence. Expecting a collapse of the three partitioners, he prepared for a Polish fait accompli. In 1915 the Germans and the Austrians drove out the Russians from Congress Poland, and on November 5, 1916, they issued the Two Emperors' Manifesto proclaiming the creation of the Polish kingdom. Its status and borders remained undefined, but the document internationalized the Polish question. Piłsudski, who refused to raise Polish troops without binding political commitments from the Central Powers, came into conflict with them and in 1917 was imprisoned in Magdeburg, Germany.

Roman Dmowski's alternative policy of linking the Polish cause with the Franco-Russian alliance appeared promising when the first formal offer of Polish autonomy and unification came from the Russian commander in chief, Grand Duke Nicholas, on August 14, 1914. Subsequent moves by the Russian government, however, revealed the hollowness of such promises. Russian concessions to the Poles, culminating in the tsar's Christmas Day 1916 order, were made only in reaction to the Central Powers' initiatives and victories.

The chances of Polish independence increased radically in 1917 when the United States entered the war and two revolutions shook Russia. U.S. Pres. Woodrow Wilson, to whom the great Polish patriot and pianist Ignacy Paderewski had gained access through Col. Edward M. House, already spoke of a united and autonomous Poland in a January 1917 address. The Russian Provisional Government, somewhat ambiguously, and the Petrograd (St. Petersburg) Soviet of Workers' and Soldiers' Deputies, more explicitly, declared their recognition of Poland's right to independence in March 1917.

At the Brest-Litovsk conference (December 22, 1917–March 3, 1918), the Bolsheviks denounced the Central Powers' handling of the Polish question. On January 8, 1918, Wilson's Fourteen Points appeared. Point 13 declared that an independent Polish state should be erected, to be composed of indisputably Polish inhabitants and with a secure access to the sea. The Inter-Allied conference (June 1918) endorsed Polish independence, thus crowning the efforts of Dmowski, who had promoted the Polish cause in the West since 1915. In August 1917 he had set up a Polish

National Committee in Paris, which the French viewed as a quasi-government. Under its aegis a Polish army composed mainly of volunteers from the United States was placed under the command of Gen. Józef Haller.

With the end of the war on November 11, 1918, Piłsudski, released by the German revolutionaries, returned to Warsaw. The German-appointed Regency Council handed over its powers to him, and Piłsudski successfully negotiated a German evacuation of the kingdom. A leftist government in Lublin headed by Daszyński resigned in his favour, but Dmowski's Polish National Committee, representing the Polish political right, did not. The danger of two rival governments was avoided through the mediation of Paderewski. Under a compromise implemented in January 1919, Piłsudski remained chief of state and commander in chief; Paderewski, who became premier and foreign minister, and Dmowski represented Poland at the Paris Peace Conference.

At that stage the Polish government controlled only Congress Poland and western Galicia. In the east the Ukrainians, having proclaimed their own republic, battled the Poles. Farther east the Poles clashed with the Bolsheviks, who were advancing into Belarusian and Lithuanian lands. A Polish uprising in Poznania led to a partial seizure of the province, but the fate of Prussian Poland lay in the hands of the peacemakers, who had also the last word about the territorial settlement.

FROM THE TREATY OF VERSAILLES TO THE TREATY OF RIGA

The Polish program at the Paris Peace Conference was affected by the Piłsudski-Dmowski dualism. Piłsudski's approach was "federalist," Dmowski's "incorporationist." The former strove to establish a bloc of states corresponding to prepartition Poland, but he was flexible on the issue of the borders of those states. The latter postulated a centralized Polish state, with its eastern border determined by the Second Partition but also including Upper Silesia and parts of East Prussia transferred from Germany in the west. France favoured strengthening Poland at Germany's expense, but Britain opposed that approach. Wilson occupied a middle position.

The borders drawn under the Treaty of Versailles (June 1919) roughly corresponded to Polish-German frontiers before the partitions, except that Gdańsk became the free city of Danzig, and plebiscites were held in parts of East Prussia and Upper Silesia to determine which nation these regions wished to join. The East Prussian plebiscite of July 1920 (at the height of the Russo-Polish War) was won by Germany. In the Silesian plebiscite of March 1921—preceded and followed by three Polish uprisings—682 communes voted for Poland and 792 for Germany. The region was formally divided in October 1921.

Poland in the 20th century and beyond. Encyclopædia Britannica, Inc.

The drawing of the southern border under the Treaty of Saint-Germain (September 1919) was preceded by an armed Czech-Polish clash in January 1919 in the duchy of Cieszyn. In July 1920 the area was divided, leaving a sizable Polish minority in Czechoslovakia. As for the embattled eastern Galicia, the Allies authorized a Polish administration and military occupation in 1919. Final recognition of Polish sovereignty came only in 1923, the delay being due to the Russian situation.

An armed struggle between the Bolsheviks and Poland resulted from Russian attempts to carry the revolution westward and from Piłsudski's federalist policy. The Great Powers failed to pursue either an all-out intervention against the Bolsheviks or a policy of peace. An Allied proposal for a temporary border between Bolshevik Russia and Poland (called the Curzon Line) was unacceptable to either side. Except for an alliance in April 1920 with the Ukrainian leader Symon

French tanks and soldiers in the streets of Katowice, Pol., during one of the Silesian uprisings, 1919–21. Encyclopædia Britannica, Inc.

Petlyura, whose troops accompanied the Poles as they captured Kiev in May, Poland fought in isolation. An offensive by the Red Army drove the Poles back to the outskirts of Warsaw, but Piłsudski's counterattack on August 16 (the "Miracle of the Vistula") saved the country from catastrophe. In the compromise Peace of Riga (March 1921), the Bolsheviks abandoned their plans to communize Poland, but the Poles had to abandon their federalist concepts. The new border, which corresponded roughly to the 1793 frontier, cut across mixed Ukrainian and Belarusian territories. In the north it included Wilno, captured by Gen. Lucjan Żeligowski, a move that opened a chasm between Lithuania and Poland.

THE SECOND REPUBLIC

With an area of about 150,000 square miles (389,000 sq km) and more than 27 million inhabitants (more than 35 million by 1939), interwar Poland was the sixth largest country in Europe. Devastated by the years of hostilities, the state had to be reconstructed of three parts with different political, economic, and judicial systems and traditions. More than three-fifths of the population was dependent on agriculture that was badly in need of structural change: agrarian reform and redistribution of land that would relieve the demographic pressure (e.g., hidden unemployment) and modernization of production that could alleviate the disparity between agrarian and industrial prices ("the price scissors"). Industrialization was essential, but local capital was insufficient, and foreign investors did not always operate in Poland's interests.

Nonetheless, the Polish economy made important strides in the mid-1920s through the reforms of Władysław Grabski. The Great Depression of the 1930s had a crippling effect on Poland's economy, but it began to recover under the guidance of Eugeniusz Kwiatkowski, whose earlier achievements included the building of a new port and town of Gdynia.

Pressing political problems, such as the issue of minorities, exacerbated economic difficulties. Ukrainians (some 16 percent of the total population, according to estimates), Jews (about 10 percent), Belarusians (about 6 percent), and Germans (about 3 percent) lived in a state that, although multiethnic, was based on a single-nation ideology. The Ukrainians never fully accepted Polish rule, and Ukrainian extremists engaged in terrorism to which the Poles responded with brutal "pacifications." In the case of the large and unassimilated Jewish population, concentrated in certain areas and professions, anti-Semitism was rampant, especially in the 1930s, though Poland never introduced anti-Jewish legislation.

Interwar politics centred to a large extent on the search for a constitutional model that would reconcile traditional Polish strivings for liberty with the need for a strong government. Piłsudski gave up his provisional powers to a Sejm elected in January 1919 but continued as the head of state under a provisional "Little Constitution." The Sejm quickly became an arena of interparty strife, with the right grouped around the National Democrats, the left grouped around the PPS and radical Populists, and the centre represented mainly by the Polish Peasant Party. The illegal Communist Party, formed in 1918, was of marginal importance. The constitution of 1921 made the parliament supreme vis-à-vis the executive. The proportional system of universal suffrage (which included women) necessitated coalition cabinets, and, except at times of national crisis, the left and the right hardly cooperated. In 1922 a nationalist fanatic assassinated the first president of the republic, Gabriel

Narutowicz, an event that underscored the extent of blind partisanship.

In May 1926 Piłsudski (who had held the title of marshal since 1920) came out of his three-year retirement. Demanding moral and political cleansing (*sanacja*), he staged an armed demonstration intended to force Pres. Stanisław Wojciechowski to dismiss the government. Fighting in Warsaw ensued and ended in victory for Piłsudski. His candidate, Ignacy Mościcki, became president and remained in office until World War II. Piłsudski rejected fascism and totalitarianism but promoted an authoritarian regime in which his former legionnaires played a key role. Worshiped by his supporters and hated by his opponents, he became a father figure for large segments of the population. The pro-Piłsudski Non-Party Bloc of Cooperation with the Government (BBWR) became his political instrument, used at first against the opposition rightist National Democrats. In 1930 Piłsudski responded to the challenge of the centre-left opposition (Centrolew) by ordering the arrest and trial of its leaders, including three-time premier Witos. The brutal Brześć

STANISŁAW WOJCIECHOWSKI

Stanisław Wojciechowski (born March 15, 1869, Kalisz, Poland, Russian Empire—died April 9, 1953, Golabki, Poland) was one of the leaders in the struggle for Polish independence from Russia in the years before World War I. He later served as the second president of the Polish Republic (1922–26).

While a student at the University of Warsaw, Wojciechowski worked for the Polish Socialist movement, which was a major force in the independence effort. He was arrested in 1891, and upon his release a year later he went to Paris and then to London. In England he helped publish the Polish Socialist periodical *Przedświt* ("The Dawn") and became friends with Józef Piłsudski. He also studied the cooperative movement, and on returning to Poland in 1906 he spent his time working to develop Polish cooperatives.

During World War I, because he saw Germany as Poland's main enemy, Wojciechowski in 1915 went to Moscow, and there in 1917 he was elected president of the Council of Polish Parties' Union. He returned to Warsaw at the end of the war and from January 1919 to July 1920 served as minister of the interior in three separate cabinets of the new Polish Republic. He was elected to the Sejm (Diet) as a member of the Polish Peasant Party in November 1922. When Gabriel Narutowicz, president of the republic, was assassinated in December 1922, Wojciechowski was chosen to succeed him.

In the new government Wojciechowski and Piłsudski, then military chief of staff, differed as to the direction the nation should take. Wojciechowski supported continued parliamentary government, while Piłsudski favoured a more authoritarian approach. In May 1926, Piłsudski staged a successful coup d'état. Wojciechowski then retired to private life.

affair (named for the fortress in which the politicians involved were imprisoned) was seen as a blot on the Piłsudski regime, even though the sentences were light and some of the accused were permitted to emigrate.

Following the 1930 elections, the BBWR had a majority in the Sejm. In April 1935 it was able to push through a new constitution, which placed the president above all other branches of government. An electoral law undercut the political parties that boycotted the 1935 parliamentary elections. In May Piłsudski died, leaving the country as a dictatorship without a dictator. His legend could not be bequeathed. A decomposition of the *sanacja* regime ensued. Attempts to pass on Piłsudski's mantle to the new commander in chief, Marshal Edward Śmigły-Rydz, were unsuccessful, as was the artificial creation of a governmental party—the Camp of National Unity. The peasant parties (now united); the increasingly chauvinist National Party (as the National Democrats were by then known), with its fascist splinter party, the National Radical Camp; and the socialists all opposed the regime and achieved success in municipal elections. Socioeconomic tension was translated into peasant strikes in the countryside and riots in towns.

Political and socioeconomic difficulties contrasted with the richness of intellectual, artistic, and scholarly life of the period. Twenty years of independence had given the Poles a new confidence that proved essential in the trials of World War II. Poland's international position between an inimical and revisionist Germany (which constantly denounced the "corridor" separating it from East Prussia) and the Soviet Union was dangerous from the start. The tasks of Polish diplomacy during the interwar period were exceedingly difficult. The only option was to remain neutral in regard to its two giant neighbours while concluding alliances (in 1921) with France and Romania. An alliance with Czechoslovakia, which might have strengthened both countries, foundered on basic differences of approach to international relations, particularly when Col. Józef Beck became Piłsudski's foreign minister in 1932.

In 1932 Poland succeeded in signing a nonaggression pact with Soviet Russia, and in 1934 it made a declaration of nonaggression with Nazi Germany. The enmity of the Nazis for the Soviets seemed to preclude a rapprochement (such as the Russo-German agreement at Rapallo, Italy, in 1922). Poland maintained its alliance with France, though the treaties of Locarno (1925) and subsequent Franco-German cooperation diminished the value of the alliance. Warsaw vainly sought to encourage Paris—through defiant gestures in Danzig and vague war-prevention overtures—to adopt a strong line against Nazi Germany. But the French did not react forcibly even to the German remilitarization of the Rhineland (1936).

Poland continued its policy of balance, but, in profiting from the German action against Czechoslovakia by gaining the disputed part of Cieszyn (October 1938), it gave the impression of being in collusion with Adolf Hitler. However, when confronted with German demands for an extraterritorial road through the "corridor" and the annexation of Danzig, as well as with an invitation to join the Anti-Comintern Pact, Beck knew that his country's independence was at stake. Accepting British Prime Minister Neville Chamberlain's guarantee of March 1939 and turning it into a full-fledged alliance with Britain, Warsaw rejected German demands. On September 1, 1939, Hitler, having secured Soviet cooperation through the German-Soviet (Molotov-Ribbentrop) Nonaggression Pact a week earlier, launched an all-out attack against Poland.

WORLD WAR II

The Poles, fighting alone against the Wehrmacht's overwhelming might, particularly in air power and armour, were doomed. On September 17, 1939, the Red Army invaded Poland from the east, and on September 28 Hitler and Joseph Stalin agreed on a final partition, the Soviets taking eastern Galicia and lands east of the Bug River (i.e., more than half of the country, where the Poles constituted about two-fifths of the population). After farcical plebiscites in October and November, these territories were incorporated into Soviet Ukraine and Belorussia. Between 1940 and 1941 about 1.5 million people were deported to the U.S.S.R. Wilno was handed over to Lithuania, which by 1940 had become one of the Soviet republics. While the Soviets singled out class enemies, the Germans—who split the area they occupied into a central region called the General Government and territories annexed to the Reich—emphasized race.

The Holocaust claimed the lives of some three million Polish Jews, herded into ghettoes and killed in extermination camps, of which Auschwitz (Oświęcim) was but one. Thousands of Jews died fighting, as in the Warsaw Ghetto Uprising in 1943. The Nazis also engaged in mass terror, deporting and executing non-Jewish Poles in an attempt to destroy the intelligentsia and extinguish Polish culture. Priests and politicians were killed; children of prominent citizens were kidnapped; and many Poles were forced into hard labour.

From 1939 a Polish underground, one of the largest in occupied Europe, resisted the Nazis through a veritable secret state and a Home Army (AK) loyal to the Polish government-in-exile. The latter was a legal successor of the government that on September 17, 1939, had crossed into Romania and was interned there. Set up in Paris and moved to London after the collapse of France, it was led by the premier and commander in chief, Gen. Władysław Sikorski. Under his command Polish troops, organized in the west, fought in all theatres of war in Europe and North Africa. Polish pilots played a disproportionately large role in the Battle of Britain (1940–41), and the small Polish navy also distinguished

AUSCHWITZ

Auschwitz (Polish: Oświęcim; also called Auschwitz-Birkenau) was Nazi Germany's largest concentration camp and extermination camp. Located near the industrial town of Oświęcim in southern Poland (in a portion of the country that was annexed by Germany at the beginning of World War II), Auschwitz was actually three camps in one: a prison camp, an extermination camp, and a slave-labour camp.

Auschwitz was probably chosen to play a central role in the "final solution"—a virtual synonym for the Holocaust—because it was located at a railway junction with 44 parallel tracks—rail lines that were used to transport Jews from throughout Europe to their death. Heinrich Himmler, chief of the SS, the Nazi paramilitary corps, ordered the establishment of the first camp, the prison camp, on April 27, 1940, and the first transport of Polish political prisoners arrived on June 14. This small camp, Auschwitz I, was reserved throughout its history for political prisoners, mainly Poles and Germans. In October 1941, work began on Auschwitz II, or Birkenau, located outside the nearby village of Brzezinka. There the SS later developed a huge concentration camp and extermination complex that included some 300 prison barracks; four large so-called Badeanstalten (German: "bathhouses"), in which prisoners were gassed to death; Leichenkeller ("corpse cellars"), in which their bodies were stored; and Einäscherungsöfen ("cremating ovens"). Another camp (Buna-Monowitz), near the village of Dwory, later called Auschwitz III, became in May 1942 a slave-labour camp supplying workers for the nearby chemical and synthetic-rubber works of IG Farben. In addition, Auschwitz became the nexus of a complex of 45 smaller subcamps in the region, most of which housed slave labourers. During most of the period from 1940 to 1945, the commandant of the central Auschwitz camps was SS-Hauptsturmführer (Captain) Rudolf Franz Höss.

Auschwitz. Encyclopædia Britannica, Inc.

Newly arrived prisoners were divided in a process known as Selektion. The young and the able-bodied were sent to work. Young children and their mothers and the old and infirm were sent directly to the gas chambers. Thousands of prisoners were also selected by the camp doctor, Josef Mengele, for barbaric medical experiments.

As Soviet armies advanced in 1944 and early 1945, Auschwitz was gradually abandoned. On January 18, 1945, some 60,000 prisoners were marched to Wodzisław, where they were put on freight trains and sent westward to concentration camps away from the front. One in four died en route. Many were shot along the way in what became known as the "death marches." The 7,650 sick or starving prisoners who remained were found by arriving Soviet troops on January 27, 1945.

Between 1.1 and 1.5 million people died at Auschwitz; 90 percent of them were Jews. The Poles constituted the second largest victim group at Auschwitz, where some 83,000 were killed or died. Also among the dead were some 19,000 Roma (Gypsies).

Although the Germans destroyed parts of the camps before abandoning them in 1945, much of Auschwitz I and Auschwitz II (Birkenau) remained intact and were later converted into a museum and memorial. Auschwitz was designated a UNESCO World Heritage site in 1979.

itself. A major Polish contribution to the war effort lay in discovering and passing on to the Allies the secret of the German ciphering machine Enigma.

The German attack on the Soviet Union in June 1941 changed Poland's position drastically, for one of its foes now became a member of the Grand Alliance. Under British pressure the Polish government-in-exile reestablished relations with the Soviet Union through the Sikorski-Maysky accord, accepting the annulment of the Ribbentrop-Molotov treaty without an explicit Soviet renunciation of annexed Polish territory. The Soviets promised to release the deported Poles—more than 230,000 Poles had been

prisoners of war since 1939—and agreed to the creation of a Polish army under the command of Gen. Władysław Anders. Difficulties appeared almost from the start, however. The Soviets sought British and U.S. approval for their territorial gains. Friction developed regarding the Polish army in Russia, which in 1942 was evacuated to the Middle East. Meanwhile, the Soviets were promoting Polish communist activity both in the U.S.S.R. and in occupied Poland, where a Polish Workers' Party (PPR) emerged in 1942 with its own small People's Guard, though this force was much smaller than the AK.

British Prime Minister Winston Churchill, not appreciating fully Stalin's hegemonic designs, believed that timely territorial concessions to the U.S.S.R. would preserve the internal independence of postwar Poland. During three visits to Washington, D.C. (1941–42), Sikorski outlined his ideas about postwar security in east-central Europe, including a Czechoslovak-Polish confederation; however, U.S. Pres. Franklin D. Roosevelt regarded Polish issues as secondary. For him, as for Churchill, the importance of the Soviet Union as an ally was crucial, and neither leader was prepared to see relations with Stalin founder on the Polish rock.

This became apparent when they were undeterred by the German announcement on April 13, 1943, of the discovery in the Katyn Forest of mass graves of more than 4,000 Polish officers who had been captured by the Red Army. The Polish search for some 15,000 missing men had previously met with a Soviet profession of complete ignorance as to their fate. Stalin accused the Sikorski government—which had asked the International Red Cross to investigate—of complicity in Nazi propaganda and severed diplomatic relations with the government-in-exile. Only in 1992 did postcommunist Moscow publicly acknowledge its guilt and furnish to Warsaw supporting documents, which also indicated the locations of other mass executions.

Sikorski's death in a mysterious plane crash in Gibraltar (July 1943) was a great blow to the Poles at a time when Soviet offensives after the victories of Stalingrad and Kursk had brought the Red Army closer to the prewar Polish borders. The new prime minister and Peasant Party leader, Stanisław Mikołajczyk, could not rival Sikorski's standing and was at odds with the new commander in chief, Gen. Kazimierz Sosnkowski. The Soviets demanded, as the price for reestablishing relations with the Polish government, territorial concessions and the dismissal of several of its members. The Soviets also provided support for Polish communist organizations such as the Union of Polish Patriots in Moscow and the National Committee of the Homeland, headed by Bolesław Bierut and set up in Poland in December 1943. At the Tehrān Conference late in 1943, Churchill's proposal that the Soviet-Polish border coincide with the Curzon Line (roughly similar to the Ribbentrop-Molotov line) and that Poland be compensated at Germany's cost was accepted by Roosevelt and Stalin. The Mikołajczyk government, which was opposed to such a territorial deal, was not informed.

Roosevelt suggested to Mikołajczyk, visiting Washington, D.C., in June 1944, that the AK show its goodwill by cooperating with the Red Army. Such cooperation, however, when attempted in areas that had been part of prewar eastern Poland, was followed by arrests and deportation or conscription into the Soviet-sponsored Polish Kościuszko Division commanded by Gen. Zygmunt Berling. On August 1, 1944, just as Mikołajczyk, prompted by the British, went to Moscow, the AK, under the supreme command of Gen. Tadeusz Bór-Komorowski, rose in Warsaw against the retreating Germans.

The Warsaw Uprising constitutes one of the most tragic and controversial events of the war. The AK planned to capture the capital and act on behalf of Mikołajczyk's government as host to the entering Red Army. It was assumed that the Soviets would not dare to disregard this demonstration of the Polish right to self-determination. In the absence of Soviet military assistance, the rising was doomed, yet, had the AK not risen, it would have been accused of inactivity by the communists. The insurgents fought alone for 63 days, because the Soviets not only halted their own offensive but also refused to allow Allied planes to help resupply the AK. When Warsaw capitulated, the city had been almost totally destroyed, and 200,000 civilians and more than 10,000 combatants had perished.

Stalin had no interest in assisting the Polish underground and did not hesitate to defy world public opinion when, in March 1945, he had 16 leaders of the underground arrested and tried in Moscow. Their elimination was linked to the process of building a communist-dominated Polish state. In July 1944 a Polish Committee of National Liberation was set up in Moscow ("officially" in Chełm), issued its Lublin Manifesto (July 22), and signed a secret territorial accord with the U.S.S.R. Mikołajczyk, caught between British pressure and the resistance of his government, resigned in November 1944.

Ignoring the socialist Tomasz Arciszewski, who succeeded Mikołajczyk as premier, Roosevelt and Churchill agreed with Stalin at the Yalta Conference (February 1945) to create a Provisional Polish Government of National Unity. Its core was the Lublin Polish Committee of National Liberation (already recognized by Stalin as the government), to which some politicians from Poland and abroad were added. Britain and the United States recognized that government on July 5, 1945, simultaneously withdrawing recognition from the government in London. A large Polish political emigration emerged as a voice of a free Poland and remained active during the next 40 years.

COMMUNIST POLAND

The postwar Polish republic, renamed in 1952 the Polish People's Republic, occupied an area some 20 percent smaller than prewar Poland, and its population of almost 30 million rose to nearly 39 million in the following four decades. The Holocaust, together with the expulsion of several million Germans and population transfers with the U.S.S.R., left Poland virtually homogeneous in its ethnic composition. The expulsion of the Germans was approved by the Potsdam Conference, but the final decision regarding the new German-Polish border along the Oder-Neisse Line was left to a future peace conference. The U.S.S.R. cleverly

Poland's territory following World War II. Encyclopædia Britannica, Inc.

capitalized on its status as the sole guarantor of this border, which gave Poland a long seacoast, with such harbours as Szczecin and Gdańsk, and such natural resources as coal and zinc in Silesia.

Despite the potential for wealth established by the redrawn borders, the fact remained that the war had devastated Poland. Warsaw, Wrocław, and Gdańsk lay in ruins, and social conditions bordered on chaos. Huge migrations, mainly to the ex-German "western territories," added to the instability. Fighting against the remnants of the Ukrainian Liberation Army was followed by the mass relocation of the Ukrainians (Operation Vistula) in 1947. Persecutions of the AK and political opponents (the National Party was outlawed) by the communists led to armed clashes that continued for several years. It was under these conditions that a Jewish pogrom occurred in Kielce in June 1946, claiming more than 40 lives.

Bierut, who was formally nonpartisan but in fact was an old communist, assumed

ODER-NEISSE LINE

The Polish-German border that was devised by the Allied powers at the end of World War II is known as the Oder-Neisse Line. It transferred a large section of German territory to Poland and was a matter of contention between the Federal Republic of Germany (West Germany) and the Soviet bloc for 15 years.

At the Yalta Conference (February 1945) the three major Allied powers—Great Britain, the Soviet Union, and the United States—moved back Poland's eastern boundary with the Soviet Union to the west, placing it approximately along the Curzon Line. Because this settlement involved a substantial loss of territory for Poland, the Allies also agreed to compensate the reestablished Polish state by moving its western frontier farther west at the expense of Germany.

But the western Allies and the Soviet Union sharply disagreed over the exact location of the new border. The Soviets pressed for the adoption of the Oder-Neisse Line—i.e., a line extending southward from Świnoujście on the Baltic Sea, passing west of Szczecin, then following the Oder (Polish: Odra) River to the point south of Frankfurt where it is joined by the Lusatian Neisse (Polish: Nysa Łużycka) River, and proceeding along the Neisse to the Czechoslovakian border, near Zittau. The United States and Great Britain warned that such a territorial settlement not only would involve the displacement of too many Germans but also would turn Germany into a dissatisfied state anxious to recover its losses, thereby endangering the possibilities of a long-lasting peace. Consequently, the western Allies proposed an alternate border, which extended along the Oder River and then followed another Neisse River (the Glatzer Neisse, or Nysa Kłodzka), which joined the Oder at a point between Wrocław (Breslau) and Opole. No decision on the German-Polish border was reached at Yalta.

By the time the Allied leaders assembled again at the Potsdam Conference in July–August 1945, the Soviet Red Army had occupied all the lands east of the Soviet-proposed Oder-Neisse Line, and the Soviet authorities had transferred the administration of the lands to a pro-Soviet Polish provisional government. Although the United States and Great Britain strenuously protested the unilateral action, they accepted it and agreed to the placement of all the territory east of the Oder-Neisse Line under Polish administrative control (except the northern part of East Prussia, which was incorporated into the Soviet Union). The Potsdam conferees also allowed the Poles to deport the German inhabitants of the area to Germany. But they left the drawing of the final Polish-German border to be determined by a future peace conference.

The German Democratic Republic (East Germany) signed a treaty with Poland at Zgorzelec (German: Görlitz) on July 6, 1950, that recognized the Oder-Neisse Line as its permanent eastern boundary. West Germany insisted, however, that the line was only a temporary administrative border and was subject to revision by a final peace treaty. West Germany continued to refuse to recognize the line until 1970. At that time, the West German government, which for several years had been striving to improve its relations with the eastern European states, signed treaties with the Soviet Union (August 12, 1970) and Poland (December 7, 1970) acknowledging the Oder-Neisse Line as Poland's legitimate and inviolable border. This recognition was confirmed in the negotiations leading to German reunification in 1990.

the presidency. In a cabinet headed by a socialist and dominated by communists and fellow travelers, Mikołajczyk became deputy prime minister. He successfully re-created a genuine Polish Peasant Party (PSL; Polskie Stronnictwo Ludowe, later also called the Polish People's Party), which was larger than the PPR and its socialist and democratic satellite parties (the PPS and the SD, respectively). Supported by all enemies of communism, Mikołajczyk sought to challenge the PPR in the "free and unfettered" elections stipulated by the Yalta accords. His opponents included the ruthless secretary-general of the PPR, Władysław Gomułka, a "home communist," and the men in charge of security (Jakub Berman) and of the economy (Hilary Minc), who had returned from Russia.

The Sovietization of Poland, accompanied by terror, included the nationalization of industry and the expropriation of privately owned land parcels larger than 125 acres (50 ha). Yet in some areas (namely, matters concerning the church and foreign policy), the communists trod lightly during this transition period. The test of strength between Mikołajczyk and the PPR first occurred during the referendum of 1946—the results of which, favourable to Mikołajczyk, were falsified—and then in the general elections of 1947, which were hardly "free and unfettered." Mikołajczyk, fearing for his life, fled the country. The victorious communists completed their monopoly of power in 1948 by absorbing the increasingly dependent PPS to become the Polish United Workers' Party (PUWP).

Over the next few years the Bierut regime in Poland closely followed the Stalinist model in politics (adopting the Soviet-style 1952 constitution), economics (emphasizing heavy industry and collectivization of agriculture), military affairs (appointing the Soviet Marshal Konstantin Rokossovsky as commander of Polish forces and adhering to the Warsaw Pact of 1955), foreign policy (joining the Communist Information Bureau, the agency of international communism), culture, and the rule of the secret police. Political terror in Poland, however, did not include, as elsewhere, show trials of fallen party leaders—Gomułka, denounced as a "Titoist" and imprisoned in 1951, was spared such a trial. Moreover, the primate of Poland, Stefan Wyszyński, could still negotiate a modus vivendi in 1950, though, as the pressure on the church increased, he was arrested in September 1953 (by which time he had been named a cardinal).

The death of Stalin in March 1953 opened a period of struggle for succession and change in the U.S.S.R. that had repercussions throughout the Soviet bloc. The interlude of liberalization that followed culminated in the Soviet leader Nikita Khrushchev's denunciation of Stalinism at the 20th Party Congress in February 1956. With the sudden death of Bierut, anti-Stalinists in Poland raised their heads; a violently suppressed workers' strike in Poznań in June 1956 shook the whole country. Gomułka, who believed in a "Polish road to socialism," became a candidate for the leadership of the party. What appeared as his confrontation with Khrushchev and other top Soviet leaders who descended on Warsaw in October and threatened intervention made Gomułka popular throughout Poland. In reality the Polish leader convinced Khrushchev of his devotion to communism and of the need for a reformist approach to strengthen its doctrine.

Important changes followed, among them Polish-Soviet accords on trade and military cooperation (Rokossovsky and most Soviet officers left the country), a significant reduction of political terror, an end to forced collectivization, the release of Cardinal Wyszyński (followed by some concessions in the religious sphere), and increased contacts with the West, including freer travel. Gomułka's objective, however, was to bridge the gap between the people and the party, thereby legitimizing the latter. Hence, the period of reform known as "Polish October" did not prove to be the beginning of an evolution of communism that revisionists at home and politically motivated émigrés had hoped for.

Within a decade economic reform slowed down, the activity of the church was circumscribed, and intellectuals were subjected to pressures. Demonstrations by students in favour of intellectual freedom led to reprisals in March 1968 that brought to an end the so-called "little stabilization" that Gomułka had succeeded in achieving. Ever more autocratic in his behaviour, Gomułka became involved in an "anti-Zionist" campaign that resulted in purges within the party, administration, and army. Thousands of people of Jewish origin emigrated.

Also in 1968, Polish troops joined the Soviet-led intervention in Czechoslovakia. In 1970 Gomułka registered a foreign-policy success by signing a treaty with West Germany that involved a recognition of the Oder-Neisse border. In December 1970, however, major strikes in the shipyards at Gdańsk, Gdynia, and Szczecin, provoked by price increases, led to bloody clashes with police and troops in which many were killed. Gomułka had to step down and was replaced as first secretary by the more pragmatic head of the party in Silesia, Edward Gierek.

The Gierek decade (1970–80) began with ambitious attempts to modernize the country's economy and raise living standards. Exploiting East-West détente, he attracted large foreign loans and investments. Initial successes, however, turned sour as the world oil crisis and mismanagement of the economy produced huge budget deficits, which Gierek tried to cover through increased borrowing. The policy of consumerism failed to strengthen the system, and new price increases in 1976 led to workers' riots in Ursus and Radom, which once again were brutally suppressed.

A Workers' Defense Committee (KOR) arose and sought to bridge the gap between the intelligentsia, which had been isolated in 1968, and the workers, who had received no support in 1970. The names of such dissidents as Jacek Kuroń and Adam Michnik became internationally known. Other committees appeared that claimed the legality of their activity and protested reprisals as being contrary to the 1975 Helsinki Accords. The PUWP responded with measures of selective intimidation.

In 1978 the election of Karol Cardinal Wojtyła, the archbishop of Kraków, as Pope John Paul II gave the Poles a father figure and a new inspiration. The coalition of workers and intellectuals, operating largely under the protective umbrella of the church, was in fact building a civil society. The pope's visit to Poland in 1979 endowed that society with national, patriotic, and ethical dimensions. A strike at the Gdańsk shipyard led by a charismatic electrician, Lech Wałęsa, forced an accord with the government on August 31, 1980. Out of the strike emerged the almost 10-million-strong Independent Self-Governing Trade Union Solidarity (Solidarność), which the government was forced to recognize. Here was an unprecedented working-class revolution directed against a "socialist" state, an example to other peoples of the Soviet bloc.

A huge movement that sought not to govern but rather to ensure freedom through a "self-limiting revolution," Solidarity could not have been homogeneous. The opponents of communism ranged from those who opposed the system as contrary to liberty and democracy to those who saw it as inimical to national and Christian values and to those who felt that it had not lived up to its socioeconomic promises. These three attitudes all resurfaced after the fall of communism and explain a good deal about the developments in Poland of the 1990s.

Gierek did not politically survive the birth of Solidarity, and he was replaced by Stanisław Kania, who was followed by Gen. Wojciech Jaruzelski. By the autumn of 1981, Jaruzelski held the offices of premier, first secretary of the party, and commander in chief. His decision to attempt to break Solidarity through the introduction of martial law in December 1981 may well have stemmed from a conviction that the constant tug of war between Solidarity and the government was leading the country toward anarchy, which had to be ended by Polish or by Soviet hands. It is likely that he could not conceive of any Poland except a communist one.

Martial law effectively broke Solidarity by paralyzing the country and imprisoning virtually all of the movement's leadership, Wałęsa included. It did not, however, destroy the movement. After the lifting of martial law in 1983, the government, despite its best attempts, could not establish its legitimacy. Severe economic problems worsened the political deadlock. In 1984 a popular priest, Jerzy Popieluszko, was murdered by the secret police, but, for the first time in such a case, state agents were arrested and charged with the crime.

In 1985 when Mikhail Gorbachev came to power as the leader of the Soviet Union, his policies of reform (glasnost and perestroika) started a process that eventually led to the collapse of communism in eastern Europe and the disintegration of the U.S.S.R. The Jaruzelski regime realized that broad reforms were unavoidable and that a revived Solidarity had to be part of them. The roundtable negotiations under the auspices of the church—Józef Cardinal Glemp succeeded Wyszyński as primate—resulted in a "negotiated revolution." Solidarity was restored and participated in partly free elections in June 1989 that brought it a sweeping victory.

POLAND AFTER 1989

Detaching the satellite (populist and democratic) parties from the PUWP, Wałęsa negotiated a compromise by virtue of which Jaruzelski was elected president, while Wałęsa's adviser, the noted Catholic politician Tadeusz Mazowiecki, became premier. This was the first government led by a noncommunist since World War II. The tasks it faced were immense. In 1990 the government adopted a "shock therapy" program of economic reform, named the Balcerowicz Plan after its author, Finance Minister Leszek Balcerowicz. It was meant to arrest Poland's financial and structural crisis and rapidly convert the communist economic model into a free-market system, thereby reintegrating Poland into the global economy. Although it proved a success, the social cost was high. The difficulties of redirecting trade previously linked to the Soviet bloc were great. The new government achieved, however, two major successes: a formal recognition of

the Oder-Neisse border by the reunited Germany and, after the dissolution of the Warsaw Pact in 1991, the evacuation of Soviet troops from the country in 1992.

Poland's reentry into western Europe, from which it had been forcibly separated since the end of World War II, was a slow process. Nonetheless, by 1996 the country had become a member of the Council of Europe, established economic ties with the EU, and been admitted to the Organisation for Economic Co-operation and Development. In 1999 Poland became a member of the North Atlantic Treaty Organization despite Russian opposition. Russia's unsettled political situation during the 1990s cast a shadow on Polish foreign policy and complicated its options. Nevertheless, Poland signed accords with Ukraine and Lithuania and established limited regional cooperation with the formation of the Visegrad Group, whose other members were the Czech Republic, Slovakia, and Hungary.

By the mid-1990s the Polish economy—more than half of which had been privatized—was making important strides, including significant reductions in the annual inflation rate and the budget deficit. Moreover, the annual growth rate of Poland's gross national product was the highest in Europe. But progress was uneven geographically, and economic sectors such as the coal-mining and building industries experienced slumps. The gap between the rich and the poor grew, adding to the bitterness and frustration reflected in a political life that was far less stable than expected.

TADEUSZ MAZOWIECKI

Tadeusz Mazowiecki (born April 18, 1927, Płock, Poland) was a journalist and Solidarity official before he became prime minister of Poland in 1989 and, as such, the first non-communist premier of an eastern European country since the late 1940s.

After graduating in law from the University of Warsaw, Mazowiecki entered journalism and became prominent among Poland's liberal young Roman Catholic intellectuals in the mid-1950s. In 1958 Mazowiecki cofounded the independent Catholic monthly journal *Więź* ("Link"), which he edited until 1981. From 1961 to 1971 he was a member of the Sejm, Poland's legislative assembly. In the 1970s he forged links with the Workers' Defense Committee, which protected anticommunist labour activists in Poland from government persecution.

When strikes in the Lenin shipyard in Gdańsk sparked the birth of the Solidarity labour movement there in August 1980, Mazowiecki became one of the principal advisers to the strikers and helped mobilize Polish intellectuals in support of them. In 1981 Solidarity's leader, Lech Wałęsa, appointed Mazowiecki the first editor of *Tygodnik Solidarność* ("Solidarity Weekly"), the new Solidarity newspaper. His ties to Wałęsa only deepened during the government's suppression of the Solidarity movement from 1981 to 1988.

In early 1989 Mazowiecki served as the mediator in talks between the government and Solidarity that resulted in Solidarity's legalization and the holding of the freest national elections in Poland since 1947. Solidarity's stunning victory in those elections in June prompted Poland's communist president, Gen. Wojciech Jaruzelski, to appoint Mazowiecki as prime minister on the advice of Wałęsa. On August 24 Mazowiecki became prime minister of a coalition government of Solidarity and communist members, as well as those of minor parties.

As prime minister, Mazowiecki undertook radical reforms aimed at moving Poland in the direction of a free-market economy. His government greatly reduced price controls, subsidies, and centralized planning while simultaneously privatizing businesses, creating a stable convertible currency, and restraining wage increases in order to reduce inflation. Through these means Mazowiecki was successful at stabilizing Poland's consumer-goods market, increasing exports, and restoring the government's finances, but only at the cost of sharply rising unemployment and a fall in real wages. Popular discontent with these negative effects became apparent in the presidential elections held in December 1990 to choose a successor to Jaruzelski: Mazowiecki finished third in a race won by Wałęsa. Just prior to the 1990 elections, he served as founder and first chairman of the Democratic Union (now Freedom Union); he left the party in 2002. In 2005 he helped found the Democratic Party (Partia Demokratyczna [PD]; not to be confused with Poland's other Democratic Party, Stronnictwo Demokratyczne [SD], founded in 1939). From 1992 to 1995 Mazowiecki represented the former Yugoslavia as a special reporter to the United Nations Human Rights Commission.

The disintegration of Solidarity, accelerated by political and personality clashes, became apparent in the 1990 election, in which Wałęsa defeated Mazowiecki for the presidency. Voters expressed their dissatisfaction by supporting the dark-horse candidate Stanisław Tyminski, a Polish émigré businessman from Canada who finished second in the balloting. The succession of cabinets in the early 1990s included one government headed by Jan Olszewski, which fell as a result of a clumsy attempt to produce a list of former high-ranking communist collaborators, and another led by Poland's first woman prime minister, Hanna Suchocka, which was unexpectedly defeated by a somewhat frivolous no-confidence vote. The centrist Freedom Union (UW), which bore the brunt of the transition to democracy, failed to communicate its vision to the masses and remained largely a party of the intelligentsia. The rightists, split into several groups, accused Wałęsa and the roundtable negotiators of selling out to communists.

Meanwhile, the communists were able to profit financially from the collapse of the economy and reorganized as the Social Democracy of the Republic of Poland (SdRP). Indeed, the SdRP exploited the increased frustration over the inequalities of a capitalist economy and the political infighting of the Solidarity camp. In 1991 the SdRP formed a coalition with the All Poland Trade Unions Alliance (OPZZ) under the banner of the Democratic Left Alliance (SLD).

Well-organized and disciplined, the coalition, along with the Polish Peasant Party (PSL), captured the most seats in the 1993 legislative election, and the two formed a coalition government. In November 1995 the SLD captured the presidency when Wałęsa was defeated by the young, dynamic former communist Aleksander Kwaśniewski, whose campaign asked voters to look to the future rather than to the past. His election may have been symptomatic of a generational change that was also visible in the attitude toward the church, whose high prestige suffered as its efforts to influence politics and to be a national rallying point in the increasingly secularized postcommunist society occasionally backfired.

After the 1993 legislative election, the SLD-PSL coalition governments—under the premiership of Waldemar Pawlak (PSL, 1993–95), Józef Oleksy (SLD, 1995–96), and Włodzimierz Cimoszewicz (SLD, 1996–97)—continued, albeit cautiously, the pro-market policies of their predecessors. They failed, however, to reform the obsolete structures of the welfare state that had been inherited from the communist regime and were inadequate in the context of a market economy.

THE CONSTITUTION OF 1997

The parliament elected in 1993 concluded its term by passing the new constitution in April 1997. The constitution's content reflected the compromise between the ruling leftist coalition and the centrist

UW, while addressing several concerns raised by the church. However, the extra-parliamentary right, since 1996 united in a loose coalition known as the Solidarity Electoral Action (AWS), challenged the draft submitted by the National Assembly and called for its rejection in a national referendum. In May 1997 the referendum approved the draft by a slim margin. The constitution came into force in October 1997.

The narrow defeat in the referendum showdown invigorated the AWS. In the September 27, 1997, legislative elections, it triumphed and formed a ruling coalition with the UW. The new government of Prime Minister Jerzy Buzek of the AWS included, among others, the leader of the UW and the architect of the shock therapy reforms, Leszek Balcerowicz, as the deputy prime minister and minister of finance. Continuing the economic policies of its predecessors since 1989, the government focused on further privatization of industries and services. It also launched a series of major reforms aimed at overhauling the state administration and welfare services.

The reform of the state structure, effective January 1, 1999, introduced a three-tier system of administration and local self-government. The health care, pension, and education systems also began undergoing reform in 1999. The policies of the government were frequently met with considerable popular opposition, as they antagonized some formerly privileged groups. Changes to agricultural policy were among the most contentious. Designed to facilitate Poland's accession to the EU, the reforms were seen by some as jeopardizing the antiquated system of farming prevalent in many regions of Poland.

POLAND IN THE 21ST CENTURY

Kwaśniewski was reelected in 2000, while Wałęsa, capturing only 1 percent of the vote as the fourth most popular candidate, announced his retirement from politics. In the 2001 parliamentary elections, a coalition of candidates from the SLD and the Union of Labour (Unia Pracy; UP) were the majority winners, with Leszek Miller of the SLD becoming prime minister. In the next set of elections, the SLD fell to the centre-right party Law and Justice (Prawo i Sprawiedliwość; PiS), with its founders, identical twins Lech and Jarosław Kaczyński, attaining the posts of president (2005) and prime minister (2006), respectively. In 2007 the PiS abandoned its coalition partners—the scandal-plagued Self-Defense Party and the League of Polish Families—and called for an early parliamentary election. In a stunning result, the PiS was defeated by the centre-right Civic Platform party, which under the premiership of Donald Tusk formed a coalition government with the PSL.

Whether the relatively frequent changes of government would lead ultimately to the emergence of a real and responsible left, centre, and right and whether the new constitution would

BRONISŁAW KOMOROWSKI

Bronisław Komorowski (born June 4, 1952, Oborniki Śląskie, Poland) became the president of Poland in 2010. Named acting president after the death of Lech Kaczyński in April 2010, Komorowski won the presidency in a special election that July.

Komorowski was born to an aristocratic family, but the communist regime in postwar Poland created a challenging environment for members of the hereditary landowning class. His family moved frequently, relocating from near Wrocław to Poznan, before settling in Warsaw when Komorowski was a teenager. He became active in the anticommunist opposition while he was still a high school student, and his dissident activities led to his first arrest in 1971. He earned a bachelor's degree in history from Warsaw University in 1977, and throughout the 1980s he taught at the Niepokalanów seminary near Warsaw. Komorowski also remained a committed dissident during this period, working as the editor of an underground publication.

With the fall of communism in 1989, Komorowski launched his political career, initially serving on the Council of Ministers before his election to the Sejm (parliament) in 1991. Over the following decade, he held a number of ministerial positions, including defense minister (2000–01) in the government of Jerzy Buzek. In 2001 he joined the centre-right Civic Platform (Platforma Obywatelska; PO), and in 2006 he was elected vice-chairman of that party. He continued his rise in the parliament, and in November 2007 he was elected speaker of the Sejm.

As speaker, Komorowski sponsored a number of pro-EU and economic reform initiatives that brought him into conflict with the more Euroskeptic Pres. Lech Kaczyński. When Kaczyński was killed, along with dozens of other prominent Poles, in a plane crash in April 2010, Komorowski was named acting president. Constitutionally obliged to call an election within two weeks of Kaczyński's death, Komorowski announced that a first round of polling would occur on June 20, 2010, and that he would run as the Civic Platform candidate. In the event, Komorowski finished first—ahead of his most prominent opponent in the race, Kaczyński's twin brother, Jarosław, who represented the conservative Law and Justice (Prawo i Sprawiedliwość; PiS) party. However, because neither candidate tallied at least 50 percent of the vote, a runoff election between them was held in July. In that contest Komorowski prevailed with 53 percent of the vote.

provide a mechanism for a smoothly functioning democracy depended in no small degree on the growing sophistication and experience of the electorate. In a nationwide referendum in 2003, the Polish electorate approved EU membership for their country, which came into force in 2004, a testimony to its successful postcommunist transition.

Although a plan to deploy a major new missile defense system in Poland was scrapped by the United States in 2009, Poland's willingness to accept the system was a thorn in the side of Russia, as was Pres. Lech Kaczyński's aggressive support for extending NATO membership to Georgia and Ukraine. On the other hand, decades of strained relations between Poland and

Russia over the Katyn Massacre, in which thousands of Polish officers were killed by Soviet troops during World War II, turned a corner on April 7, 2010, when Prime Minister Vladimir Putin became the first Russian leader to participate in commemoration ceremonies at the massacre site. Three days later, on April 10, en route to another memorial ceremony, a plane carrying Kaczyński crashed near Smolensk, near the Katyn site, killing the president, his wife, the army chief of staff, the head of the national security bureau, the president of the national bank, and a number of Polish government officials and evoking widespread mourning in Poland. In June in the special election to replace Lech Kaczyński, interim president Bronisław Komorowski of the Civic Platform party edged out Jarosław Kaczyński at the head of a 10-candidate field, though neither polled the 50 percent necessary to prevent a runoff election between them. In that contest, held in July, Komorowski won the presidency with 53 percent of the vote.

Poland weathered the global economic downturn that began in 2008 better than most of its EU partners, and the Polish electorate returned the Civic Platform party to power in the 2011 parliamentary elections, making Tusk the first prime minister since the end of communism to serve a second consecutive term. Civic Platform captured about two-fifths of the seats in the Sejm and was poised to continue coalition rule with its junior partner, the PSL.

Given the geographical proximity of Poland and the three Baltic states—Estonia, Latvia, and Lithuania—it is not surprising that the histories of the four countries followed a similar trajectory and, at times, were closely interwoven. Throughout the centuries, the prominence and degree of independence of the precursors to the four modern-day countries waxed and waned. Estonia and Latvia were dominated by foreign powers through much of their histories. Poland, on the other hand—once a collection of small principalities and townships that were subjugated by successive waves of invaders in the early Middle Ages—evolved into what was the largest state in Europe at the time and perhaps the continent's most powerful nation. Yet two and a half centuries later, during the partitions of Poland (1772–1918), it disappeared, parceled out among the contending empires of Russia, Prussia, and Austria. Lithuania was also a powerful empire and dominated much of eastern Europe in the 14th–16th centuries in close alignment with Poland; then, from 1569, it was part of a confederation with Poland until the aforementioned partitions broke the commonwealth apart.

All four countries were under some form of communist rule for much of the 20th century; Estonia, Latvia, and Lithuania as part of the U.S.S.R., and Poland as a communist satellite state closely aligned with the U.S.S.R. After the fall of communism in the late 1980s and early 1990s, Poland and the newly independent Baltic states had to shift their economic and governmental policies. Poland, after hard-won political reforms and an economic austerity program, had transitioned into a market-based democracy by the turn of the 21st century. The Baltic states struggled to make a transition to a market economy from the system of Soviet national planning that had been in place since the end of World War II, all while embracing democratic reforms to their governments. All four countries were successful enough in their transformations that they were able to gain admittance into the European Union (EU) in 2004. Since then, they have seen economic growth and weathered economic storms while continuing to operate under the common economic, social, and security policies of the EU.

Glossary

AUSTERITY Enforced or extreme economy.

BILATERAL Affecting reciprocally two nations or parties.

BLOC A combination of persons, groups, or nations forming a unit with a common interest or purpose.

CEDE To yield or grant typically by treaty.

COALITION A temporary alliance of distinct parties, persons, or states for joint action.

COLLECTIVISM A political or economic theory advocating collective control especially over production and distribution.

COLONIZE To establish a settlement in a new territory while retaining ties with the parent state.

COMMODITY An economic good, such as a product of agriculture or mining, an article of commerce, or a mass-produced unspecialized product.

COMMUNISM A totalitarian system of government in which a single authoritarian party controls state-owned means of production

COUNTEROFFENSIVE A large-scale military offensive undertaken by a force previously on the defensive.

COUP D'ETAT The overthrow or alteration of an existing government by a small group.

DISSOLUTION The dissolving of an assembly or organization.

EPISCOPAL Of, having, or constituting government by bishops.

FASCISM A tendency toward or actual exercise of strong autocratic or dictatorial control.

INDIGENOUS Produced, growing, living, or occurring naturally in a particular region or environment.

LEGISLATURE An organized body having the authority to make laws for a political unit.

MOAT A deep and wide trench around the rampart of a fortified place (as a castle) that is usually filled with water.

MUNICIPALITY A primarily urban political unit having corporate status and usually powers of self-government.

OCCUPATION The holding and control of an area by a foreign military force.

OIL SHALE A rock (as shale) from which oil can be recovered by distillation.

PARISH A subdivision of a county often coinciding with an original ecclesiastical parish and constituting the unit of local government.

PATRIARCHAL Social organization marked by the supremacy of the father in the clan or family, the legal dependence of wives and children, and the reckoning of descent and inheritance in the male line.

PODZOLIC Any of a group of zonal soils that develop in a moist climate especially under coniferous or mixed forest and have an organic mat and a thin organic-mineral layer above a light gray leached layer resting on a dark horizon that is marked by illuviation and enriched with amorphous clay.

PROVINCE An administrative district or division of a country

SUBSIDY Money granted by one state to another or by a government to a private person for assistance.

TREATY A contract in writing between two or more political authorities (as states or sovereigns) formally signed by representatives duly authorized and usually ratified by the lawmaking authority of the state.

UNICAMERAL Having or consisting of a single legislative chamber.

BIBLIOGRAPHY

ESTONIA

Estonia's geography is surveyed in publications prepared by the Institute of Geography at Tartu University and by the Estonian Geographical Society (EGS). Since 1972, the EGS has issued English-language texts every four years on the occasions of International Geographical Congresses, such as *Estonia: Geographical Studies*, vol. 11 (2012). Estonia's cultural heritage is addressed in Ivar Paulson, *The Old Estonian Folk Religion* (1971); Endel Nirk, *Estonian Literature*, 2nd ed. (1987; originally published in Estonian, 1983); and Monika Topman, *An Outline of Estonian Music*, trans. from Estonian (1978). Developments of the late 1980s are found in Pia Pajur, *Hello, Perestroika: Nine Interviews with Individual and Cooperative Workers* (1989; originally published in Estonian, 1989).Toivo U. Raun, *Estonia and the Estonians*, 2nd updated ed. (2001), is a comprehensive survey of Estonian history, spanning the period from the first human settlements to the end of the 1970s. A good survey of Estonian history in the 20th century is John Hiden and Patrick Salmon, *The Baltic Nations and Europe: Estonia, Latvia, and Lithuania in the Twentieth Century* (rev. ed. 1996). An older but still important work is Evald Uustalu, *The History of Estonian People* (1952). Works focusing on specific periods and topics include J. Selirand and E. Tõnisson, *Through Past Millennia: Archaeological Discoveries in Estonia*, trans. from Estonian (1984); Juhan Kahk, *Peasant and Lord in the Process of Transition from Feudalism to Capitalism in the Baltics* (1982); Igor Sedykh (compiler), *Estonia: Choice of a Path, 1917–1940: A Documentary Survey* (1987); and Villem Raud, *Developments in Estonia, 1939–1941*, 2nd ed. (1987). The impact of Soviet occupation is discussed in Vello Salo (ed.), *Population Losses in Estonia, June 1940–August 1941* (1989). A popular and well-written history of the Baltic states, mainly focusing on the period after glasnost, is Anatol Lieven, *The Baltic Revolution: Estonia, Latvia, Lithuania, and the Path to Independence*, 2nd ed. (1999, reprinted 2005).

LATVIA

General information on Latvia's physical and human geography is available in a brief illustrated survey by Monika Zile, *Latvia*, trans. from Russian (1987), from the series of commemorative booklets *Socialist Republics of the Soviet Union*. More-detailed, though older, studies are found in J. Rutkis (ed.), *Latvia: Country and People* (1967); Vaira Vikis-Freibergs (ed.), *Linguistics and Poetics of Latvian Folk Songs* (1989); and Rolfs Ekmanis,

Latvian Literature Under the Soviets, 1940–1975 (1978). Vito Vitauts Simanis (ed.), *Latvia* (1984), is useful as a reference source.

Andrejs Plakans, *Historical Dictionary of Latvia*, 2nd ed. (2008), provides a general overview of Latvian history. Alfred Bilmanis, *Latvia as an Independent State* (1947, reprinted 2007); and Visvaldis Mangulis, *Latvia in the Wars of the 20th Century* (1983), provide historical surveys. Juris Dreifelds, *Latvia in Transition* (1998), discusses the formative events that led up to Latvia's passage to independence. Andrew Ezergailis, *The Holocaust in Latvia, 1941–1944: The Missing Center* (1996), is a comprehensive study of the Holocaust in Latvia.

LITHUANIA

Simas Sužiedēlis (ed.), *Encyclopedia Lituanica*, 6 vol. (1970–78), though older, is a comprehensive work, with many of the articles translated from Lithuanian. Jonas Zinkus (ed.), *Lithuania: An Encyclopedic Survey*, trans. from Lithuanian (1986), was published in the U.S.S.R. and presents the Soviet point of view; it is informative but has no index. Histories of the Lithuanian church contribute significantly to a characterization of the people in Antanas Musteikis, *The Reformation in Lithuania: Religious Fluctuations in the Sixteenth Century* (1988); and Michael Bourdeaux, *Land of Crosses: The Struggle for Religious Freedom in Lithuania, 1939–78* (1989).

A general treatment of Lithuanian history is provided in Simas Sužiedēlis, *Historical Dictionary of Lithuania*, 2nd ed. (2011). A broad historical survey is offered in Albertas Gerutis (ed.), *Lithuania, 700 Years*, 6th ed. (1984). More-specialized histories include Leonas Sabaliūnas, *Lithuanian Social Democracy in Perspective, 1893–1914* (1990); and Robertas Ziugza, *Lithuania and Western Powers, 1917–1940* (1987; originally published in Lithuanian, 1983). Robert A. Vitas, *The United States and Lithuania: The Stimson Doctrine of Nonrecognition* (1990), examines the diplomatic history of the 1940s. The history of the Polish-Lithuanian confederation is brilliantly covered in Norman Davies, *Europe: A History* (1996). Analysis of the independence movement is presented in Richard J. Krickus, *Showdown: The Lithuanian Rebellion and the Breakup of the Soviet Empire* (1997).

POLAND

Glenn E. Curtis (ed.), *Poland: A Country Study*, 3rd ed. (1994), provides a balanced treatment. Grzegorz Weclawowicz, *Contemporary Poland: Space and Society* (1996), discusses the changes since 1989. Zbigniew Landau and Jerzy Tomaszewski, *The Polish Economy in the Twentieth Century*, trans. from Polish by Wojciech Roszkowski (1985), offers an uncritical treatment. Aspects of cultural life are dealt with in Bolesław Klimaszewski (ed.), *An Outline History of Polish Culture*, trans. from Polish by Krystyna Mroczek (1979, reissued 1984), covering the main cultural trends from medieval times to 1982. *The Polish Review* (quarterly) focuses on current cultural events.

The history of Poland is presented in W.F. Reddaway et al. (eds.), *The Cambridge History of Poland*, 2 vol. (1941–50, reissued 1978); Jerzy Lukowski and Hubert Zawadzki, *A Concise History of Poland*, 2nd ed. (2010); Norman Davies, *God's Playground: A History of Poland*, new ed., 2 vol. (2003; also published as *A History of Poland, God's Playground*, 1981); Norman Davies, *Heart of Europe: The Past in Poland's Present*, new ed. (2001; originally published as *Heart of Europe: A Short History of Poland*, 1984); Adam Zamoyski, *The Polish Way: A Thousand-Year History of the Poles and Their Culture* (1987, reissued 1994); Jerzy Lukowski, *Liberty's Folly: The Polish-Lithuanian Commonwealth in the Eighteenth Century, 1697–1795* (1991, reissued 2004); Józef Garliński, *Poland in the Second World War* (1985, reissued 1987); and Jacek Jedruch, *Constitutions, Elections, and Legislatures of Poland, 1493–1993: A Guide to Their History*, rev. ed. (1998). George J. Lerski, *Historical Dictionary of Poland, 966–1945*, ed. by Piotr Wróbel and Richard J. Kozicki (1996), is a useful companion to historical readings. Communism and its collapse and aftermath are examined in Timothy Garton Ash, *The Polish Revolution: Solidarity, 1980–82*, 3rd ed. (2002); Grzegorz Ekiert, *The State Against Society: Political Crises and Their Aftermath in East Central Europe* (1996); Jan Kubik, *The Power of Symbols Against the Symbols of Power: The Rise of Solidarity and the Fall of State Socialism in Poland* (1994); Michael H. Bernhard, *The Origins of Democratization in Poland: Workers, Intellectuals, and Oppositional Politics, 1976–1980* (1993); and Raymond Taras, *Consolidating Democracy in Poland* (1995).

Index